"Teachers know the difficulties inherent in their profession, we live them daily. Hughes and Badley describe this book as a love letter for the difficulties and the joyful moments of teaching. Indeed, this is a letter of love to our labor of love as teachers. This volume brings together a wide assembly of educators whose stories will inspire and challenge teachers while revealing the joy of teaching. Each chapter describes the work of teaching as immensely challenging and rewarding. Teachers do find hope in the struggle. This book affirms that reality and invites the reader into a community of hope, not in avoiding the struggle, but in recognizing the challenges and accepting the realities while flourishing in the midst of it all."

Scot Headley, Professor of Educational Leadership, George Fox University, Newberg, Oregon

"This is an inspiring collection, full of the joy that its title promises. Hughes and Badley have assembled these essays as a 'love letter' to teachers at a time when so many pressures can drain educators' energies or ideals. Quite admirably, the writers face the current challenges squarely, but they avoid overworn platitudes and offer a valuable blend of seasoned wisdom and recent research to help teachers renew their spirits and their strategies. There are some rousing words here, yet the writers also respect that teachers are at their core learners themselves and will welcome new ideas to revitalize their craft. They will find all that in this thoughtful panorama."

Mark Sargent, Former Provost, Westmont and Gordon Colleges, Santa Barbara, California

"For teachers who have become dismayed by the myriad of challenges encountered in education, *Joyful Resilience in Educational Practice* will lift their souls. The authors have thoughtfully reframed the deficit model of teaching to reveal how the great rewards of the profession are most often hidden within the challenges. This insightful compilation is the perfect gift to inspire and encourage your favorite teachers!"

Stella Erbes, Divisional Dean, Humanities & Teacher Education; Associate Professor, Teacher Education, Pepperdine University, Malibu, California

"Not since Parker Palmer's *The Courage to Teach* has there been such an inspirational book on teaching as a calling. Authors in this book describe the positive energy they experience when they resolve challenges with attention to the animating forces that first drew them to the profession."

Jodi Nickel, Past-President, Canadian Association for Teacher Education; Professor, Mount Royal University, Calgary, Alberta

"I very much appreciate the heart and the expertise of the editors and chapter authors of *Joyful Resilience*. Many of us who have been involved in education for more than just a few years are very concerned about its direction, especially as it relates to the life (or lack of it) of the teacher. This book includes many personal accounts from those who are obviously passionate about the education enterprise and the future of education. The result is a hopeful volume that not so much prescribes as encourages, providing timely inspiration and refreshment for its readers."

Paul Shotsberger, Professor of Graduate Faculty at Southern Wesleyan University, Central, South Carolina

"In the midst of a global pandemic, *Joyful Resilience as Educational Practice*, challenges teachers, who operate in one of the most difficult professions even in the best of times, that joy and resilience are matters of choice. This collection of essays from a wide range of experienced professionals at all levels of the teaching profession, explores the rich treasure of resources for self-renewing flourishing that surrounds them in their daily work if they only have eyes to see, and the courageous discipline to receive them as gifts."

Shirley A. Mullen, President and Professor of History, Houghton College, Houghton, New York

JOYFUL RESILIENCE AS EDUCATIONAL PRACTICE

Joyful Resilience as Educational Practice: Transforming Teaching Challenges into Opportunities invites teachers to remember some of the gifts that teaching gives back to teachers. The contributors to this volume recognize that teaching is hard and demanding work, but they remind educators that their colleagues, their supervisors, their students' families, and even the textbooks they use all serve to make their work more rewarding.

Michelle C. Hughes has served as a junior high teacher, high school administrator, and Education Department faculty member at Westmont College in Santa Barbara, California. Michelle embraces promoting the teaching profession with Westmont students and the larger educational community. She is passionate about equipping teachers for long-term career success with dispositions such as resilience, compassion, empathy, and gratitude.

Ken Badley lives in Calgary, Alberta, and teaches foundations of education at Tyndale University in Toronto, Ontario. He has taught in secondary, undergraduate, graduate, and doctoral programs in Canada and the United States, and has worked extensively with teachers in Kenya. He is the author of many books and articles related to curriculum, instruction, and the teaching vocation.

JOYFUL RESILIENCE AS EDUCATIONAL PRACTICE

Transforming Teaching Challenges into Opportunities

Edited by Michelle C. Hughes and Ken Badley
Illustrations by Kristen Badley

NEW YORK AND LONDON

First published 2022
by Routledge
605 Third Avenue, New York, NY 10158

and by Routledge
2 Park Square, Milton Park, Abingdon, Oxon OX14 4RN

Routledge is an imprint of the Taylor & Francis Group, an informa business

© 2022 Michelle C. Hughes and Ken Badley

The right of Michelle C. Hughes and Ken Badley to be identified as the authors of the editorial material, and of the authors for their individual chapters, has been asserted in accordance with sections 77 and 78 of the Copyright, Designs and Patents Act 1988.

All rights reserved. No part of this book may be reprinted or reproduced or utilized in any form or by any electronic, mechanical, or other means, now known or hereafter invented, including photocopying and recording, or in any information storage or retrieval system, without permission in writing from the publishers.

Trademark notice: Product or corporate names may be trademarks or registered trademarks, and are used only for identification and explanation without intent to infringe.

Library of Congress Cataloging-in-Publication Data
Names: Hughes, Michelle C., editor. | Badley, Kenneth Rea, 1951- editor.
Title: Joyful resilience as educational practice : transforming teaching challenges into opportunities / [edited by] Michelle C. Hughes, Ken Badley ; illustrations by Kristen Badley.
Description: New York, N.Y. : Routledge, 2022. |
Includes bibliographical references and index.
Identifiers: LCCN 2021013352 (print) | LCCN 2021013353 (ebook) |
ISBN 9780367644185 (hardback) | ISBN 9780367644192 (paperback) |
ISBN 9781003124429 (ebook)
Subjects: LCSH: Teachers--Psychology. | Teaching--Psychological aspects. | Teachers--Professional relationships.
Classification: LCC LB2840 .J69 2022 (print) | LCC LB2840 (ebook) |
DDC 371.102--dc23
LC record available at https://lccn.loc.gov/2021013352
LC ebook record available at https://lccn.loc.gov/2021013353

ISBN: 978-0-367-64418-5 (hbk)
ISBN: 978-0-367-64419-2 (pbk)
ISBN: 978-1-003-12442-9 (ebk)

DOI: 10.4324/9781003124429

Typeset in Bembo
by Taylor & Francis Books

To teachers everywhere, who, in the face of adversity, invite students into joy-filled learning every day.

CONTENTS

List of Illustrations	*xi*
Preface	*xii*
Acknowledgments	*xiv*
List of Contributors	*xvi*

1 The Teaching Vocation and the Interior Lives of teachers 1
   Ken Badley and Michelle C. Hughes

2 Reciprocities with Students 11
   Michelle C. Hughes

3 When Students Become Our Teachers 26
   Joy A. Chadwick

4 Is there a Class in this Text? 38
   Ken Badley and Dana Antayá-Moore

5 Sustainable Teaching: Reflective and Responsive Practices 47
   Sunshine R. Sullivan

6 Minding the Gap: Seeing, Valuing, and Using the Theory–
   Practice Tension in the Classroom 58
   Paige A. Ray

7 Colleagues 71
   Tiana Tucker

8	The Power of Gifts from Supervisors who Share *Jay Mathisen*	80
9	A Long and Rewarding Apprenticeship: The Sustaining Inspiration of Our Mentors *Andrew Mullen*	90
10	Families *Michelle C. Hughes and Ken Badley*	101
11	Joyful Resilience through Dissonance, Doubt, and Disillusionment *Carrie R. Giboney Wall*	111
12	Navigating Political, Economic, and Curriculum Constraints with Joyful Defiance *Dana Antayá-Moore and Joanne Neal*	124
13	Teacher–Student Reciprocities within Three Educational Models *Daniel H. Jarvis and April E. Jarvis*	136
14	Uncovering Joyful Resilience *Ken Badley and Michelle C. Hughes*	158

Index   *163*

ILLUSTRATIONS

Figures

6.1	Schlechty's Five Levels of Engagement	60
6.2	The Recursive Relationship between Theory and Practice	67
13.1	Jarvis Family Teachers and Learners (l to r: Dan, April, Clara, Thea, Ella, Anna, Rose)	137
13.2	Ella in her Independent Reading-time Tree	142
13.3	Cabin Renovated as Collaborative Family Learning Project during Summer 2020	153

Table

13.1	Student Experiences within the Three Different Educational Models	145

PREFACE

Co-editors Michelle C. Hughes and Ken Badley met at George Fox University, where Ken served on the faculty in the Educational Leadership and Foundations Department, and where Michelle earned her doctorate in 2014. Sometime in 2015 during regular collegial email exchanges about writing projects and teaching, Ken suggested writing a book together about the reciprocities of teaching. He noted that, as teachers, we know of the many reciprocities, gifts, and rewards that come from students and our relationships with them, but what about the textbooks, families, curriculum, our own stories, the doubts and disillusionment, and the political and financial influences? Together we engaged in dialogue about how so many aspects of educators' work—from students, the most significant part of the job, to less significant matters, such as seating charts—have impacts on both our work as educators and how we feel about that work. Building on our conversations and at Ken's urging, Michelle agreed to write a chapter about the reciprocities and rewards that students give to teachers.

With full teaching schedules in education departments in higher education, and despite the fact that Ken lives in Alberta and Michelle lives in California, the conversations continued. After a few exchanges of Michelle's Chapter 2 drafts, both the book idea and the writing were tabled. After a few more years of correspondence, we committed in the early spring of 2020 to move the book idea forward—at the start of the Covid-19 crisis. Ironically, it took lockdowns and a global pandemic for this book to come to fruition; Ken finally felt he had the time to tackle the book proposal and used Michelle's Chapter 2 draft on students as a template. We then reached out to colleagues across the United States and Canada, inviting them to contribute chapters. Not one of our requests was turned down—from Alberta to Ontario, and from California to New York. Each potential contributor we approached chose a topic from the list we suggested and dove into writing, eager to research, write, and reflect on the joyful rewards that teaching offers, in each case acknowledging those rewards in full view of the sometimes harsh realities of teaching. It essentially took a pandemic for us to hunker down and write about the resiliency of teachers—another irony—especially during a time when teachers everywhere have demonstrated oodles of resilience and grit in the midst of the most unusual and difficult context for teaching that most living educators have ever experienced.

Ken and Michelle have worked in higher education for many years, both teaching pre-service teachers. Each of us has told prospective teacher candidates that teaching is hard work. It is courageous work; it is not for the meek or weak. Teaching is intellectual work that requires decision-making, research, organization, and commitment. It is also physical work and emotional work that asks a teacher to sit on the floor and read with students, organize relay races and model push-ups for physical education, and at the same time attend to our students' emotional states, their mental health needs, and even their economic circumstances. Teaching is meaningful work that challenges all of us, authors and readers alike, individually and collectively, to do better, not for ourselves but for our students.

As we dove into writing with our team of contributors, our focus on reciprocities revealed an even greater emphasis on vocation and why we chose to teach. In this book, you'll see how each contributing author weaves together personal experiences, anecdotes and stories, and research, while showing personal and professional strength. Hence the title, *Joyful Resilience as Educational Practice: Transforming Teaching Challenges into Opportunities* emerged, highlighting the flexibility, courage, adaptability, strength, wisdom, and grit that every teacher must develop and demonstrate.

We hope that you, our readers, will be inspired by the words on the pages of this book. We hope you will be reminded not only of the rewards that teaching gives and the resilience that teaching requires, but also of the joyful resilience that the art and acts of teaching bring to light. We hope that you will be encouraged to keep showing up, keep learning, keep reflecting, and keep growing alongside your students.

As a journey, teaching requires pruning and growth. We mean to capture what we have said in this Preface in the cover design: a rose growing and blooming from a crack in the sidewalk. *Joyful Resilience as Educational Practice: Transforming Teaching Challenges into Opportunities* is our love letter to all teachers. It is our love letter for the joyful moments and for the moments when we deal with thorns: the late nights of grading, the parent conferences, the report cards, the curricular disagreements, the tight funding, the lack of recognition, and the district disputes. These thorns are particulars in our daily work that don't immediately bring to mind great rewards or reciprocities. Yet the consistent work that we all do in classrooms for students day in and day out reveals why we keep showing up and why we keep making the best of the challenges—and why we keep transforming hurdles into opportunities. This book is our thank-you to you, our expression of gratitude for and to all teachers who encourage and empower us. May it remind you that your work is meaningful, joyful, and inspiring.

Michelle C. Hughes, Santa Barbara
Ken Badley, Calgary
February, 2021

ACKNOWLEDGMENTS

We begin by acknowledging the contributions of the colleagues who wrote the chapters in this volume. It was a joy to receive their 'yes' answers to our original queries about their interest in this project. As do all educators, they already had more than enough to do. They work as teacher educators in undergraduate, graduate, and doctoral programs, as school and district administrators, as classroom and home educators, and as educational consultants. In their spare time—whatever and whenever that may be—they willingly worked through our questions and editorial suggestions, giving us the joy of thinking more deeply about our own work as educators. This book would literally not exist were it not for these colleagues. We acknowledge their work with deep gratitude. We are thankful for the hours they devoted to writing, editing, and sharing ideas. We are all better when we work and learn together.

Together, we are grateful for the encouragement and guidance of both our editor at Routledge, Matthew Friberg, and Jessica Cooke, at Taylor & Francis. As we said about our contributors, this book would not have come into being without them. We also acknowledge the work of the editors, typesetters, and designers at Routledge who worked behind the scenes to bring our work to fruition.

MCH: Thank you first to Ken Badley. For years, you have mentored and encouraged me as a writer and colleague and I am grateful to have learned from you and with you through this project. Thank you to Kristen Badley for creatively bringing the cover of *Joyful Resilience as Educational Practice* to life. I extend heartfelt appreciation to the Westmont College community for the opportunity to learn and grow professionally over the last 12 years, long after I completed my BA and teaching credential on the same campus. I am grateful to my Westmont Education Department colleagues who work hard for teacher candidates every day. It takes a village to grow a teacher and I am honored to engage in meaningful work together. Thank you to my Westmont students. You inspire me every day with your curiosity, humility, grit, and compassion. I consider myself blessed to be your professor. I am grateful to my dear friends who continue to encourage me and affirm K-12 teachers. Finally, thank you to my parents, sister Nicole, and my immediate family (whom I call Team Hughes) for your consistent support. Thank you to my husband, Chris, who cheers for me—and his own junior high students—every day, and to my beautiful grown-up children, Haley and Grant, who inspire me to keep trying new things.

KB: As always, I am grateful to the members of Team Ken who encouraged me to keep going on this project. You know who you are. I am grateful to Kristen Badley, who continues to support my writing problem with her amazing graphic work, even when I have yet to learn how to load MSPaint. I am grateful to my wife, Jo-Ann, whose influence runs through all my thinking about education and whose insights appear uncredited in this volume. Without her encouragement, I might be sitting in a coffee shop every morning complaining about the government or pretending to solve world problems. I acknowledge the role of my BEd students at both Tyndale University in Toronto and Mount Royal University in Calgary who, over the last several years, have inspired me to keep discovering what Parker Palmer calls the heart of teaching and to laugh with them at my pedagogical flops and then carry on. They taught me so much while on campus and have given me joy as I have watched them emerge into teaching as competent and visionary beginning professionals who show resilience and find joy in teaching. Finally, I acknowledge the brilliance, hard work, and organizational skills that my colleague Michelle C. Hughes has brought to this project. When she signed on, this project had languished for some years. She brought it back to life and completed the chapter we submitted with the proposal, Chapter 2.

CONTRIBUTORS

Dana Antayá-Moore lives in Edmonton, Alberta. She teaches an introduction to inclusive education course at the University of Alberta. She has taught in elementary, secondary, and undergraduate programs in Canada, and has worked extensively with teachers in Kenya.

Joy A. Chadwick is an assistant professor in the Department of Education at Mount Royal University in Calgary, Alberta. She has extensive K-12 school experience as a teacher, resource teacher, curriculum leader, system specialist, coordinator, assistant principal, and principal. Her research interests focus on students with exceptionalities and the exploration of the pedagogical understandings that support effective learning environments for all students.

Daniel H. Jarvis lives in Corbeil, Ontario, Canada, and currently teaches graduate and mathematics education courses in the nearby Schulich School of Education at Nipissing University in North Bay. His research interests include instructional technology, mathematics of the workplace, curriculum integration, and innovation education.

April E. Jarvis lives in Corbeil, Ontario, Canada and has experience as both an international school classroom elementary teacher and a home-schooling mom of nearly 20 years. She is a music major, plays—and has taught—piano and violin, and has enjoyed providing a caring learning environment for her five daughters, Clara, Anna, Rose, Thea, and Ella.

Jay Mathisen lives in Bend, Oregon and serves as the Director of Educational Leadership at George Fox University. He has taught at the middle and high school levels and served as an assistant principal, principal, assistant superintendent, and deputy superintendent over 25 years in public education in Oregon. He has worked extensively over the last 11 years with educators in Rwanda on best teaching and leadership practices.

Andrew Mullen taught elementary-age children in nature centers and public and private schools before venturing into teacher education. His professional interests include children's literature and curriculum history. He joined the education faculty at Westmont College, where he currently serves, in 2001.

Joanne Neal has been an active K-9 teacher, professor, researcher, and writer in Edmonton, Alberta for the past 35 years. Her own love for learning has been the inspiration for working with undergraduate and graduate students, as well as with the larger teaching community. Recently retired from Alberta Education, she continues to teach with the Graduate Theological Foundation in the United States and to act as an associate faculty member with St. Stephen's College in Edmonton.

Paige A. Ray currently serves as Associate Professor of English at the College of the Ozarks, where she teaches in the Composition Sequence and instructs pre-service teachers in secondary English education. Before coming to the College of the Ozarks, she taught for several years at the secondary level. She sees her combined experience in both high school and undergraduate classrooms as essential to the preparation of teacher candidates.

Sunshine R. Sullivan has been an educator for 24 years. She currently serves as a professor and Associate Dean of the Department of Education at Houghton College. She enjoys teaching literacy and inclusive education courses as well as mentoring student teachers. Her research centers on communities of practice, multiple literacies, and place-based pedagogies in rural contexts.

Tiana Tucker currently serves as Human Resources Director for the Lincoln County School District on the central Oregon coast. She previously taught English and served as an assistant principal and principal in her district. In her current role, she is driven to strengthen the educational workforce through diversity, equity, and inclusion work with all staff in the district.

Carrie R. Giboney Wall began her career in education as a secondary math teacher before earning a degree in School Counseling along with a Pupil Personnel Services credential. She is now serving as an associate professor of teacher education at Pepperdine University in Malibu, California. She comes from a long line of educators and has worked in the field of education for the last 34 years. Her research interests include pre-service teacher learning, resilience in education, community-based learning, and trauma-informed practices.

1
THE TEACHING VOCATION AND THE INTERIOR LIVES OF TEACHERS

Ken Badley and Michelle C. Hughes

Teaching is hard work. But it is immensely rewarding work. An abundance of research on teachers' mental health, teacher burnout, and attrition in the profession has proven the truth of the first claim. And, without reading a word of academic research, teachers know the truth of the second claim: teaching is immensely rewarding work.

In this introduction, we dive into the tension between those two claims. All the chapters that follow work in this tension, and teachers work in this tension in classrooms all over the world. Teachers work and live in this tension in Alberta and California, the jurisdictions where we live. And educators in Bulgaria, Kenya, Costa Rica, and the Philippines, where we have worked with teacher colleagues, also do their day-to-day work in this tension. Our purpose and that of our contributing colleagues is to focus on one part of that tension—on what teaching gives back to teachers. While recognizing the challenges teachers face and the sacrifices teachers make, we have made it our purpose in this book to identify what we receive in return—on what we get back—from facing the challenges and making the sacrifices. In other words, in this volume, we want to focus on the reciprocities of teaching and on how joyful, resilient teachers transform challenges into opportunities.

Of course, the word "reciprocity" itself is intriguing. Its connotations range from a strictly legal and sometimes negative sense to a rather positive sense that has emerged in social psychology in recent decades. On the legal end, party A has agreed to meet one set of conditions if party B meets another set of conditions. Search "Reciprocity Treaty 1854" or 1911 online and you will find that Canada and the United States signed trade treaties long before the North American Free Trade Agreement or its successor agreements were part of the conversation. Search "Reciprocity Treaty 1875" and you will find that the United States once signed an agreement with a kingdom in the Pacific known as Hawaii. In these paradigm cases, appropriately named treaties, the two parties each took on a legal obligation to permit specified goods to cross their borders in both directions without penalty.

DOI: 10.4324/9781003124429-1

The recent use of "reciprocity" in the social sciences has a greater sense of moral obligation than did the 1854, 1875, and 1911 legal meanings of the word. In this case, nothing is signed, no documents are filed away or displayed in a museum. Some in the field go further than that, using it in the sense popularized in the feature film *Pay it Forward* (Leder, 2000). In this understanding, one does good to others not in expectation of an exchange or of getting something back but because one simply wants to contribute to the well-being of others, giving in the hope that others will likewise give.

With the range of connotations available to us, where do we categorize the reciprocities, rewards, and opportunities teaching gives teachers? Most teachers sign a contract with a school or school district and that contract specifies the professional duties which they are to carry out and what salary they will receive for the successful completion of those duties. We might consider that if the work that teachers do and the salary they receive stop there, we would have a perfect parallel to the kinds of legal and binding trade agreements the United States signed with Canada and Hawaii over a century ago. The legal contract between a teacher and a school or board of trustees does not address the matter of working weeknights after dinner, the necessity of doing class preparation or grading papers on the weekends, the worries about the success of a student who finds school challenging, or the deep questions about the teaching vocation itself. Interestingly, nor does that contract mention the joy teachers experience when their students graduate or when a student warmly greets them on the street months or years after leaving their classroom.

In short, while teachers engage with their boards and districts in a form of legal reciprocity, we usually do not think about teaching contracts as exchanges (except during a work-to-rule campaign, walkout, or other labor action). In this book, we want to recognize reciprocities, the moral and non-legal connotations, whether one is paying back or paying forward. For example, Chapter 4 examines our relationship with and use of printed and online resources, including textbooks. The two authors of that chapter have worked on many textbook projects (some of them together—and they have remained friends). Textbooks are essential resources for teachers to use in their classrooms, yet all teachers have had to make compromises with the textbooks they chose or the jurisdiction specified for them; they have had to come to terms with the weaknesses of their textbooks as well as with their students' responses to the contents of the texts and the texts' approaches to the content. Teachers might be unhappy about the treatment of a topic, about the level of critical thought demanded by the questions provided, or even about the layout. When teachers are unhappy in these ways, they compromise and supplement. They come to terms with the reality that they must use an imperfect—and possibly expensive—textbook. Chapter 4 recognizes the weaknesses inherent in textbooks (because they are produced by human beings), but it asks teachers to recognize what textbooks give back to us. Textbooks are just one example of many that the contributors to this volume believe give back to teachers. All the authors want readers to understand that we keep coming back to a single truth: yes, we compromise, sacrifice, work hard, face challenges and complexities, but we are resilient and teaching reciprocates. The challenging aspects of our work as teachers are only part of the story; teaching creates opportunities for growth and gives back to us in surprising ways.

The Context of this Book

We return to textbooks at the end of this chapter when we introduce the other chapters, noting in each case the reciprocities of the various aspects of teachers' work. Before we introduce the other chapters, however, we want to set our project in a slightly larger context: the teaching vocation. We view this volume as a contribution to the larger conversation about the calling to teach. Unlike some other issues of interest to educators—for example, the relationship between socio-economic status and school achievement—the teaching vocation conversation, while ongoing, is not robust. Most of our readers will know about Parker Palmer's distinct contributions to this conversation, especially his best-selling *The Courage to Teach* (Palmer, 1998). Some of our readers will have received as gifts various inspirational books meant to encourage teachers, such as *Chicken Soup for the Teacher's Soul: Stories to Open the Hearts and Rekindle the Spirits of Educators* (Canfield & Hansen, 2002). A few other titles focus on vocation rather than inspiration, although none of these has achieved the popularity of the two mentioned above (Fried, 1995; Friedman & Reynolds, 2011; Nieto, 2005; Spotts, 1963). We note this small body of literature because we want you to understand how we see our book fitting into and contributing to this area.

We want *Joyful Resilience in Educational Practice: Transforming Teaching Challenges into Opportunities* to encourage teachers and motivate them. We hope this book will serve as an inspirational volume that students, their parents, and teachers' friends give to teachers. Books in this genre usually include stories meant to illustrate the joys of teaching. Some include quotations meant to reinforce the importance of teachers' work. The contributors to this book regularly include stories from classrooms but these stories are not the primary focus; we want to open these stories up to discover what they mean for us and the vocation. Some of the other books mentioned above dig deeply into the meanings of the word "vocation" (from *voce*, the Latin word for "voice") and the challenges teachers face as they respond throughout their working lives to having heard a call or voice. We do some of that digging here too, although, again, this kind of analysis is not our focus.

Research into teacher burnout, disaffection, and attrition has grown in recent decades, producing a large collection of academic articles but not many books. Our volume recognizes the realities that researchers have studied but, again, the hard aspects of teaching are only our starting point; they are not our priority or our ending point. We address the challenges of teaching but we always focus on and revisit the reciprocities, the joys, the challenges and opportunities, and the professional and often personal resilience that these challenges produce. We do so with the conviction that if we can show how teaching pays us back then we can inspire teachers to keep teaching. If we achieve that, we will have met one of our goals: to inspire. We write with the conviction that if we can demonstrate how teaching fills, challenges, transforms, and rewards us, we can also help teachers understand more deeply their calling to the profession. We can help teachers believe that they were not crazy when they heard a voice or felt a nudge pushing them toward this profession. If we achieve this, we will have met one of the purposes of the aforementioned books that explore the teaching vocation in depth.

In short, we understand that as teachers we work with our own doubts, failures, and weaknesses. We also work with our strengths, successes, and, for most of us, an abiding sense of vocation. In the significant daily tasks we complete and in our interactions with students, we receive daily confirmation that we have heard a voice and that we are, in fact, called to teach. Palmer (1999) frames this voice as listening to your true self, your values and truths, as well as your limitations and potential.

In the chapters that follow, our contributors will note such sobering objective factors as the increased, nearly obsessive concern about assessment, the tightened budgets that we hear about almost daily, the increasing numbers of students in (or missing) class who are not prepared for school, or who have not eaten that day, and the increasing degree to which schools need to support the mental health of students and their families. Teachers face uncharitable and even hateful student evaluations of our courses (and, for many educators, the most negative comments get rent-free space in our heads for years afterward). Teachers also face personal and subjective challenges. Some wake up in the middle of the night, worrying about students (and some have nightmares about coming to class unprepared, or without materials, or without clothes!). Teachers recognize that at the end of a class, or at the end of a day, or at the end of a course, they could have done things better. Some teachers become deeply weary because they're tired at the end of each workday and cannot seem to find or make time for any restoration on the weekend. Teachers feel the weight of additional responsibilities that include meetings, remote learning (and technology that keeps changing), unexpected and uncontrollable challenges such as fires and floods, and, recently, even a pandemic that demanded that teachers suddenly move their programs online for over a year. We hesitate to list even the few items above but we want you, our readers, to understand that this book's contributors know all about these challenges and complexities. We all have first-hand experience in the trenches in K-12 classrooms. We get it.

For us, knowing about and living with such challenges is not the last word; we have no desire to write a book on teacher burnout and attrition. Instead, we recognize the challenges and we want to shift our thinking. We want to reframe teaching—toward the joys, opportunities, resilience, and successes that teaching produces professionally (and personally). For example, we hear from students—sometimes years later—that for them our class was life-changing, or that they learned "so much." We hear that our class was the best course they ever took. We have students express surprise and even disappointment that a session has ended, that the bell has rung, or that they were absent from yesterday's class because they were sick. They even express disappointment when we ourselves are absent due to illness or needed to serve in another role at school. Sometimes our colleagues and supervisors pass along that they have heard about the quality of our classes. These are just a few of the joys and reciprocities of teaching. We do not expect such gifts but when we recognize and receive them we feel validated for doing the work we do.

Teachers' work has negatives and positives, and teachers at all levels struggle; some throughout their entire careers come to terms with the contrast between these aspects of teaching. In *A Hidden Wholeness*, Parker Palmer (2004) helps his readers navigate the tension between these two sides of fulfilling our vocations. We see our volume specifically as a contribution to the effort he began there. We believe that if we can not only see but actually notice—take note of and somehow grasp—the reciprocities or what teaching gives back, we will be able to fulfill our vocation with greater joy than if we default in our thinking to the challenges. We have called our book *Joyful Resilience in Educational Practice: Transforming Teaching Challenges into Opportunities* because we want our readers to begin each new academic term, or semester, or year, knowing that this term, semester, or year is another opportunity to fulfill a vocation, a calling. And we gave it that title because we believe that remembering what teaching gives back to teachers will help us all grow professionally, strengthen our practice, and teach each day with less apprehension and more joy.

The Chapters that Follow

We now offer an overview of the aspects of teaching that we and our colleagues examine throughout the book. We know you can look at the Table of Contents, but we want to introduce the chapters to give brief snapshots about their respective authors. We want our readers to know that all the contributors are live educators. Individually and collectively, we have spent most of our professional lives in classrooms; in some cases, all our working lives.

We begin, appropriately, by asking about students (Chapter 2). Michelle C. Hughes comes from California and has been an educator for 32 years. She has served as a high school administrator, a junior high school teacher, and a college professor, so from a variety of angles she recognizes the significant need to support teachers. In her chapter on students, Michelle acknowledges the obvious requirement that teachers expect to give great amounts of energy to their students. She catalogues some of the reciprocities, the unexpected rewards that students give back to teachers, noting that these reciprocities are often long delayed—until after a teacher has finished teaching a student or a class. You may be interested to know that this chapter was the first any of the contributors completed for the book, perhaps reflecting both Michelle's long-term commitment to students and her enthusiasm for this project.

In Chapter 3, Joy A. Chadwick follows Michelle's treatment of students in general by noting some of the reciprocities of teaching students with special needs and other students who face challenges related to their gender, socioeconomic, cultural, or family factors. Joy is now a professor but as someone who has worked as a classroom teacher, a special education teacher, and a school principal, she knows firsthand that teaching students requires teachers to adjust and reframe their teaching methodology continually in ways not required in the past. She knows that those necessary adjustments can lead to feelings of futility and failure, yet she points to the benefits and reciprocities. She believes that the requisite reframing and rethinking can also contribute to teachers' ongoing professional development. In her view, when teachers view all children, with their myriad gifts and challenges, as their own potential teachers, each day becomes an opportunity for teacher growth. She calls on teachers to focus less on what students can and cannot do and more on how their learning needs can inform our teaching practice. For her, these gifts of teacher learning foster spaces of hope, new opportunity, and moments of success for teachers and their students.

Including Chapter 4 on learning resources and textbooks may surprise some readers; when most educators think about the challenges and complexities of teaching they typically default in their thinking toward students, parents, administrators, time pressures, and budgets. But, as we noted earlier, teachers know the imperfections of printed and online resources and they know that any given textbook rarely meets every student and teacher need. In fact, at the college and university level, those imperfections are one of the reasons there are so many textbooks addressing the same material. A professor finds the available texts unsatisfactory for a course and decides to produce a new one, presumably one that another professor up the road will, in turn, deem to be imperfect. Ken Badley has worked with several publishers on junior high, secondary, and university textbooks. He has worked with Dana Antayá-Moore on student resources and teacher resource guides, and she has worked on several others. They have personal knowledge of the challenges of developing resources that will engage students well, support teachers' work, and meet the curricular requirements for the jurisdiction that has contracted with the publisher. Both authors recognize what resources demand from teachers; they focus on what such resources give back to teachers and what new teaching opportunities emerge from them. In doing so, they write both as classroom teachers and as textbook authors.

Higher educators and K-12 educators regularly need to deal with new curricula, new instructional initiatives, new forms of assessment, new educational trends, new buzzwords, new school and district policies, changing demographic trends among students, and so on (this list *is* exhausting). In our better moments as educators we know these changes help us keep our brains alive. But such changes also have the potential to wear us down, and may even produce cynicism. In Chapter 5, Sunshine R. Sullivan examines curriculum changes. As a classroom teacher and now the chair of an education program, she knows that educators swim in water where the currents are always changing. Intellectual currents shift and societies evolve. Educational stakeholders identify new concerns, forcing curricular change. Students' attitudes change along with those of society. Hence, teachers must change and adapt. Such adaptations, while they usually involve work, are not always negative. Sunshine argues that teachers who embrace change rather than avoid it stand to benefit. They are resilient. When they commit to adaptation, they grow intellectually, essentially as artists who teach, and they increase the likelihood that they will remain professionally vital throughout their careers. In short, change entails work, but adapting to change is transformative; teachers who embrace change receive more than they might ever expect.

The theme of shifting intellectual currents continues in Chapter 6, where Paige A. Ray identifies a strong link between theory and practice. Indeed, she believes that there is nothing more practical than a good theory. Think about that for a moment. Instead of theory being nonsense produced by out-of-touch people at the university or at the Department of Education, what if it is an attempt to understand and explain something that is happening in practice? Maybe the car won't start because of X. Maybe the roses won't grow because the soil lacks Y. Maybe these students have difficulty reading because of their home environment or because the reading approach I've been using doesn't take Z into account. All of these examples represent theorizing at its best. Paige has taught both secondary and college English, and she knows about the demands that are regularly placed on teachers because of new theories and new attempts to understand teaching and learning, yet she argues that embracing theory—and seeing the recursive links between theory and practice—pays back teachers.

Chapter 7 focuses on colleagues. Every teacher would love to have perfect colleagues. Except in Utopia, no teacher does. Teachers know, given enough meetings, emails, and lunch breaks, our colleagues—likely the ones with the sharpest elbows—will rub off some of our corners. However, if we keep our eyes and ears open, we can gain untold wisdom from those colleagues. The contributors to this volume—and, we suspect, all our readers—have had many colleagues who supported our work, told us to keep going, gave us ideas and teaching materials, and shared our professional and perhaps personal joys and sorrows. We have also had some colleagues we wished taught somewhere else, in a galaxy far, far away. Tiana Tucker, who has worked as a teacher, an assistant principal, a principal, and a human resources director, knows many of the joys and sorrows that colleagues can bring teachers' way. She reminds us of our colleagues' gifts and calls on us to value them, support them, and allow them to support us.

In Chapter 8, which may be seen as a counterpart to Chapter 7, Jay Mathisen argues that teachers' supervisors also offer them great gifts. Only teachers who run their own single-teacher schools enjoy the luxury of not reporting to a supervisor (and even they report to parents and, in a sense, students). The rest of us in the teaching profession have to report to supervisors. (And, yes, we can all think of a supervisor who we wish would seek employment elsewhere.) Jay has taught for many years and has reported to supervisors who ranged from great to not-so-great. This long and rich experience inevitably shapes his perspective. Jay argues that teachers who come to terms with their supervisors and the institutions in which they have found themselves have much to gain; they too can find opportunities to experience resilience and to grow professionally.

Many teachers chose the profession because of their own teachers. Andrew Mullen wrote Chapter 9 as a kind of thank-you letter to teachers' teachers in recognition of the fact that our own teachers gave and continue to give to us. He notes how the models of teaching we are exposed to at every stage of our development affect us powerfully, at both conscious and subconscious levels. Our own teachers and mentors may serve as models—or, at times, as counter-models—in our ongoing journey of professional self-definition. Andrew argues that cultivating awareness of the ways our own teachers and mentors have shaped us is essential as this liberates us from any subconscious tendency to emulate those mentors in new contexts that may call for different pedagogies. His chapter explores his life-long efforts—as both a K-12 teacher and a university professor—to capitalize on the modeling he witnessed with effective (and sometimes less effective) educators. He draws attention to specific applications of his own and others' practices and dispositions, and highlights the need for discernment in attempting to re-create—across cultural and generational boundaries—what might have been effective in our own education.

In Chapter 10, Michelle C. Hughes and Ken Badley address the issue of families and how we connect with our students' home environments. A school is traditionally a venue that hosts students, yet what happens when families tell teachers and principals they know a better way to run a school or classroom? What happens when members of students' families call teachers idiots for choosing the path we did in this or that situation? Michelle and Ken recognize the hard moments and conversations (and even the rants) but move quickly and steadily toward the reciprocities, to the families that ask, "How can we help?" or "How can my family serve your school community?" or "What do you need, what can we can do, what can we give?" They explore several stories where families and schools became partners, fostering community and helping pay it forward. The relationships between teachers, schools, and families will often be challenging, yet they can produce rich benefits—and strengthen a teacher's backbone.

At the start of this chapter, we acknowledged that teaching is hard work. We also noted that teachers face myriad challenges, complexities, and disappointments on their vocational journeys. In Chapter 11, Carrie R. Giboney Wall addresses these difficult—and sometimes intimidating—aspects of teaching. In her view, teaching is a multifaceted, dilemma-ridden journey that forces educators to ask questions with complicated answers. Clashes between expectations and reality seep into all aspects of the teaching process, fueling emotional dissonance, cognitive dissonance, contextual dissonance, and identity dissonance. Though educators' first responses may be to avoid dissonance, Carrie suggests cognitive disequilibrium can be a catalyst for healthy educator development by challenging assumptions, promoting deep learning, and igniting transformational change. From the perspective of someone with many years in both K-12 and university classrooms, she argues that reciprocities may be found in these harsher aspects of the amazing—and sometimes amazingly difficult—vocation called teaching.

In his 1762 book *Émile*, Rousseau pictured a "school" with one teacher (really a tutor) and one wealthy, engaged, rather self-directed student. Check the catalogue in your local library to see if *Émile* is shelved in Philosophy of Education or Fiction. We think of it as a work of fiction. In the real world of education, schools invariably operate in political and financial contexts. And most educators exercise their vocations in institutional settings. To be rather blunt, departments of education, school boards, and schools tell teachers what to do. In Chapter 12, Dana

Antayá-Moore and Joanne Neal, both experienced public servants from the Department of Education in Alberta, Canada, address these contextual realities. They begin by noting that government departments of education and school board offices are not usually populated by evil bureaucrats who devise new regulations simply to make life difficult for teachers and students. Almost always, these individuals have teachers' and students' best interests at heart, and they go to work each day wanting to support teaching and learning. Nevertheless, budget constraints are real, and the concern for accountability is legitimate. Teachers must come to terms with the reality that, at this point in history, accountability has become an obsession, expressed largely through expanded programs of standardized assessment. Dana and Joanne conclude that constant assessment and new levels of accountability have the potential to give back to teachers (as unlikely as that conclusion may seem to some contemporary educators). They survey strategies that several creative educators have used to meet institutional expectations while remaining true to their own educational missions.

Many teachers serve throughout their careers without even changing buildings; many others teach in several schools, perhaps in different jurisdictions, or even in different countries. In Chapter 13, April E. Jarvis and Daniel H. Jarvis draw on their experience teaching in several settings to explore teacher–student reciprocities in a number of educational contexts. Both Daniel and April have taught in an international K-12 school setting, in Chiang Mai, Thailand, and they have supervised a home-schooling program for their five daughters. Daniel has also taught in a public secondary school for five years, and in a university context as a teacher-educator for 18 years. Based on research and personal observations, this chapter specifically focuses on comparing public school, home school, and international school contexts, all in relation to the overall teacher–student experience. April and Daniel identify some of the perceptions of and misconceptions about the challenges and rewards of teaching in multiple settings and conclude that the challenges bring their own joyful opportunities.

In Chapter 14, Michelle C. Hughes and Ken Badley conclude that teaching pays teachers (and, yes, we know about the website with a similar name). We revisit the concession we made at the start of this chapter—that teaching is hard, challenging work—but then argue that its reciprocities make it worthwhile and keep us and countless other teachers in the profession. Yes, it is one of the most demanding professions on earth. Notwithstanding those demands, we believe—and know many of our readers also believe—that it is one of the most rewarding professions. Our goal is to remind our teaching colleagues of the reciprocities, the rewards, the unexpected paybacks. In essence, we offer this book as a love letter—a "hang in there, you've got this" message—to our teaching colleagues everywhere. We offer Chapter 14 as our signature to that love letter.

Because we want you to enjoy teaching with full confidence that it is your calling, we invite you to read, wrestle with, and find joyful resilience in the professional challenges outlined in this book. Thank you for reading this far. We hope you will enjoy and take courage from all that follows.

References

Canfield, J. & Hansen, M. V. (2002). *Chicken soup for the teacher's soul: Stories to open the hearts and rekindle the spirits of educators.* Health Communications.
Fried, R. L. (1995). *The passionate teacher.* Beacon.
Friedman, A. A. & Reynolds, L. (Eds.) (2011). *Burned in: Fueling the fire to teach.* Teachers College Press.
Leder, M. (Director) (2000). *Pay it forward.* Warner.
Nieto, S. (Ed.) (2005). *Why we teach.* Teachers College Press.
Palmer, P. (1998). *The courage to teach.* Jossey-Bass.
Palmer, P. (1999). *Let your life speak: Listening to the voice of vocation.* Jossey-Bass.
Palmer, P. (2004). *A hidden wholeness.* Jossey-Bass.
Spotts, C. D. (1963). *Called to teach.* United Church Press.

2
RECIPROCITIES WITH STUDENTS

Michelle C. Hughes

Teaching is traditionally regarded as a profession where trained professionals give of themselves and their expertise to cultivate young minds. Teachers are the translators of knowledge, content, and example; students are the recipients. Teachers invest wholeheartedly in their students hoping for a noble return or acknowledgment that students will give back and contribute to society in meaningful ways. Because teaching remains a complex interpersonal activity (Hargreaves, 2000; Hill-Jackson, Hartlep & Stafford, 2019; France, 2019), the significance of the teacher–student relationship brings a unique facet to classroom life that benefits not only the student, but the teacher.

Years ago, I began using the phrase "teaching is about the business of students." Teaching begins with relationships, and fostering connections between teachers and students is essential. Sir Ken Robinson once proclaimed that education must be recognized as a human business (*Education Week*, 2015). Similarly, Parker Palmer (1983) has consistently recognized that relationships are two-way. He writes of relationship as a kind of mutuality. He suggests that teachers not only know but must allow themselves to be known, noting that true relationships are richer when those involved allow and invite mutual exchange and accountability. Although teaching is typically viewed as a profession where knowledge is given from the teacher and by the teacher, when a teacher sets foot in a classroom, she quickly realizes that teaching is reciprocal. At its best, teaching requires active participation and exchange by both teacher and student (Palmer, 1983; Sanger & Osguthorpe, 2013; Schwartz, 2016).

Reciprocity connotes mutual relationship, corresponding, or complementing. Throughout my 32-year career in education I have often wondered about the reciprocal nature of teaching and why teachers do not take more time to recognize and reflect on the hidden treasures in the mutual teacher–student relationship. As a former junior high teacher and high school administrator, and presently as a faculty member in a pre-service program, I have heard teachers say, "I learn from my students" or "The students are why

DOI: 10.4324/9781003124429-2

I teach." Ironically, educators are not often prompted to recognize and acknowledge the unspoken gifts revealed in daily classroom life. Consequently, my goal for this chapter is to explore the unexpected and often surprising reciprocities that students impart to teachers. Using a combination of research, personal stories, and anecdotal evidence, I will unpack and name four themes or rewards that shine a light on the mutual relationship between teacher and student.

To frame the chapter, I need to point out that teachers are human; teachers are relational and interpersonal. Davis (2006) concluded that teaching remains an interpersonal activity. He examined relationships between students and teachers, noting that influences such as students' beliefs about teachers, motivation, and social behaviors all shape relationship quality in the classroom, and pointed to the importance of the social-emotional component that links student and teacher interactions. He suggested that balance is needed in a good relationship and that this includes components such as support, attention to academics, and even conflict. This conclusion reinforced earlier research (Johnson & Miller, 1993) that identified the complexities of the teacher–student relationship. Teachers' acceptance of students and student attraction—or pull toward a particular teacher—were identified by these authors as essential ingredients in positive classroom relationships. France (2019) recently affirmed that investing in a teacher's humanity makes learning more personal and sustainable, strengthening the idea that building students' interpersonal skills through social-emotional learning validates the unique nature of the teacher–student relationship (Kress & Elias, 2020; Weissberg & Cascarino, 2013).

Additional research promotes cultivating positive teacher–student relationships as the most important factor in fostering the right climate for learning, offering practical ways to foster teacher–student relationships, and recognizing that how a teacher responds to students in both positive and negative contexts is critical (Pigford, 2001). Teachers can honor the significance of this relationship by consciously investing in the teacher–student relationship. Research suggests that if teachers choose to embrace the relational complexities along with the ethical responsibilities of teaching, they can foster student development (Fallona & Canniff, 2013; Sanger & Osguthorpe, 2013). Another perspective includes framing a teacher's role as that of moral companion (Wineberg, 2004), and yet another recognizes that teaching is both a moral endeavor and a relational practice that requires response and responsiveness (Stengel, 2013). Because students are social beings, the feeling of belonging in the classroom leads to greater connectedness as well as to positive learning outcomes (Nichols, 2006; Zins, Weissberg, Wang, & Walberg, 2004).

Most teachers, myself included, typically recognize that the relational aspect of teaching remains central to the profession. Before content, standards, syllabi, and instruction can even begin to take shape, teacher–student relationships need to be prioritized, pursued, and valued. The popular phrase "Students don't care what you [a teacher] say about content until we know that you care about us, the students" rings true with this perspective.

Having worked with pre-service teachers for over a decade, I feel a significant burden to prioritize cultivating the student–teacher relationship. This means getting to know students, implementing team-building activities to create safe spaces for learning, listening to students, providing routines and structures, and valuing students' opinions. Colleagues I have interacted with through the years have modeled these and countless other approaches that cultivate connection with students, not only inside the four classroom walls, but most recently on Zoom, as well as outside the classroom at sporting events, school plays, exhibitions, and concerts. These efforts are foundational to cultivating trust, respect, and care between a student and a teacher; they reveal genuine benefits that produce motivated, engaged, and academically successful students. Furthermore, Dweck's (2006) research on growth mindset reveals that mistake-making and risk-taking in the classroom can develop grit and foster teacher–student relationships.

Building on this notion that relationships are a classroom prerequisite, I will explore the unexpected gifts and rewards that teachers uncover in their relational work with students.

Reward 1: Recognizing a Teacher's Ability to Laugh at Herself

Humor has been long recognized as one of the methods through which teachers embrace the profession and then sustain career longevity. It can help a new teacher stay afloat, bolster a veteran teacher on difficult days, and increase satisfaction during what sometimes feels like the monotonous ebb and flow of the school year.

From my classroom experience, I can testify that humor often elicits a student response in the form of a smile, small giggle, or deep belly laugh. Humor and laughter are not only good for a person's health but can raise spirits and play a role in building relationships. When a teacher laughs, students often laugh in response. Classroom humor and laughter can cultivate joy and positive space for students to learn and grow (Hughes, 2018). Tomlinson (2015a) intentionally shares funny and happy stories to encourage student laughter. Such stories create memories and a shared experience; the subsequent laughter can serve as an important indicator of a positive classroom community. Humor can also be a means by which students and teachers cultivate connections with each other. Davis (2006) concluded from her research that, while students appreciate and identify humor as a way to gain interest in academic study, teachers appreciate students who use humor in positive ways. Others have found that students prefer teachers who can laugh with them and make them laugh (Silver, Berckemeyer, & Baenen, 2015). Hence, humor is an important conduit for relationships and connections in the classroom. Other researchers have concluded that students enjoy classroom playfulness, which simultaneously helps build teachers' positive attitudes toward their own teaching and classroom work. (Sherman, 2013; Silver et al., 2015). Good-spirited and inclusive humor can lighten a student's spirits as well as remind a classroom community of some of the incongruities in life. Evans-Palmer (2016) concluded that humor builds resilience, noting that dispositions that are linked with humor lead to greater teacher self-efficacy and that teachers' and students' collective laughter helps build relationships and positive classroom culture.

Ziv (1988) recommended employing humor in teacher-training programs. He suggested that teachers should choose the type of humor that best serves their teaching objectives and argued that spontaneous humor enhances the climate for teaching. Another scholar went so far as to encourage "humorless" teachers to leave the profession if they found themselves unable to embrace the complexity, spontaneity, and inconsistencies of the classroom (Hall, 1969). Wandersee (1982) affirmed that wisely used humor enhanced classroom learning and identified two distinct categories: spontaneous and prepared. He found that either type could motivate a student's curiosity and desire to explore a new facet of content, but added the caution that poorly deployed humor can undermine or even derail a lesson. Other researchers have identified practical ways to introduce joy and humor into the classroom (e.g., Minchew, 2001). Minchew cautions that humor should not be used solely as entertainment; it must remain a means to engage students and hook them into learning.

Humor can give a teacher permission to take a deeper look at herself. Using humor and laughter in the classroom may give students a unique opportunity to observe their teacher in a different light. One of my personal experiences underscores this idea. In my first year of teaching junior high school, I enthusiastically stood at my classroom door and greeted the students. One morning, as I high-fived and welcomed the class, a quirky seventh-grader called John[1] skirted into the classroom and handed me a note. I opened the note and was immediately embarrassed to read, "Will you kiss me after class? Will you French kiss me after class?" I blushed instantly and struggled to keep my jaw from dropping to the ground. I was first uncomfortable and then overwhelmed because John had clearly crossed a professional line.

Looking back on this incident, I am amazed at the mileage I have managed to extract from it. I have told, embellished, and retold this story on countless occasions. I may not have found it funny at the time, but it has become progressively funnier over time and now forms part of my teaching repertoire that I always share with a smile. Reflecting on the humor of this interaction gives me permission to laugh at myself as well as take a step back and gain a new perspective. The day after John gave me his note, the school counselor and I met with him to inquire about his intentions and explain the inappropriateness of his message. The memory of this humorous incident serves as a continual professional reminder not to take myself too seriously. The encounter nudged me to grasp and embrace the humorous moments that teaching presents. I will continue to relate the story, listen for the deep belly laughs among my audience, and share this early career lesson with a smile.

Most teachers, like me, have discovered the need for a professional sense of humor in the classroom. Humor helps foster rapport between students and teachers. It enables students and teachers to develop connections, build rapport, and even meet learning goals (Davis, 2006). One researcher (Cornett, 1986) advocated using humor as an instructional resource, listing a number of ways in which it can stimulate creative and critical thinking. She described humor as a three-step process—arousal, problem-solving, and resolution—that serves to enlarge an individual's perspective, motivate, improve health, enhance communication, energize, and foster reciprocal relationships between teachers and students. On the other hand, she warned that, although humor is widely used in social situations, it can be dangerous and become a distraction. Evans-Palmer (2016) echoed Cornett's argument when recommending the use of humor in teacher training to increase self-efficacy and career longevity. Connections grow between student and teacher when learning is maximized with humor and fun, and students flourish as a result (Wormeli, 2019).

Humor in the teacher–student relationship leads me next to unpack the idea that this relationship can widen a teacher's lens.

Reward 2: A Teacher's Efforts to Stretch, Reflect, and Look Within

Over several decades, educational activist and author Parker Palmer has encouraged educators to engage in inner work within community. He has consistently suggested that examining the self and the inner life are vital for the developing professional (Parker, 1983; 2000; 2004). He has also emphasized the need for mentors to ask probing questions that allow their fellow professionals to develop self-awareness and self-understanding. He has encouraged professionals to tell stories that name the good, the bad, and the ugly throughout their careers in order to foster the awareness that is needed for long-term teaching. Farrell (2014) extended these ideas and encouraged open-mindedness by asking teachers to listen to students and receive their input with an open mind and heart. Stated more simply, intentional listening is a critical pathway to hearing others' stories and, most significantly, to hearing a student's story. On these accounts, hearing others' stories requires a willingness not only to reflect but also to take action. Aguilar's (2018) recent writings encourage teachers to cultivate habits and dispositions to build resilience. She urges teachers to uncover and understand their emotions for building a classroom community. That is, knowing and sharing ourselves as teachers helps us know our students.

Teachers listen intently as they answer questions, observe students, and instruct thoughtfully. Developing open-mindedness and a desire to listen is a crucial aspect of successful teaching. Skilled teachers go so far as to lean in physically to listen to individual students, even when they are presenting a lesson on Zoom. Researchers affirm that listening intently leads to enhanced and deeper relationships between students and teachers (Dearborn, 2015; Schwartz, 2016). I experienced this first hand on my college campus a few years ago. Nancy, a first-generation college student, and I met to get to know each other over lunch. During the meal, I asked her to tell me about her family and education. When she disclosed the details of her story, I laughed and cried along with her. As the first person in her family to attend college, she was sincerely grateful that her parents had sought a better life for her and that she had received generous financial support for her undergraduate education from college donors. She was fully embracing college life and truly appreciated the opportunity. That afternoon, I sent Nancy an email to thank her for her time and trust; I was honored that she had trusted me and agreed to share her story with me. She replied, "Thank you for caring to get to know me."

Reflecting on this now, I realize that our lunchtime conversation provided essential space for Nancy to feel heard and seen. Additionally, the exchange reminded me of the value of investing in relationships with my students. Currently, as teachers all over the globe engage in dialogue with students regarding the Black Lives Matter movement, mental health concerns, and the lack of contact in remote learning environments, a teacher's ability to listen has become more important than ever. Brown's (2012; 2018) research on leadership, courage, and vulnerability underscores the need for teachers to demonstrate vulnerability, self-awareness, and a desire for the kind of personal growth that fosters professional growth.

Nancy's story broadened my perspective. Since meeting her, I have leaned in closer and tried to listen more carefully to my students and colleagues. Similarly, a friend of mine—Jessica—told me about an experience with one of her students. As a novice high school teacher, she wrestled with her school's attendance policy. One student in particular ignited professional tension within her after missing ten consecutive days of school. Jessica contemplated giving the student all zeros or a failing grade, as the school's regulations stipulated. Feeling conflicted, she looked within, reflected, and asked: "Am I going to give you [the student] zeros on all the stuff you have missed and can't make up? Or am I going to bestow compassion on you and choose to praise you whenever you walk through the door?" She chose the latter option after becoming deeply convinced that one of her roles as a teacher was to show genuine care for her students. She recognized the need to commend the student for the things she had done well.

Unexpectedly, Jessica's encounter prompted her to reflect on her role as a professional. She chose to dig deep within herself and was able to offer a greater deal of empathy and compassion to her student. She told me that she acquired a new lens through which to view the student's attendance record and personal story. This new perspective overshadowed school policy, and required Jessica to listen and reflect on her student's needs and struggles. By doing so, she was able to shift her response (Hughes, 2014).

Similarly, when I made a career change from K-12 to higher education, I questioned how I could connect my career in K-12 public education to the scholarly environment of a private liberal arts college. I wondered about the impact I could have in this new professional setting. As I pondered these and other questions, Shelly arrived in my office and passionately told me about her roommate, who was in a state of deep depression. I listened attentively, discussed the next steps Shelly might take, and helped her create an action plan. This unexpected visit to my office validated my role as a teacher, even though I was new to higher education (Hughes, 2015).

While reflecting on Shelly's visit, I realized that students need teachers to serve as both educators and mentors. Students like Shelly need teachers to engage with their joy and their pain. I often recall our conversation and am struck by the teachable moment that reminded me to listen, care for, love, and guide my students through the twists and turns of academia and life in general. Every teacher can choose to lean in, listen, and broaden their perspective. When teachers ask questions of students and themselves, they may be prompted to think differently and reflect on their own interests, actions, and concerns.

The incidents outlined above are from my own experience, but they typify the interactions most teachers have with their students. Such experiences demonstrate that teaching is emotional, intellectual, and courageous work (Day, 2004). Teaching—specifically passionate teaching—is vital. Teachers commit to and care for their students, and they are often sustained by a sense of moral purpose in their work. As countless authors have noted, both in this volume and elsewhere, many teachers choose to teach in the hope of influencing others. They repeatedly make students feel important. They inspire and believe in their students, and go the extra mile for them (Day, 2004). One eighth-grade teacher assured her graduating students of this when encouraging them to get to know their teachers in high school. In a letter of advice, she stated: "[W]e [teachers] actually like when students share their private lives with us. Most of us also like to share our lives with you. It is those people [students] who come in to talk with me because they want to, not because they have to, who I will stay close to" (Holst, 2015: p. 34).

Building on the reciprocal nature of the teacher–student relationship, it is essential to note that there is a basic need for what some researchers call 'relatedness' in every relationship (Spilt, Koomen, & Thijs, 2011). Noddings (1984) first examined and identified this type of connection as an ethic of care. Highlighting care for the other, she validated the significance of the caring exchange. In her account, teaching requires teachers to view their work through a caring lens. When they take the time to invest in, learn about, and listen to their students, they reap substantial dividends, including internal satisfaction and even joy for their efforts. Likewise, when students feel cared for, their motivation, engagement, and achievement improve (Schat, 2020).

This second reward—this reciprocal benefit—affirms the notable work teachers do and reminds them of the reasons why they chose the profession in the first place. Such reciprocities, identified in the teacher–student relationship, lead directly to the third reward: improved classroom practice.

Reward 3: Shifting Perspective to Improve Classroom Practice

Students watch teachers. Students hold teachers accountable as they observe, learn, engage with, and even when they call out teachers about something that causes tension in their thinking or if they perceive something to be incorrect. Ask any teacher and they will tell you, "Students remember teachers and they find us!"

Over the years, I have had the pleasure—and sometimes the surprise—of former students appearing in unexpected places. When this happens, they remind me of what they read and wrote in my class or of how I performed as a teacher. They find me—and probably you—in the grocery store. They stop us. And even when we cannot recall their names, they remember ours. Students I run into tell me about the impact—either good or bad—that I had on their lives. They rehash the stories, the lessons, and even the detentions and time-outs I assigned.

My husband, Chris, regularly finds unexpected messages on his phone and Facebook page from past students who have taken the time to thank him for the impact he has had on their lives as a physical education teacher and coach. A few years ago, he stumbled across another unexpected tribute in a high school yearbook. Three volleyball players were asked who they look up to in professional volleyball. Two of the three named Olympic legends, but the third named Chris. This surprising recognition was an unexpected and joyful dividend. Throughout his career, Chris has demonstrated his passion for teaching, kids, and coaching, yet he does not teach and coach to be recognized or honored. When I asked him about the yearbook, he replied, "I love the surprise recognition, but I was just doing my job. I am happy I made a positive impression and became a role model for my players."

Most teachers can relate to Chris's story and I am reminded of a treasured impromptu visit I had with one of my former junior high school students. Years ago, Nicole stopped by my office when I was serving as a high school administrator. She was by then a college graduate and was working as a substitute teacher at my school. She entered my office with a smile, sat down, and enthusiastically presented me with a homemade certificate of merit. It read, "I went into teaching because of you!" She proceeded to tell me that, as a student in one of my first English classes, she had loved my clothes, shoes, and demeanor, and that I had inspired her to become a teacher. I chuckle when I think of that moment, especially as the details she remembered most had nothing to do with my teaching, lessons, or the fact that I had passed on a love for literature.

Years later, as I reflected on that conversation, I boldly decided to call Nicole and ask her what I had done to make such an impact on her. I was curious to see if only my shoes and clothes had made all the difference. To my surprise, we had a lengthy conversation during which she explained that she had given me the certificate at a time when she was questioning whether she should continue her own teaching career:

> I seized the moment and chose to reach out to you and two other people that inspired me. Giving the award, at that particular time, was a way to honor and express the difference that you had made in my life and career. I wanted you to know that I carried you with me. When I was in seventh grade, you were the person I wanted to be like. Even as I continue to see you in my life as our paths continue to cross, your professional presence made and makes a difference. I was grateful to have you as an appropriate role model who shared my interest in literature and writing.

That phone call with Nicole was a delayed gift that brought me joy and an unexpected professional reward. I was a grateful beneficiary. It is worth noting that we have continued to cross paths professionally over the years: Nicole served as director of the high school program that my daughter attended. Her unexpected presence in my daughter's life was an additional gift that further endorsed the unique reciprocal relationship between teacher and student. I can personally testify that the surprising mutual exchanges between the two are both satisfying and soul-filling.

Here, I am reminded of another student's interaction with one of her teachers. Sally told me that during her senior year of high school, her English teacher, Mr. Ramirez, was so inspired by his students that he gave a graduation speech in which he thanked them and listed what they had taught him as a professional. I was captivated by this story and enlisted Sally's help to track down Mr. Ramirez. We spoke over the phone about his speech, his relationship with his students, and what he had learned from them. During this conversation, Mr. Ramirez enthusiastically declared, "What drives, energizes, and sustains teachers like me is the natural back and forth with students. I don't know that there is any other way to be."

He then recalled an occasion when Sally was late to class. He was frustrated and confronted Sally in front of the rest of the class about her tardiness. Sally tried to explain why she was late, but Mr. Ramirez chose not to listen and continued with the lesson. After class, Sally boldly told Mr. Ramirez that he had been rude and disrespectful because he had intentionally chosen not to listen to her. Perhaps surprisingly, Mr. Ramirez humbly admitted that Sally did indeed have a legitimate reason for her tardiness. He explained to me: "She got me thinking about who I was not listening to. Was I listening to my students? Was I listening to my own kids at home?" He continued, "I am a better parent and teacher now because I listened to, was challenged by, and reflected on what Sally had to say."

Sally's courageous response to Mr. Ramirez became "a stand-out moment" for him. He elaborated:

> I am grateful Sally took the time to stand up to me and do it appropriately. She was right. As a result, that particular year, I gave the high school's commencement speech. In my speech, I highlighted Sally and two other students who had clearly taught me about myself, my relationships with students, and even my relationships with my own children. Sally's actions have since encouraged me to build more listening strategies into the structure of my classroom. Furthermore, the exchanges with Sally pushed me to seek new ways to listen and care for my students.

Teachers like Mr. Ramirez who are prepared to invest in relationships demonstrate a genuine openness to learning from their students. Mr. Ramirez modeled working alongside students as co-learners and mutual participants, further substantiating the view that student–teacher exchanges can lead to improved professional practice for the teacher. His willingness to listen, reflect, and adjust his perspective confirms the notion that good teacher–student relationships produce powerful benefits. In addition, his "stand-out moment" with Sally validates the claim "I teach students, not subjects," suggesting that teachers derive meaning from their interactions with students and that those interactions affect a teacher's decision-making about content and instruction in the classroom (Moje, 1996). Moreover, it illustrates that candid teacher–student exchanges can alter teachers' perspectives, with a consequent positive effect on their decision-making and their approach to teaching and students. Steeg Thornhill and Badley (2021: p. 84) claim that teachers' decisions to change during a lesson or plan can produce "pedagogical fruit"—what Csikszentmihalyi (1990) calls "flow." Following van Manen (2016), they use the term "tact" to refer to the kind of understanding or ability to decide in the moment what is needed to support student learning.

Although all of these examples relate to secondary students (as that is where most of my personal experience lies), teachers have an impact on students of all ages—from pre-K through college—and their students give back to them, too. My mother and friends who taught elementary school have shared some of their ups and downs and unexpected rewards—found in a holiday card, a chance meeting at the grocery store, or a surprise note in the mail. The relational work is significant between teachers and students of all ages, yet is foundational to student development and socialization in the early years of school (Bohlin, Durwin, & Reese-Weber, 2018).

Teachers like Mr. Ramirez do not always see immediate results from the seeds that are planted in daily teacher–student exchanges in the classroom; they do not always see the fruits of their labor or realize the impact they have had. Students finish a school year and move on to the next grade, the next teacher, the next classroom; they attend another school, graduate, head off to college or work. They forge careers, start families, sometimes move away. Yet, when the unexpected meeting, delayed gift, or surprise note arrives, their teachers are instantly reminded of the honorable work they did—and continue to do—in the classroom.

One contemporary educator highlights the connection and impact of reciprocal exchanges on classroom climate, affirming the practice of standing at the classroom door and greeting students each day (Anderson, 2015: p. 33). "It doesn't really matter to them [students] that I teach them about the formula for experimental probability—they just want to know that someone is truly interested in them and their lives." Thus, the simple daily practice of standing at the door to greet students can produce powerful benefits that help build long-term relationships with those students. It can also give the teacher greater motivation and energy. Caring for students includes adapting our thinking to their needs, even though this can be both humbling and difficult (Tomlinson, 2015b).

Just as the reciprocal teacher–student relationship (the third reward) can shift a teacher's perspective, mutual exchanges can prompt her to revisit her decision to teach, which, in itself, can be another reward.

Reward 4: Revisiting the Decision to Teach

Teachers often embrace the profession and choose to teach in hopes of making a positive contribution to the lives of others; such educators are intrinsically motivated and eager to pour into their students (Ryan, Cooper, & Bolick, 2016). Other teachers choose to teach because of their love for a particular discipline, love for the teacher's lifestyle, or love for students. Hence, while teaching is almost always considered a calling or a vocation, this can take several different forms. Palmer (2000: p. 2) traces the etymology of "vocation" to the Latin word for voice and suggests, "When I do not know myself, I cannot know who my students are." He also links vocation to self and service (Palmer, 2000: p. 16): some individuals may connect the notion to a calling or career path in which they are inspired to become, for example, lawyers, teachers, or doctors; others may think of it as a spiritual response to an invitation from a higher power.

Choosing to teach is ultimately a decision to walk alongside and equip children in their learning (Badley & Van Brummelen, 2012). Many aspiring professionals choose to teach because they want to impart knowledge, serve students, and make an impact. Some enter the profession with a strong sense of vocation and service; their commitment to see students grow often serves as sufficient motivation to do the work (Day & Gu, 2007). Other novice educators may choose to teach in the hope of changing the system or because they possess a desire to "save" or "fix" students.

The rewards may be insufficient to keep some teachers in the profession; but for many others, they remain a driving force to continue. Research has shown that a large number of teachers leave the profession within the first five years (Cruickshank & MacDonald, 2018), but also that they are much more likely to remain if they are given the necessary professional support (Martin, 2012; McCoy and Mashburn, 2017). Therefore, finding the space and time to reflect on and name teaching's reciprocal rewards can help maintain a teacher's career. Goodwin (2019) suggests that teachers do not leave their students; they leave unproductive school communities. He argues that overwhelming workloads, classroom management struggles, and unsupportive school cultures mean that new teachers need more training to engage in better relationships and more contact with students. As already noted, some teachers are inspired to teach because they see the profession as a moral practice (Day 2004; Sanger & Osguthorpe, 2013; Santoro, 2011). This viewpoint suggests that individuals enter the teaching profession because they believe it is significant: they want to serve and contribute to the moral development of students. Many educators possess an intrinsic desire and moral responsibility to invest in their work for their students. They choose to invest in their students' futures in the hope that those students will give back to society and make positive contributions to humanity (Taulbert, 2006). Moral rewards can provide intrinsic motivation that can validate a teacher's calling as well as enhance and sustain her career (Murrell, Diez, Feiman-Nemser, & Schussler, 2010; Santoro, 2011).

Initially, a new teacher may take time to ponder and consider her future or long-term influence. By doing so, she may discover untapped rewards and wisdom in the relational facet of teaching that can fuel her career. Some research suggests that relationship building is life changing; hence, teachers should pay significant attention to relationships (Silver *et al.*, 2015). If students energize teachers, then investing in relationships with students will surely serve as a major contributor to career satisfaction. Moreover, some researchers note the need for teachers to sustain a commitment to life-long learning throughout their careers. Of course, this commitment may be deeply dependent on the school environment and professional development opportunities. The kind of support teachers receive can have considerable positive or negative effects (Day & Gu, 2007).

From March 2020, in the United States and across much of the globe, the coronavirus pandemic demanded a historic pivot to remote learning for teachers and students. Although this was new territory for all involved, teachers were quickly reminded of the power of the relationships they had already established with students. For many, these relationships enabled them to continue teaching through the complex challenges created by the pandemic and remote learning. Because trust and relationships had already been formed, such teachers had one less hurdle to negotiate when the pandemic arrived.

It is important to note that some teacher–student exchanges can challenge even the most seasoned teacher to examine why she chose teaching in the first place. Teachers typically embrace the profession and make an unspoken promise and commitment to shape students into learners and thinkers. Creating a relational culture encourages relationship-building to be taught and practiced so that learning content and critical thinking can flourish (Silver et al., 2015). In particular, when teachers foster relationships with attention and intention, they share who they are with their students and give those students a chance to use their personal voices and express their opinions. Students often work harder for teachers with whom they maintain a good relationship; in turn, raising students' expectations can be a prime source of motivation for teachers (Davis, 2006). This underscores the need to identify the benefits of mutual exchanges between students and teachers.

Four Rewards ... So What's Next?

This chapter has identified four significant professional rewards that produce joy in teachers: the first recognizes a teacher's ability to laugh at herself; the second and third encourage a teacher to stretch, reflect, and shift perspective to improve classroom practice; and finally, a teacher needs to revisit her decision to teach. In a complex and ever-changing educational landscape, it is necessary—and surprisingly invigorating—for teachers to examine the heartfelt interpersonal exchanges and discoveries that are inherent in teacher–student relationships. It is my hope that this discussion of four of the reciprocities that are found in such relationships will serve to encourage all educators who are in the process of investing and persevering in a challenging profession. Additionally, it is my hope that teachers will take time to reflect on the reciprocities and rewards that are highlighted in this chapter. May they serve as fuel for your practice.

So, what's next? Because intentional teacher attention to interactions and exchanges with students can lead to increased student confidence and improved academic performance (Zins et al., 2004), I recommend further reflection and investigation, both formal and informal, to identify and uncover additional reciprocal benefits in the teacher–student relationship. I also recommend creating informal and formal time and space for reflection as professionals, both individually and with colleagues. In addition, I hope that efforts to elevate the importance of and mutuality in the teacher–student relationship will inspire and empower teachers and teacher leaders. Let us, as professionals, commit to amplify, share, and uncover all of teaching's unexpected rewards and joys. May we uplift, support, cheer for, and give back to our students and the profession in a spirit of hope and joy.

Note

1 All students' and teachers' names have been changed throughout this chapter.

References

Aguilar, E. (2018). *Onward: Cultivating emotional resilience in educators*. Jossey-Bass.
Anderson, G. (2015). Connecting with students: Where do you stand? *Association of Middle Level Education*, 3(2), 32–33.
Ayers, W. (2000). A teacher ain't nothin' but a hero: Teachers and teaching in film. www.taylorfrancis.com/chapters/teacher-ain-nothin-hero-teachers-teaching-film-william-ayers/e/10.4324/9781410600509-18.
Badley, K. & Van Brummelen, H. V. (2012). *Metaphors we teach and live by*. Wipf and Stock.
Bohlin, L., Durwin, C. C., & Reese-Weber, M. (2018). *EdPsych modules*. Sage.
Brown, B. (2012). *Daring greatly: How the courage to be vulnerable transforms the way we live, love, parent and lead*. Random House.
Brown, B. (2018). *Dare to lead: Brave work, tough conversations, whole hearts*. Random House.
Cornett, C. E. (1986). *Learning through laughter: Humor in the classroom*. Phi Delta Kappa Educational Foundation.
Cruickshank, V. & MacDonald, A. (2018). Teachers who feel appreciated are less likely to leave the profession. https://theconversation.com/teachers-who-feel-appreciated-are-less-likely-to-leave-the-profession-89864.
Csikszentmihalyi, M. (1990). *Flow: The psychology of optimal experience*. Harper and Row.
Davis, H. A. (2006). Exploring the contexts of relationship quality between middle school students and teachers. *Elementary School Journal*, 106(3), 193–223.
Day, C. (2004). *A passion for teaching*. Routledge Falmer.
Day, C. & Gu, Q. (2007). Variations in the conditions for teachers' professional learning and development: Sustaining commitment and effectiveness over a career. *Oxford Review of Education*, 33(4), 423–443.
Dearborn, G. (2015). Compassionate discipline: Dealing with difficult students. *Association of Middle Level Education Magazine*, 3(1), 8–11.
Dweck, C. (2006). *Mindset: The new psychology of success*. Random House.
Education Week (2015). Q and A with Sir Ken Robinson: Education has to be a human business. www.edweek.org/go/ken_robinson.
Educators Rising (2016). *Educators rising standards*. Phi Delta Kappa International.
Evans-Palmer, T. (2016). Building dispositions and self-efficacy in pre-service art teachers. *Studies in Art Education*, 57(3), 265–278.
Fallona, C. & Canniff, J. (2013). Nurturing a moral stance in teacher education. In M. N. Sanger & R. D. Osguthorpe (Eds.), *The moral work of teaching and teacher education: Preparing and supporting practitioners* (pp. 75–91). Teachers College Press.
Farrell, T. S. C. (2014). Teacher you are stupid! Cultivating a reflective disposition. *Teaching as a Second Language Electronic Journal*, 18(3), 1–10.
France, P. E. (2019). The value of vulnerability. *Educational Leadership*, 77(1), 78–82.
Goodwin, B. (2019). Keep the romance alive: How can we help new teachers maintain a long-term love of their jobs? *Educational Leadership*, 77(1), 84–85.
Hall, C. L. (1969). Humor in teaching. *Peabody Journal of Education*, 47(1), 3–5.
Hargreaves, A. (2000). Mixed emotions: Teachers' perceptions of their interactions with students. *Teaching and Teacher Education*, 16, 811–826.

Hill-Jackson, V., Hartlep, N. D., & Stafford, D. (2019). *What makes a star teacher: Dispositions that support student learning.* ACSD.

Holst, J. (2015). A letter to my eighth graders. *Association of Middle Level Education Magazine,* 2(9), 33–34.

Horwitz, E. K. (2000). Students and teachers: An ever-evolving partnership. *Modern Language Journal,* 84(4), 523–535.

Hughes, M. C. (2014). One pre-service program's dispositional efforts revealed. Ed.D. diss, George Fox University. http://digitalcommons.georgefox.edu/edd/31/.

Hughes, M. C. (2015). Dispositions and the Christian teacher. *Christian School Educator,* 18 (3), 30–32.

Hughes, M. C. (2018). Three ideas for infusing joy into the classroom. www.amle.org/BrowsebyTopic/WhatsNew/WNDet.aspx?ArtMID=888&ArticleID=990.

Johnson, G. M. & Miller, P. J. (1993). Field theory applied to classrooms: Toward a bidirectional paradigm of teacher–student relationships. *Journal of Classroom Interaction,* 28(2), 15–21.

Kress, J. S. & Elias, M. J. (2020). *Nurturing students' character: Everyday teaching activities for social-emotional learning.* Taylor and Francis.

Martin, K. L. (2012). New teacher induction: Research summary. www.amle.org/TabId/198/ArtMID/696/ArticleID/302/Research-Summary-New-Teacher-Induction.aspx.

McCoy, D. & Mashburn, T. (2017). Providing leadership and a structure of support. www.amle.org/providing-leadership-and-a-structure-of-support/.

Minchew, S. S. (2001). Teaching English with humor and fun. *American Secondary Education,* 30(1), 58–70.

Moje, E. B. (1996). I teach students, not subjects. *Reading Research Quarterly,* 31(2), 172–195.

Murrell, P. C., Diez, M. E., Feiman-Nemser, S., & Schussler, D. L. (2010). *Teaching as a moral practice: Defining, developing, and assessing professional dispositions in teacher education.* Harvard Educational Press.

Nichols, S. L. (2006). Teachers' and students' beliefs about student belonging in one middle school. *Elementary School Journal,* 106(3), 255–271.

Noddings, N. (1984). *Caring: A feminine approach to ethics and moral education.* University of California Press.

Palmer, P. J. (1983). *To know as we are known: Education as a spiritual journey.* Harper.

Palmer, P. J. (2000). *Let your life speak.* Jossey-Bass.

Palmer, P. J. (2004). *A hidden wholeness: The journey toward an undivided life.* Jossey-Bass.

Phegley, M.N. & Oxford, J. (2010). Cross-level collaboration: Students and teachers learning from each other. *English Journal,* 99(5), 27–34.

Pigford, T. (2001). Improving teacher–student relationships: What's up with that? *The Clearing House,* 74(6), 337–339.

Reeve, J. (2006). Teachers as facilitators: What autonomy-supportive teachers do and why their students benefit. *Elementary School Journal,* 106(3), 225–236.

Rogers, C. R. (1969). *Freedom to learn.* Merrill.

Ryan, K., Cooper, J. M., & Bolick, C. M. (2016). *Those who can, teach* (14th ed.). Cengage.

Sanger, M. N. & Osguthorpe, R. D. (Eds.) (2013) *The moral work of teaching and teacher education.* Teachers College Press.

Santoro, D. A. (2011). Good teaching in difficult times: Demoralization in the pursuit of good work. *American Journal of Education,* 118(1), 1–23.

Schat, S. (2020). The successful communication of education care. In P. Shotsberger & C. Freytag (Eds.), *How shall we then care: A Christian educator's guide to caring for self, learners, colleagues, and community* (pp. 17–34). Wipf and Stock.

Schwartz, K. (2014). What's your learning disposition? How to foster students' mindsets. ww2.kqed.org/mindshift/2014/03/25/whats-your-learning-disposition-how-to-foster-students-mindsets/.

Schwartz, K. (2016). *I wish my teacher knew: How one question can change everything for our kids.* Da Capo Press.

Scott, K. (2020). Back to school: Managing the emotions of virtual learning during the pandemic. https://6abc.com/back-to-school-coronavirus-virtual-learning/6363429/.

Sherman, S. M. (2013). Let's lighten up! Play and important roles in learning. *Virginia Journal of Education, 4,* 13–15.

Silver, D., Berckemeyer, J. C., & Baenen, J. (2015). *Deliberate optimism: Reclaiming the joy in education.* Corwin.

Spilt, J. L., Koomen, H. M. Y., & Thijs, J. T. (2011). Teacher well-being: The importance of teacher–student relationships. *Educational Psychology Review, 23*(4), 457–477.

Steeg Thornhill, S. M. & Badley, K. (2021). *Generating tact and flow for effective teaching and learning.* Taylor and Francis.

Stengel, B. S. (2013). Teaching moral responsibility. In M. N. Sanger & R. D. Osguthorpe (Eds.), *The moral work of teaching and teacher education* (pp. 44–59). Teachers College Press.

Taulbert, C. (2006). *Eight habits of the heart for educators.* Corwin.

Tomlinson, C. A. (2015a). Being human in the classroom. *Educational Leadership, 73*(2), 74–77.

Tomlinson, C. A. (2015b). The caring teacher's manifesto. *Educational Leadership, 72*(6), 89–90.

van Manen, M. (2016). *Pedagogical tact: Knowing what to do when you don't know what to do.* Routledge.

Wandersee, J. W. (1982). Humor as a teaching strategy. *American Biology Teacher, 44*(4), 212–218.

Weissberg, R. P. & Cascarino, J. (2013). Academic learning + social-emotional learning = national priority. *Kappan, 95*(2), 8–13.

Wineberg, T. (2004). Metaphors for teachers. In K. Badley & H. Van Brummelen (Eds.), *Metaphors we teach by* (pp. 32–51). Wipf and Stock.

Wormeli, R. (2019). Humor? Yes, please! Embracing humor in the classroom invites creativity, reduces stress, and enhances retention. *Association of Middle Level Education Magazine, 7*(1), 32–37.

Zins, J. E., Weissberg, R. P., Wang, M.C., & Walberg, H. J. (2004). *Building academic success on social and emotional learning: What does the research say?* Teachers College Press.

Ziv, A. (1988). Teaching and learning with humor: Experiment and replication. *Journal of Experimental Education, 57*(1), 5–15.

3
WHEN STUDENTS BECOME OUR TEACHERS

Joy A. Chadwick

It is my strong belief that the students who keep us up at night, who worry us, and who at times exasperate us are the students who teach us the most about our best and worst teaching selves. These are the students who just do not fit into our wonderfully engaging and well-thought-out learning experiences. Earlier in my teaching career a colleague described the students who do not fit into our general class expectations as "students on the margins." This idea has stayed with me, and these are the students that I would like to consider in this chapter. I suggest that as we reflect on the successes and challenges of our teaching days we look to our students on the margins of our classrooms because these amazing human beings are our best and most important teachers.

One Size Education Does Not Fit All Students

There was a time when teachers opened a textbook to a certain page and all students were expected to read the same content, solve the same math problems, and write responses to the same questions on the end of the chapter quiz. Students who could not fit into this expectation were graded lower, considered unmotivated, unable, unwilling, or failures. These were the students on the margins. Often these students were identified with specific learning exceptionalities, and the failure to meet the expectations of the classroom was placed squarely on their shoulders. Thankfully, we are moving away from the one-size-fits-all approach to learning and from the negative labels of "deficit," "disability," "disorder," and "dysfunction." In many of today's classrooms teachers are working to embrace a strength-based approach to learning to help students achieve success in school and in life in general. This paradigm shift has come, in part, from decades of political influence, including three significant pieces of US legislation—*Education for All Handicapped Children* (1997), *No Child Left Behind* (2001), and *Every Child Succeeds* (2015)—and from our growing understanding of the brain and learning.

To help us appreciate this perspectival shift from disability to ability, it would be wise for us to look at the growing body of research related to neurodiversity (Armstrong, 2019, 2012, 2010; Murdock, 2020; Rentenbach, Prislovsky, & Gabriel, 2017). Neurodiversity is a model of thinking about diversity that acknowledges that all brains are unique in some way (Armstrong, 2012). In fact, from a neurodiversity standpoint, there is no such thing as a normal brain (Armstrong, 2010). As stated by Murdock (2020: p. 5), "the symptoms and behaviors of the people who would ordinarily be classified as non-neurotypical are simply expressions of human function rather than disorders to be diagnosed and treated." The neurodiversity movement values human differences and negates approaches that pathologize and diminish individual worth (Armstrong, 2012; Rentenbach et al., 2017). Just as society has grown to embrace cultural, economic, and gender diversity, educators must begin to recognize and appreciate the neurodiversity of the students they teach (Armstrong, 2010).

Unfortunately, the practice of labeling some students as disabled and different has created silos of students who are considered either able or unable in our classrooms. Sadly, I have experienced this sorting of students at the beginning of a school year when teachers receive their new class lists. In my experience the first thing some teachers do is count how many "IPP/IEP students" or "ELL/ESL students" they have on their class lists. At that very moment teachers are imagining who will be the easier students to teach and who will be the more challenging students in their classrooms. And as teachers contemplate the year ahead, they worry about whether they have the ability and skill to support the complexity of student needs represented by those lists. Those more challenging students become the students on the margins. This simple counting and sorting ritual perpetuates teachers' perceptions of themselves as people able to meet the learning needs of some students and not those of others. How might a teacher's perception of the upcoming year be different if they embraced the students on that class list as windfalls rather than handicaps to the year ahead? Just as we want students to embrace the start of each school year with excitement and anticipation of the potential learning opportunities that lie ahead, we want teachers to begin each year with that same anticipation and excitement. Embracing students as opportunities at the start of each year opens, rather than closes off, the potential gifts of learning that each student can give us. A neurodiverse lens permits teachers to focus less on pathologizing their students (Armstrong, 2012) for their different ways of being in the world and to focus more on exploring the potential and ability of each student in their classroom.

The neurodiversity perspective has a significant impact on how we must reimagine our classrooms. When we embrace a neurodiverse stance on teaching, we recognize that students come to us with unique ways of thinking, and with untold gifts, talents, and abilities. It is our responsibility, then, to create classroom environments that recognize the uniqueness and potential in each and every student. We must also acknowledge that at some point in their learning journey all students will challenge our professional knowledge and instructional choices. If we are open to the inherent learning needs of all our learners, we invite the possibility for all students to teach us something about who we are and about who we could and should become as educators. From a neurodiversity perspective, all students have the potential to become our teacher. In van Manen's (2002: p. 11) words, "All that is required is that we watch and listen to the children and learn from them. In this, children are our teachers."

My image of the students on the margins of our classrooms has shifted over my teaching career. As I consider the many diverse individuals that create our classroom communities, I see the margins differently. They are no longer occupied with students with identified behavioral or learning challenges. The students whom I now see on the margins are those who—through their voices, silence, or actions—are communicating to me that I need to stop and pay attention. I believe that these are our best teachers as they show us our own wonderful abilities and our unending potential as teachers.

A Moment's Response Makes a Difference

The complexity of today's classrooms compels us to know more about the effectiveness of our instructional choices in order to meet the needs of the students before us. The adage "We don't teach curriculum, we teach students the curriculum" symbolizes an important pedagogical shift: to do this well, we must be open to what our students are telling us about themselves and our teaching. A student telling you they hate school is telling you something. A student who falls asleep in class is telling you something. A student who puts their head down and tells you they are stupid and will never figure out how to compute a math problem is telling you something. In teachers' efforts to manage the many complexities of the day, it is sometimes easier to look at the student as the problem rather than to consider that, again, they need to adjust and reconsider their instructional choices. Becoming observant and responsive to students in the moment-to-moment experiences of the classroom is a powerful learning opportunity for every teacher.

In *Hanging In*, a fascinating book about teaching challenging adolescents, Jeffrey Benson (2014) describes how his school community worked together to meet the needs of very complex adolescent learners. One compelling story describes how Riley, a student in Benson's math class, asks Benson to explain a math problem. After several failed attempts, and Riley's continued blank stare, indicating that the concept is still not making sense, Benson calmly assures Riley that his lack of understanding of the math concept is not his fault. Benson shares with Riley that this challenge is his failure to know the right way to teach the equation, not Riley's failure to learn it. Benson promises to do his homework that night and assures Riley that he will have a better explanation for him the next day. This is an example of a teacher actively and thoughtfully responding to the learning needs of a particular student. Benson was not afraid to admit that he was failing at teaching Riley and he was able to place his student's sense of efficacy ahead of his own. Teachers' fear of failure and perceived ineffectiveness can have an impact on their instructional choices (Liston, 2000). It is so easy to place the failure of learning on the student's shoulders and not consider changes in our own teaching choices. However, we need to reframe moments of perceived failure to moments of opportunity. Continuing to focus on the students as the issue forecloses the potential of a pedagogical relationship with our students (van Manen, 2002; 2015) and profoundly impacts our confidence in our teaching ability.

We often struggle to find a way to teach students who do not always understand what we are trying to teach them on the first or second try. Because Benson paid attention to Riley's body language and nonverbal responses, he understood that he needed to adjust his instructional technique. He recognized that repeating failed attempts would not support Riley's learning. In Benson's (2014: p. 23) words: "Too many students internalize a belief that our failure to know how to teach them in the moment is actually their failure to learn." It is important that we are open to our students' verbal and nonverbal cues so that we adjust our teaching choices in ways that affirm that they are capable and able individuals. It is also critical that we are not afraid to admit that we are learners of our teaching craft and that we do not have all the answers all the time.

Benson's ability to improvise in the moment affirmed that he was there to support Riley in his learning and that Riley did not have to fit into a preconceived teaching plan. We often focus exclusively on what needs to be covered in a specific lesson. We have our visual schedules, our plans for the day, and (if we are really organized) our plans for the week or month ahead. We focus on covering the intended learning goals, creating engaging experiences, and gathering formative and summative assessment data to address reporting responsibilities. It is a subtle and important reframing of our teaching when we acknowledge that children are not there primarily to follow our plans, goals, and agendas; rather, and more importantly, we are there to support their learning. When we can carefully attend to our students, we are able to respond effectively to their learning needs. The rewards of their successes become our successes. A good teacher knows how to respond tactfully to a classroom experience. They know what to attend to and what to pass over (van Manen, 2002; 2015; Steeg Thornhill & Badley, 2020).

In their most vulnerable moments, students need trusting teachers to guide them through their learning challenges. "Students need relationship (connection) in order for them to want to learn" (Carrington, 2019: p. 19). Knowing how to respond to any given classroom situation requires us to be observant, curious, and responsive educators. Tactful educators are attentive to the uniqueness of each child and the uniqueness of the situation (van Manen, 2015). Opening ourselves to our students' stories invites us to learn along with the unique young people in our care.

One of the classic responses to inappropriate behavior is to send the student to the principal's office (or, in larger schools, to the vice or assistant principal or whoever oversees discipline). When I was a school-based leader, I was not always a great disciplinarian. I confess when a student was sent to my office, I pulled out the jujubes more than a few times. I waited for the student to calm down while they munched away on the candies (not the healthiest choice, I admit), then engaged them in a conversation to strategize how we might move forward, rather than rehash what had already been done. I recall an incident when a grade-one teacher sent a student to my office because she had placed her hands around the neck of another student and choked her. This occurred in the library when the student had stepped in front of the offending student as they were lined up waiting to sign out library books. The teacher abruptly deposited the offending student in my office and then dashed off to attend to her now distraught class. This student had recently arrived in our school community from a refugee camp. Since I didn't speak his first language and he did not understand English, we spent some time looking at each other; then I offered him some jujubes, which he readily accepted. I also supplied him with some puzzles. Then I got on with some paperwork. The teacher arrived during recess and was not impressed that her student was not suffering any consequences for his behavior. Even worse, he was eating candy. She was quite certain that this student had significant behavioral issues and that I therefore needed to squelch his unruly behavior promptly. I pointed out that, short of pantomiming the experience with other students stepping in as actors, I was sure I was not going to get that point across. I also suggested a potential reframe for this teacher. What if it was the child's responsibility while in the refugee camp to hold a spot in line for water or food each day? What would he have learned about the life-and-death consequences of someone stepping in line in front of him? If we focus only on the behavior, we miss the story.

I love Ross Greene's (2014: p. 11) phrase: "Kids do well if they can." When we are faced with a student who tells us, "I hate math, I hate you, and school sucks!" it is so much easier to focus on the outburst rather than what is behind it. In that moment we often respond reactively with the quickest fix to the problem. It is much harder to shift our focus from the student's behavior to a true understanding of what caused it. If we believe the student is "doing well if they can," then we respond differently in that moment. We focus less on the student as a problem and more on the context and situation that need our attention. In Chapter 2, Hughes shares the idea of "leaning in" to a student's story. She suggests that it is important to take the time to be attentive to what our students are doing and not doing in our classrooms because these moments provide us with valuable information that can shift our perspectives and result in our own professional growth and personal satisfaction. If we see our students doing the best that they can at any moment, then we too must do the best that we can. Listening to our students' stories and being attentive to what they are saying in their interactions with us, in their engagement with tasks, or in their relationships with peers can change the narrative that they are disabling our classes and our ability to teach.

Children Listen to What We Say and Watch What We Do

Children listen to what we say and watch what we do. If you really want to know about your teaching presence in a classroom, ask your students to role-play and teach a lesson for you. When you sit back and watch, you will see the amazing things you say and do, and you will see all your quirky gestures, phrases, and instructional choices. In other words, you will see the good, the bad, and the ugly of your teaching practice.

If you are a primary teacher, you know that it is not easy for many of your students to keep track of their belongings. Think of the student who has lost their shoes for the second time that day and the fifth time this week. Read the following sentences in the tone of exasperation that you no doubt feel while your other 25 students are waiting to start the lesson. "You've lost your shoes again, Susie! You just had them before recess. What are we going to do about this?" Now take a breath and say it again, this time with care and invitation. What do each of these responses say to Susie and to the rest of the class about Susie? Easy to say, harder to do! Maybe Susie's experience is telling you something about your classroom organization? Maybe Susie needs a visual schedule, a peer to support her, or just a second pair of shoes? Unfortunately, this is a true story that happened in my school. Susie's teacher and I were very frustrated because we felt we were always being taken away from our teaching responsibilities to look for Susie's shoes. With some detective work and close observation, we learned that the fault was not at all with Susie. Students had been taking her shoes and hiding them throughout the school. We were devastated because of the times we had shown our frustration and disappointment in front of her. If we focus only on the behavior, we miss the story. Our students are very aware when we miss their story.

For some students, it is important to have a plan of what will happen in their moments of frustration and loss of control. Leaving a classroom can be a positive strategy for students who need time to cool down. However, having a proactive plan of what this looks like for students is critical. At all times, the worth of the student–teacher relationship must be at the forefront of any action taken. As teachers, it is critical that we model self-control and effective management of our emotions when these incidents arise. We can have the situation where, in exasperation, we send Joey out of the room. Or we can say to Joey, "I can see you are feeling frustrated, and I am too. Let's give ourselves some time so that we can ensure we can solve this problem together." Or, another scenario might look like: "I care for you and our relationship and I can feel that I am not my best self right now. Let's take a break and then when you are ready and I have the class working, I really want to listen to you and find out what we can do together to fix this problem." What do these interchanges say to the student about the value we are placing on our relationship with them? What does this say to the students who are watching and listening to everything we are saying and doing at that moment?

Resilience-promoting teachers make themselves available to their students, show empathy for students' adversity, provide positive strategies that help students deal with adversity, and develop positive and caring relationships with their students (Hutchinson & Specht, 2020; Unger, 2013). There is significant benefit for students and teachers when educators respond in proactive and caring ways to classroom challenges. When we respond to these situations with intention and care, students view their classroom as a safe space where individuals are respected and valued. Teachers promote resilience in their students and model effective problem-solving processes. There is also a reciprocity of care that occurs in these situations. Our care for students promotes our own sense of efficacy, resilience, and worth. We are less likely to go home feeling exhausted or defeated when we feel we have navigated these challenging moments successfully.

Children watch what we do and what we don't do. Most teachers have the ability to give students the look. This is a very handy strategy for classroom management. It can be the cue for students to move on to something new, to stop what they are doing, or to continue on course. Our presence, our stature, our voice, and our eyes create moments of invitation and moments of exclusion. Sometimes what we say and what we are doing do not match, and our students are witness to that. If we say we believe everyone in our classroom is important, but we are not visibly seen working with all students, then our words and actions do not match. If we say "Good job!" but our voice and eyes do not enforce the meaning of the phrase, students will know it. If we ask students to be patient with a classmate who struggles with following classroom rules, but students see us becoming frustrated with that student, then what we are asking of students and what we are modeling for students are quite different. Students watch what we do and say and what we don't do and don't say. It is important that our body language matches our tone of voice and the direction of our gaze. Again, because we are frantically keeping up with the myriad demands that are placed on us throughout the day, this is not easy. However, it is critically important that we remain aware of the impact our choices have on the students in our classrooms.

We are the models for our students, and how we respond to any given situation tells them the worth we place on them and their classmates. If we believe in the infinite worth of each individual (Hoffman, 2015) we respond to challenges differently. We want to protect our pedagogical relationship with our students at all costs. Showing frustration can shame a student and embarrass them in front of the class. Showing patience, understanding, and empathy demonstrates that we value the relationship and uniqueness of each student. We come to school to share our best selves with our students. The more we demonstrate our care, love, and respect for students, the more successful our students will be in managing those challenging moments. Their successes become our successes. Students are constant observers of what we are saying and what we are doing.

How Full is Your Bucket?

Think about a time when you had infinite patience for a student. What allowed for that patience? Was it that you were well rested? Did you step away from teacher mode and have fun the previous night? Or perhaps you just came from an inspiring staff meeting (that example might be a bit of stretch). Most likely, at that moment, you were working from a half-full or even nearly full emotional bucket. Yes, the great book *How Full is Your Bucket?* (Rath, Reckmeyer, & Manning, 2009) that we read to students also applies to teachers. We have to watch our buckets. If we are struggling with patience, endurance, or even creativity, we need to ask ourselves the question: how full is my bucket at this moment?

Most professionals can leave their professional responsibilities and expectations when they leave their workplace. Not so in teaching. Literally and figuratively, we bring our work home with us at the end of the day. We find it challenging to confine our responsibilities to the school and school day and to distance ourselves from our work when at home. For most teachers, teaching is more than a job and more than a way to earn a living (Hansen, 1996). Teaching is truly an emotionally taxing profession (Danilewitz, 2017). It is both heart and head work that can cause significant challenges with work–life balance (Kutsyuruba, Godden, & Tregunna, 2013). Even an excellent juggler does not have the endurance to keep all the balls in the air indefinitely. "But teachers do what they do because of one thing: they love their students, and they believe in the power of education" (Herman, Hickmon-Rosa & Reinke, 2018: p. 97). However, life becomes complex as we race home to care for our families, support extended families, volunteer, attend to our relationships, and plan for the next teaching day.

Our ability to care for ourselves has a significant impact on our capacity to be attentive and responsive to our students' learning needs and our capacity to be open to the moments in which they bring us feelings of joy and success. It is critical that we have the strength, fortitude, and grace to be available for our students each teaching day. I know that when my emotional bucket has been low, I have laughed less, blamed more, and focused significantly on what was not working rather than acknowledging what was working in my teaching practice. Conceptually we know that when we have more energy and are more confident in our ability to attend to the needs of our students, we are more likely to be effective as teachers (Tschannen-Moran & Hoy, 2007). Alternatively, emotional exhaustion "is likely to interfere with a teacher's efforts to implement effective instructional practices and may influence the development of negative attitudes about and interactions with students" (Herman et al., 2018: p. 91). A positive feedback loop develops in our teaching when we feel our instructional choices are having an effect. When we perceive we are being effective, we are more likely to be effective in our future practices (Han & Weiss, 2005; Herman et al., 2018). The more attentive we are to the state of our emotional bucket, the more open we can be to the feedback our students are giving us about their learning and our teaching. Being attentive to our interactions with students is an important professional and personal balance check for all of us.

How are we filling our bucket and who can we turn to for support in this endeavor? We need to call on colleagues, family, and friends to help us be our best selves. Whether it is a book club, walking, cooking, time in nature, or quiet meditation we are better for our students when we are fulfilling our passions and interests. Filling our bucket will help us focus on our successes and on the potential of even our most challenging classroom experiences.

It is also important to remember to celebrate our successes. We must ensure that we take the time each day to share with our colleagues something great that happened in our teaching day. It is critical that we acknowledge our good work, because there is always good work with students each day. As a teacher educator, I wonder if it might be wise to include a gratitude component in the lesson plans that we ask our teacher candidates to complete when they are student teaching. This could include what they are grateful for in the lesson they just completed or they could express gratitude for what a student said or did. I wonder if this might help teacher candidates ensure that they celebrate one aspect of a lesson or teaching day. Our student successes are our successes, and sharing them with others is an affirmation of who we are and who we want to be as teachers.

As teachers, we also need to reframe conversations in the staffroom, shifting from what is ineffective to what is working well. Focusing on negativity or what is not working does not fill our emotional bucket. It is so easy to take the path of negativity. When teachers focus on what is not going well with students, they are more apt to perpetuate their perception of their students' inadequacies and, by reflection, the inadequacies of their instructional practices (Zierer & Hattie, 2018). Our confidence, self-efficacy, and growth mindset are enhanced when we focus on our strengths and our potential as teachers. This does not mean we cannot talk about our frustrations, challenges, and worries about students or our teaching. Without this uncertainty in our abilities as educators our "teaching would be reduced to a set of techniques, recipes, or rules" (van Manen, 2015: p. 33). Debriefing our challenging teaching experiences with colleagues who are helping us improve our teaching practice helps to focus conversations so that we keep moving forward instead of staying stagnant or, sadly, even moving backward. We have all experienced the powerful changes that occur in our practice when we engage in critical conversations with our colleagues that are centered on student learning (Hadar & Brody, 2010). Our conversations with colleagues need to focus on the impact and effects we are having on our students (Zierer & Hattie, 2018). Having proactive conversations with our colleagues keeps us in a growth mindset and in turn has a positive impact on our teaching and our emotional well-being. I appreciate the wise advice from Jody Carrington (2019: p. 187) when she states, "Sit with the winners. The conversation is different."

Just as we provide students with formative feedback to reach their learning goals, we should be more proactive about looking for and inviting student feedback on their perception of their classroom experiences and our teaching. As we look around our classrooms, students do give us feedback by means of a curious look or a vacant stare, a smile or a scowl, pride in a project or shame in one not submitted, the friendly banter or angry tension of the classroom. We must get into "the habit of kid watching" (O'Keefe, 1997). So much affirmation of our teaching can come from taking the time to observe the actions and interactions of our students. "Kidwatching is not for the faint of heart. It requires commitment, risk taking, and valuing the good in each child. However, kidwatching is its own reward" (O'Keefe, 1997: p. 5). We are missing great opportunities for professional growth and authentication of our instructional practice when we do not specifically look for and invite students to give feedback about their classroom experiences. When teachers ask, "What did I do that helped you with your learning today?" or "How might I do this differently to support you?" they can grow in their teaching practice. I wonder, as teachers, if we fear asking these questions because we do not want to hear about more things we need to change. However, we should be open to what we might hear from our students. As Palmer (1997: p. 2) suggests, "We must enter, not evade, the tangles of teaching so we can understand them better and negotiate them with more grace, not only to guard our own spirits but to serve our students well." I think we would be surprised by the wonderful generosity of our students' feedback.

It is important we take the time to celebrate the small victories and successes in our teaching days. Our students can often see our successes far clearer than we can see them ourselves. Inviting student feedback about our teaching brings new authenticity to our perceptions of our best and not-so-good teaching selves. Keeping our emotional bucket full allows us to arrive at school each day ready to meet the moment-to-moment challenges in our classrooms. Jody Carrington (2019: p. 187) sums up these ideas perfectly when she states, "[Bring] your best self to work every day. Show up as authentically as possible, every damn day and you will create your own kind of magic." Seeking opportunities to celebrate our students' successes and our own successes creates the magical moments that keep our buckets full and keeps us in love with this wonderful gift of teaching.

Know Thy Impact!

At the end of the teaching day teachers reflect on the impact they have made on student learning. They consider the gains they have made in supporting their students' acquisition of new knowledge, understanding, and skills related to a particular lesson or area of study. They also reflect on their moment-to-moment interactions with some of their students and the missed opportunities for connections with other students. They wonder about their overall impact on their students' emotional wellbeing and where today's lessons and interactions will lead to the next day. When teachers reflect on their impact on their students' lives and learning, they are committing to a continual adjustment and refinement of their teaching practice (Zierer & Hattie, 2018).

"Knowing thy impact" (Zierer & Hattie, 2018) requires teachers to be open to the stories behind their students' behaviors and to what they can learn about their instructional choices through these stories. To do this well, we must ensure that we work to build trusting and caring relationships with all our students. Students watch what we do and don't do, and listen to what we say and don't say. When we model care, they see care. When we model patience, they see us as open and available to their learning needs. Effective teaching requires "finesse, subtlety and elegance. It requires the most nuanced and careful action and—at times—inaction" (Causton-Theoharis, 2009: p. 37). When we accept that our students are doing the best they can at any moment, we are able to see them and classrooms in a different way. We look less at a student's faults and more at what we might need to adjust or change to create increased opportunities for success. Our students' successes are ultimately our successes. Thus, students and teachers become learners together.

It is also critical that we shift our attention to the potential in each of our students. Focusing on the abilities of all our students will help us see them less as disabled and dysfunctional and more as unique and—in their own ways—complete. Our students on the margins can give us feedback—both direct and indirect—on our teaching successes and they can direct us toward where we need to improve and grow. Embracing the diversity of our students as a natural and expected part of our teaching experience can lead to a powerful shift in how we see them and how we see ourselves as educators. As Kohl (1995: p. 64) states so eloquently,

> Teaching well means encouraging the widest diversity and greatest depth of learning possible, and always being open to adding a new dimension or theme to what one is doing in order to tease the genius out of one more child.

The diversity of our classrooms also offers significant potential to tease out the genius in each teacher as they seek to build deep and caring relationships with their students.

Above all else we must take care of ourselves. Our work is complex and all-encompassing. Our love and passion for learning and for our students can have a negative impact on our ability to keep a healthy work–life balance. Maintaining the energy and stamina to attend to our work with patience, courage, and grace is not easy. We must invite our colleagues to support us in this endeavor. Sharing the chaos of each teaching day with a teacher who can understand the nuances and quirks of your classroom is critical. As Hughes suggests in Chapter 2, we must remember to laugh, too. Humor can help us "stay afloat" even on our most challenging days. Celebrating and collecting artifacts of success is also important. I still have a file of notes, drawings, and stories that students have given to me over the years. They are the greatest affirmation that I have been successful and that I remain an effective teacher. These files are important to collect and to review often. They are reminders of the heart and soul that we invest in our teaching practice.

Our commitment to being lifelong learners is at the heart of our profession. Each day is an opportunity to grow and learn. How we invite and experience students' gestures, voices, and behavior can also lead to opportunities for growth. If we believe our classrooms are learning communities, then it seems natural that our students will become our best teachers. In van Manen's (2002: p. 86) words, "We must be even better learners than they are, because they in turn must learn from us." Ultimately, just as we are scaffolding and supporting our students' learning journey, they are providing opportunities for us to move along our learning journey as educators.

References

Armstrong, J. (2010). Your brain is a rain forest. *The Optimist Daily*, May 1. www.optimistdaily.com/2010/05/your-brain-is-a-rain-forest/.

Armstrong, J. (2019). Teaching kids about their brain forest. American Institute for Learning and Human Development. www.institute4learning.com/2019/12/12/teaching-kids-about-their-brain-forests/.

Armstrong, T. (2012). *Neurodiversity in the classroom: Strength based strategies to help students with special needs succeed in school and life*. ASCD.

Benson, J. (2014). *Hanging in: Strategies for teaching the students who challenge us most*. ASCD.

Carrington, J. (2019). *Kids these days: A game plan for (re)connecting with those we teach, lead, & love*. Impress.

Causton-Theoharis, J. N. (2009). The golden rule of providing support in inclusive classrooms: Support others as you would wish to be supported. *Teaching Exceptional Children*, 42(2), 36–43.

Danilewitz, J. (2017). Quality of life and sources of stress in teachers: A Canadian perspective Thesis, University of Western Ontario. https://ir.lib.uwo.ca/cgi/viewcontent.cgi?article=6279&context=etd.

Greene, R. (2014). *Lost at school: Why our kids with behavior challenges are falling through the cracks and how we can help them.* Scribner.

Hadar, L. & Brody, D. (2010). From isolation to symphonic harmony: Building a professional development community among teacher educators. *Teaching and Teacher Education,* 26(8), 1641–1651.

Han, S. & Weiss, B. (2005). Sustainability of teacher implementation of school-based mental health programs. *Journal of Abnormal Child Psychology,* 33(6), 665–679.

Hansen, D. T. (1996). *The call to teach.* Teachers College Press.

Herman, K. C., Hickmon-Rosa, J., & Reinke, W. M. (2018). Empirically derived profiles of teacher stress, burnout, self-efficacy, and coping and associated student outcomes. *Journal of Positive Behavior Interventions,* 20(2), 90–100.

Hoffman, K. (2015). Every person has infinite worth [video]. TedxSpokane. www.youtube.com/watch?v=E9fHCrP8hZM.

Hutchinson, N. & Specht, J. (2020). *Inclusion of learners with exceptionalities in Canadian schools: A practical handbook for teachers.* Pearson.

Kohl, H. (1995). *I won't learn from you: And other thoughts on creative maladjustment* (2nd ed.). The New Press.

Kutsyuruba, B., Godden, G., & Tregunna, L. (2013). Early career teacher attrition and retention: A pan-Canadian document analysis study of teacher induction and mentorship programs. https://educ.queensu.ca/sites/webpublish.queensu.ca.educwww/files/files/People/Faculty/Kutsyuruba%20-%20Pan-Canadian%20Document%20Analysis.pdf.

Liston, D. P. (2000). Love and despair in teaching. *Educational Theory,* 50(1), 81–102.

Murdock, J. (2020). Autism: A function of neurodiversity? *Journal of Human Services: Training, Research, and Practice,* 5(1), 1–17.

O'Keefe, T. (1997). The habit of kid watching. *School Talk,* 3(2), 4–6.

Palmer, P. J. (1997). *The courage to teach: Exploring the inner landscape of a teacher's life.* Jossey-Bass.

Rath, T., Reckmeyer, M., & Manning, M. J. (2009). *How full is your bucket? For kids.* Gallup Press.

Rentenbach, B., Prislovsky, L., & Gabriel, R. (2017). Valuing differences. *Phi Delta Kappan,* 98(8), 59–63.

Steeg Thornhill, S. & Badley, K. (2020). *Generating tact and flow for effective teaching and learning.* Routledge.

Tschannen-Moran, M. & Hoy, A. W. (2007). The differential antecedents of self-efficacy beliefs of novice and experienced teachers. *Teaching and Teacher Education,* 23, 944–956.

Unger, M. (2013). The impact of youth–adult relationships on resilience. *International Journal of Child, Youth & Family Studies,* 4(3), 328–336.

van Manen, M. (2002). *The tone of teaching: The language of pedagogy* (2nd ed.). Althouse Press.

van Manen, M. (2015). *Pedagogical tact: Knowing what to do when you don't know what to do.* Routledge.

Zierer, K. & Hattie, J. (2018). *10 mindframes for visible learning: Teaching for success.* Routledge.

4

IS THERE A CLASS IN THIS TEXT?

Ken Badley and Dana Antayá-Moore

In the last few decades educators have heard plenty of confident predictions that the end of the printed textbook was drawing near. It turns out that reports of textbooks' death were premature. Although paper texts remain in widespread use, electronic resources have grown more popular, especially in higher education. Both of us expect educational use of electronic resources to increase, in part because school boards must regularly replace hard-copy textbooks (despite teachers' prodigious use of tape). More importantly, perhaps, electronic textbooks can be updated easily and they adapt themselves more readily to assistive technologies, such as converting text to speech.

All the contributors to and readers of this book have used hard-copy textbooks as students and we have likewise all used them as teachers or professors. In one or both roles, many of us have also used electronic texts. As educators, what do we make of these books, whether paper or digital? How do we use them? We know what they demand of us. We have all had to come to terms with the constraints texts place on us and our students. And we can all recall weaknesses of various texts we have used. Our purpose in this chapter is to remind ourselves and our readers how textbooks help us in our work as educators … what they give us.

As authors of this chapter, our own work with textbooks—as both textbook authors and educators—leads us to want to defend them. We do not sense any need to defend those we worked on ourselves because of course they are all perfect. But we want to offer some insights into how textbooks come into being that may help others view them as the gifts we think they can be to educators.

Together, we worked on three junior high texts and their accompanying teacher resource guides for courses in ethics and world religions for the Canadian province of Newfoundland. In that case, Ken asked Dana to join the project with Canadian educational publisher Nelson Thomson. Those books appeared in 2004 with these titles: *Expressions of Faith* for grade seven, *Who am I?* for grade eight, and *My Place in the World* for grade nine (Badley, Antayá-Moore, & Kostelyk, 2004a; 2004c; 2004b). We

DOI: 10.4324/9781003124429-4

also wrote the teacher resource guides for those three textbooks (Badley and Antayá-Moore, 2004a; 2004c; 2004b). Those titles had been on teachers' desks and in students' hands (or at the bottoms of their lockers) for only a few months when Dana asked Ken to participate in a grade-eight social studies text and teacher guide Pearson was contracted to complete for the Canadian province of Alberta. This text, *Worldviews, Contact and Change*, appeared in 2007 (Antayá-Moore et al., 2007b; 2007c). Independently of each other, we have both worked on other texts and teacher guides for K-12 and university classrooms (Antayá-Moore et al., 2007a; Badley, 1996; Badley et al., 2007; Edmunds, Nickel, & Badley, 2015). We provide this information not to boast but rather to point out that we know both sides of the textbook equation. As authors, we have worked hard to make textbooks clear, accessible, and suited to the course objectives for which they were developed. We know how much work goes into textbooks. And as K-12 teachers and university professors, we have both assigned textbooks to our students and we know the strengths and weaknesses of the books we have used. But to our point in this chapter, we have also worked with Departments of Education, subject-area committees, pilot-classroom teachers, publishers, editors, and artists to produce absolutely the best books we could.

As educators, we can all recognize what textbooks offer us, even with the weaknesses that we and our students discover as we work with them year after year. Certainly, on our own and often with our students' help, we discover the flaws in the textbooks we use. We wish that the authors had included this topic or that topic, given more attention to this other topic, omitted a third topic altogether, or nuanced another topic a bit differently. We might wish for different artwork. We would like more questions and topics for further exploration … or fewer. We would like more suggestions for adaptations and accommodations … or fewer. Of course, we wish that school authorities and post-secondary students could afford them more easily.

But we believe educators can achieve a kind of reciprocity with our textbooks; they can come to terms with the shortcomings and find creative ways to use texts as the learning resources they are meant to be. As have our readers in K-12 classrooms, we have used texts assigned by the jurisdictions in which we were teaching. As have our readers in higher education, we have used texts that we chose. We have used purpose-written textbooks and we have used trade books that suited our purposes in specific courses. In short, despite having been on all sides of textbooks—students, teachers, authors—we have not become jaded or cynical about them. We believe that, when used creatively, textbooks can play a central and very helpful part in our students' learning.

You, our readers, may be able to come to terms with textbooks more easily if we very briefly review how they come into being. In K-12 education, a state or provincial Department of Education announces to educational publishers that curriculum revisions in a subject area will require new textbooks for specified grades. Publishers then submit textbook proposals to the department based on the same curriculum documents (general learning outcomes or standards for the subject area and specific learning outcomes or standards for specific grades) that teachers will later use to guide their instructional planning. Based on the proposals they receive, including cost projections, sample chapters, and the profiles of the editorial and writing teams, the Department of

Education awards contracts to one or more publishers. From that point on, members of the department's subject-area committee, the publisher(s), and the writers work closely together to ensure that the book takes shape in ways that meet the specified learning outcomes for that subject area and grade. Following a tightly prescribed schedule, writers produce chapters, editors edit, graphic artists produce proofs, editors and writers check the proofs, editorial assistants write to other publishers for permission to use photos and other copyrighted materials, and, eventually, the publisher produces spiral-bound copies of individual chapters or book sections for use in pilot classrooms. Teachers and students in those pilot classrooms use the draft materials and give their feedback to the editorial team, who then work with the writers to make the suggested changes to the evolving book. Editors and writers do another round of proofing and, finally, the book is printed and shipped to school districts. To save space, we have purposely omitted many small parts of the process, and we have not described the process for higher education textbooks. But we have included enough information here for someone unfamiliar with the process to understand that textbooks do not simply fall out of the sky. Also, we have no desire to shill for publishers, but our description of the complexities of the process may help some understand that textbook cover prices reflect much more than the final printing and shipping costs of the books themselves.

One final comment is warranted about the textbook production process. This may sound a bit like an article of faith more than a statement of fact, but in our experience as textbook authors, we have seen how much textbooks improve between the pilot-taught draft and the final published resources. More times than either of us wish to remember, we have submitted what we considered perfectly brilliant material to a publisher only to have it come back from the pilot classrooms with dozens of criticisms. We neglected this. We gave poor instructions for that. We misunderstood this other matter. Our editor at Nelson Thomson used to say "sigh" about some of the challenges that arose during the editorial and production stages of textbook production. We will honor her here by pointing out that when textbooks arrive in teachers' and students' hands, they are largely post-sigh.

How Teachers Use Textbooks: Four Postures

Decades ago, in response to a student's otherwise innocent question about textbooks, English professor Stanley Fish (1982) wrote a famous essay and book of the same name, *Is There a Text in This Class?* He used the student's question to raise philosophical questions about the written word, especially about the nature of written text and how we read. We want to turn his question around by asking: "Is there a class in this text?" That is, how do teachers and professors use textbooks and resources in their courses? We have observed that, having chosen or been required to assign a given text or resource, teachers adopt one or two of four distinct postures:

- teaching *from* the text;
- teaching *with* the text;

- teaching *against* the text;
- teaching *to* the text.

After exploring each of these independently, we will argue that teachers sometimes shift back and forth between postures and sometimes even combine two or three postures as they use a particular textbook with their students. What do we mean by these four postures?

It is perhaps easiest to describe and understand teaching *from* the text, although somewhat less easy to understand why people continue to do it. The textbook is there. We organize the course in the same order that the text's authors organized the text. We begin at page 1 and work our way through to page 368. Classes consist of explanations of difficult passages, or of examples not provided in the text, or of discussion with students about points of interest or points in need of clarification.

Periodically, one hears about a class where the teacher or professor actually reads from the text. In some of the poorest places on earth, where only one copy of the textbook is available per classroom, the teacher reads aloud so that students can copy down the text's contents. We have both worked as volunteers with colleagues in severely under-resourced settings where each classroom has just one copy of the text and we do not criticize those teachers' practices. Still, such settings and practices should sadden any educator's heart. More saddening is the picture of a class in a well-resourced country where all students have access to the text and yet the teacher gives over valuable class time to reading aloud what students already have in front of them. This practice is most discouraging in higher education, where the financial value of one clock hour of class time is so easy to calculate (number of students in the room × tuition paid by each student for the course ÷ number of hours of class time in the term). To be clear, that formula takes into account only the students' direct contribution to the course costs, not the other sources of university income. Without wanting to be overly mercenary in our calculations, we must note that classes in public universities can easily run to $20 or more per clock minute. Calculations are similarly simple—and just as sobering—for K-12 classrooms (total cost per student per year to operate the school system ÷ instructional hours in the school year × number of students in the room). We trust this somewhat harsh excursion into educational budgeting reinforces our argument that educators should not ordinarily read a textbook to their students.

Of course, there are exceptions to our assertion about reading the text. Educators sometimes want a class to engage in close examination of a problematic or key passage. In small groups or as a whole class, students may need to outline an important argument, unpack a writer's nuancing of an argument, or explore their use of irony, understatement, or some other device. K-12 educators commonly use the phrase "checking for comprehension," which may involve such close reading. Students may perform portions of a text as readers' theatre. We recognize such exceptions but we repeat our general claim that no educator in an adequately resourced classroom should be reading aloud what students have in front of them.

Our claim notwithstanding, publishers have made the situation more complicated than we have presented it so far. Many textbooks are published as part of a package that may include teacher resource guides, exam question banks, and slide decks to support instruction. University students regularly report on professors who, day after day, simply show the published slide decks that accompanied the textbook—a practice that, in our view, raises sobering questions about why students should attend class at all. In some cases, these packaged programs include a complete examination program, including the grading function. In this case a teacher needs simply to book a computer lab on the day of the exam or have students sign in to a website on their own computers. Students write the exam and the teacher or professor is furnished with a class set of grades. Faced with the easy availability and (usually) the quality of such resources, and given their busy schedules, some educators cannot resist using textbook programs like those we have described.

With reference to these complete textbook packages, we quote a prescient passage from Alfred North Whitehead's *The Aims of Education*, written almost a century ago:

> [E]ducation is the acquisition of the art of the utilization of knowledge. This is an art very difficult to impart. Whenever a text book is written of real educational worth, you may be quite certain that some reviewer will say it will be difficult to teach from it. Of course it will be difficult to teach from it. If it were easy, the book ought to be burned; for it cannot be educational. In education, as elsewhere, the broad primrose path leads to a nasty place. This evil path is represented by a book or a set of lectures which will practically enable the student to learn by heart all the questions likely to be asked at the next external examination.
>
> *(Whitehead, 1929: pp. 4–5)*

Imagine Whitehead's wording of this criticism if he could see the sophisticated, packaged resources that publishers provide now. In our view, it is absolutely unnecessary to teach from the text as creative educators know how to bring a packaged textbook and curriculum to life. But the temptation is strong. Many educators have found ways to use the text to maximum advantage, some of them by adopting the next posture we address here: teaching *with* the text.

By teaching *with* the text, we mean that educators view the textbook as a resource—perhaps the main resource and perhaps one of several resources. The key point is that the educator in this case shapes the course, and the textbook serves her purposes. In Alberta K-12 schools (where both of us have worked for many years), the Department of Education approves two textbooks for each course and grade. For example, both Oxford and Pearson may be awarded contracts to custom-publish the mathematics textbooks in a given grade. Individual school boards can then choose which approved textbook they wish to adopt. In some cases, those school boards turn the adoption decision over to individual schools. The key point for teachers and students in this scenario is that the texts are written to address the learning outcomes specified by the province. The textbooks developed by publishers are meant to aid teachers and students in their study of the specified topics for each grade and subject. But the textbooks do not determine the contents, the pedagogy, or the assessment. They are student resources and they are called that by the publishers. Thinking of the textbook as a student resource and thinking of a teacher guide as a teacher resource guide may help both parties remember that the textbook is there to help meet the province's learning outcomes, not to determine the order of instruction or to reduce teachers' agency (to anticipate Sunshine Sullivan's argument in Chapter 5). With this *resource* vocabulary in place, it is easier for Alberta's teachers to remember both that they are teaching *with* the text (as opposed to *from* the text) and that they are educational professionals, not robots.

In an age when both teachers and students have access to myriad online resources, this vocabulary also frees educators to treat the text as one resource among many. Granted, because it may have been custom-written to suit a particular subject and grade, it may remain the dominant resource for a class. But whatever the status of the text, perhaps teachers can use it more effectively in conjunction with online sources. And textbook publishers and writers should already be producing textbooks that recognize and take full advantage of the ubiquity of online information.

By teaching *against* the text, we mean those situations where teachers regularly point out a textbook's flaws. If done carefully, this posture toward the textbook can lead to more critical engagement by students. For example, when teaching *against* the text, a teacher could require students to write 200 words on how they would have explained the topic on page 174; or they could require the students to conduct research and then rewrite the 50-word sidebar on page 60. Such assignments increase critical engagement by saying, in effect, "There are multiple ways to address this topic," as opposed to "Our textbook got this wrong." By contrast, the teacher who criticizes the text by noting persistently how the authors omitted important content or covered this or that topic in the wrong way may ultimately undermine students' confidence in the text (and possibly in the teacher who chose it). Students may ask under their breath or aloud, "Why are we using this textbook if you are so unhappy with it?" In higher education, teachers may question why they spent as much money as they did on a fundamentally flawed resource.

By teaching *to* the text, the fourth and final posture on our list, we mean that the teacher cedes too much authority to the textbook and allows it to shape the course. This posture is easier to understand when we remember that many texts are custom-written to suit specific learning outcomes. That is, the text may match the course objectives so well that the teacher and possibly the students begin to see it as the ultimate authority, rather than a resource. This posture toward the textbook thus contains the danger that teacher and students alike will not think critically about ideas, will not do further reading, and will not research the course's topics more broadly.

The Gifts Textbooks Give Educators

We have noted some of the struggles teachers have with textbooks and we have listed four ways educators use or work with textbooks. Now we want to catalogue some of the gifts textbooks give teachers.

Most obviously, textbooks save time because their contents are organized to foster learning. In fact, with custom-published textbooks, the contents already match the learning outcomes a state or province has specified for that grade and subject. Imagine for a moment that you have proposed a brand-new elective course—for example, an art history course for ninth-graders titled *Impressionism and Post-Impressionism: From Claude to Vincent*. Your principal agrees that you have the expertise to develop this course and that your school's students would benefit from it. The school could easily fill another ninth-grade elective every second day in Block 4. In short, you receive the go-ahead. After scouring libraries and the internet you decide that no text is really suited to your purposes. Scholarly studies and coffee-table books about the Impressionists abound, but you can find nothing suited for school use with early adolescents. As interesting as you find Season 5, Episode 10 of *Doctor Who*—"Vincent and the Doctor"—it will simply not suffice as curriculum content for a course that will meet 45 times for 82 minutes each time. So you set to work.

- Which paintings will we focus on?
- What published resources can we use?
- Which websites are best for what?
- What assessments should I develop?
- How many units should there be in this course?
- Will the course involve painting itself or only the study of paintings?
- To what degree should we attend to the painters' biographies?
- How do I get my students to study some of the lesser-known Impressionists?
- Who were the main influences on the painters and whom did they influence?

We write as Canadians, so, if this were our course, we would ask about French Impressionism's influence on Canadian painting. A similar question could be asked about American, British, or German painting. We have provided enough questions to make our point: course development and assembling curriculum materials demand a great deal from those who would take them on. To reiterate our earlier confession, we know that a textbook written for a ninth-grade course on French Impressionism would not be perfect. Every teacher who used it would be able to think of one way or another that it might be improved, and of additional resources to supplement it. But we want to repeat our earlier claim, too: that textbook would save a teacher dozens or even hundreds of hours of course design and instructional planning time.

When we make that claim, we assume that, like most textbooks, our textbook—let's call it *The French Impressionists*—contains much expository text. It has suggested extension activities. It contains sidebars and textboxes featuring interesting contents that don't fit smoothly into the running text. Again, our point is that all this material and all these resources are already in our own—and our students'—hands, between two covers. Done. Ready to use. Imperfect, yes, but in our hands and ready to use. Like us (the authors), every reader of this chapter has developed classroom activities from scratch or adapted materials from a website or a supportive colleague. We all know how much time it takes to develop a new activity, or even adapt an existing one. Inasmuch as textbooks have developed so much material for us, they act like a second teacher or a teacher's assistant. We repeat what we said above: pages and pages of expository text, illustrations, suggested activities, and questions are gathered together, ready for use. In the case of custom-written texts, all these resources are suited directly to the course's learning outcomes. Teachers can base a class plan on something in the text without needing to develop new material from scratch. Furthermore, because most texts provide more resources than any one teacher could use or any one class could complete during the hours available in a typical course, texts allow teachers to pick and choose contents and activities. We view that freedom to select from among a variety of activities as a gift.

Let us suggest another. Textbooks, especially those that are custom-published, give students a tangible sense of the course and their progress through that course. We note this despite our earlier concern about educators who shape their course too closely to the textbook. Students measure their own experience of a semester or year by the number of weeks already gone and/or the number of weeks that remain on the calendar. This is a system of measurement that leads to a range of emotions—from despair to joy and hope. Students also measure their progress by the number of pages or chapters they have completed and/or have yet to complete in their textbook.

We have already confessed that we approached this chapter as textbook authors ourselves, doubtless bringing our biases to the question of what textbooks give educators. With those biases acknowledged, we consider textbooks as gifts to both educators and students. But we want to remind you, our readers, that our work as textbook authors means we have experienced more than our quota of slings and arrows. We ask you to consider whether our experience on all sides of the textbook equation entitles us to at least a temporary hall pass.

Conclusion

We have been forthright about the imperfections of textbooks, and, for those readers who have borne with us this far, we admit that even our own textbooks are not, in fact, perfect. Indeed, they contain clear signs of having been written by mere mortals. As K-12 and higher educators, we, like you, have identified many flaws in the textbooks we have used. In short, all educators know that texts have shortcomings, and we often wish they were different than they are. We see these problems ourselves and our students point them out to us. In this chapter, we have mentioned—but not expanded upon—some of the usual complaints students and teachers make about textbooks.

Still, notwithstanding their evident shortcomings, we maintain that textbooks give much to teachers for which teachers should be thankful. They are, in short, a gift to educators—and, without a microgram of sarcasm, we welcome anyone who disagrees with us to write one. More positively, with the increased attention given to gratitude practices in recent years (Howells, 2012), we encourage all educators to list, in writing, some of the aspects of the textbooks they use for which they are grateful. And we encourage classroom teachers to slip regular praise of their textbooks into conversation with their students. It is not too burdensome to say to a class that "Questions 4 and 5 on page 211 are such great questions. I want you to select three from the others on that page but you must include those two."

Including notes about a textbook in a gratitude journal or praising parts of a text in front of students does not in any way undermine critical engagement with the textbook. As with any book, we may consider a textbook good and worth reading and still note how the author's perspective might have led to an omission. We can agree with a book's conclusion but not with the arguments the author used to reach it. Or we can agree with an author's arguments but disagree with where that author insists they logically lead. In fact, noticing our textbooks' weaknesses or disagreeing with their authors' conclusions makes for better, more engaged pedagogy. Using textbooks in that way—teaching *with* the text—can become a central element in the high-functioning classroom.

We believe that textbooks, be they perfect or flawed, are a gift to teachers and students alike, and we invite you, our readers, to view them in that way too.

References

Antayá-Moore, A., Smith, T. A., Goodman, D. M., & Harding. J. C. (2007a) *Voices of Canada: People, places, and possibilities*. Pearson.

Antayá-Moore, D., Cunningham, D., Duguay, M., Harding, J. C., & Kleitsch, C. (2007b). *Worldviews, contact and change*. Pearson.

Antayá-Moore, D., Badley, K., Cunningham, D., Duguay, M., Fitton, A., Harding, J. C., Kleitsch, C., Plishka, K., & Reed, M. (2007c). *Worldviews, contact and change: Teacher resource*. Pearson.

Badley, K. (1996). *Worldviews: The challenge of choice*. Irwin.

Badley, K. & Antayá-Moore, D., (2004a). *Expressions of faith: Teacher's guide*. Nelson Thomson.

Badley, K. & Antayá-Moore, D. (2004b). *My place in the world: Teacher's guide*. Nelson Thomson.

Badley, K. & Antayá-Moore, D., (2004c). *Who am I? Teacher's guide*. Nelson Thomson.

Badley, K., Antayá-Moore, D., & Kostelyk, A. (2004a). *Expressions of faith*. Nelson Thomson.

Badley, K., Antayá-Moore, D., & Kostelyk, A. (2004b). *My place in the world*. Nelson Thomson.

Badley, K., Antayá-Moore, D., & Kostelyk, A. (2004c). *Who am I?*Nelson Thomson.

Badley, K., Colyer, J., Perry-Globas, P., Tonn, D., Weeks, P., Yoshida, D., Zelinski, V., & Zook, D. (2007). *Perspectives on globalization: Teacher's resource*. Oxford.

Edmunds, A., Nickel, J., & Badley, K. (2015). *Educational foundations in Canada*. Oxford.

Fish, S. (1982). *Is there a text in this class? The authority of interpretive communities*. Harvard University Press.

Howells, K. (2012). *Gratitude in education: A radical view*. Sense.

Whitehead, A. N. (1929). *The aims of education*. Macmillan.

5
SUSTAINABLE TEACHING
Reflective and responsive practices

Sunshine R. Sullivan

In the middle of their regular writers' workshop, Maria notices that one of her students has their head heavy in their palm, pencil down, staring at a clean piece of notebook paper. She quietly walks over and asks questions, listens, and asks more questions, re-engaging the writer. She notices and notes the questions that appeared to spark the ideas for this writer as she walks back to her conference space, where another writer is waiting for her. At the end of the day, Maria reviews her notes and considers how tomorrow's plans should be adjusted. In her notes she notices that one student has not stuck with a text for their independent reading for more than two days. Maria's attempts to connect her students with genres and authors that she thought would connect meaningfully for this student have failed so far. She reaches out to her grade-level team as well as her friends who teach in other contexts—central members of her professional landscape of practice—for ideas.

In response, Maria's colleagues provide encouragement and concrete ideas for tomorrow, as well as challenges with resources and strategies for Maria to review and selectively add to her teaching repertoire. A week later, Maria's administrator comes to observe a lesson. At the end of the day, Maria meets to discuss the observation with her administrator and is questioned primarily about why she didn't use the curriculum during the lesson. She provides reasons with supporting evidence about her students' growth as well as the research and resources in which her approach to teaching is grounded. The administrator responds with a clarified expectation that she is to use the curriculum because it will make her work easier, adding a note that the district spent large amounts of money on the new curriculum in the expectation that teachers would maintain fidelity to it. Maria leaves the meeting and reaches out to some of the colleagues she heard from the previous week but also extends her reach to others from another community that is part of her landscape of practice, sharing her confusion and frustration about her role as an inclusive, culturally responsive educator who is being directed to follow a purchased curriculum more closely.

DOI: 10.4324/9781003124429-5

Conversations about Sustainable Teaching

Maria's experience is and has been common across US schools. Unfortunately, preservice and practicing teachers are often recruited to do the work of a teacher with calls for creative, inclusive, and responsive practices. The gulf between this open language that is used when recruiting new teachers and the narrower language that is used to align teachers with mandates often contributes to teacher burnout. When teachers are confronted with challenges, mandates, and prescribed curricula that restrict their teaching repertoires they can experience frustration, anxiety, isolation, and tension between what they thought teaching was and what is now required of them. Yes, teachers and learners should have standards. But how learners and teachers are supported in their efforts to meet those standards depends on individual areas of potential growth, passions, and ways of knowing.

The purpose of this chapter is to name and illustrate realities of how reflective practice can support educators in their work day to day, week to week, semester to semester, and year to year. I invite you to join me as I reflect critically on parts of my own growth as a reflective educator practicing and learning across four decades, three states, and four distinct educator roles. However, before we can dialogue here, it is important for you to know that this critical reflection is rooted in my experience and readings related to key traits of sustainable teaching: teacher agency, reflective practice, and participation in a landscape of practice.

Teacher Agency

Teachers' responses to the challenges and tensions they face in their practice are directly linked to their sense of agency. That sense of agency will determine how national, state, and district mandates and prescribed curricula are understood and used to shape their teaching and learning responsibilities. Ahearn's (2001) review of multidisciplinary scholarship demonstrates the complexity of defining and understanding agency. She begins by explaining that "agency refers to the socio-culturally mediated capacity to act" (Ahearn, 2001: p. 112). Agency is a combination of:

- the ability to recognize the constitutive power of discourse;
- the ability to catch discourse/structure/practice in the act of shaping desire, perception, knowledge; and
- engagement in a collective process of re-naming, re-writing, and re-positioning oneself in relation to coercive structures (Davies, 2003: p. 201).

On Davies' (2010: p. 56) account, agency is "linked to the opening up of new ways of being." Johnston (2004: p. 29) defines agency as "a sense that if you act, and act strategically, you can accomplish your goals." These definitions are enhanced by Freire's (1970, 1973) and Finn's (2009) clarifications that such agency does not mean people must abandon who they are; rather, they gain understanding of power and privilege and work toward social justice through their diverse literacies. When I use the term "agency," I am referring to a person's ability to recognize that the choices and decisions they are faced with both influence and are influenced by their socio-cultural selves and their willingness and ability to act on those choices and decisions. Maria engaged her agency both in her classroom and in her post-observation meeting with her administrator. Instead of simply progressing to the next day's lesson, she used her student assessment data and teaching repertoire to inform her instruction and adjusted her plans in response. In her conversation with her administrator, she clarified her purposes and processes supported by educational research and theory as well as her deep knowledge of her students as learners. Those agentive actions were supported by her reflective practice and communities of practice.

Reflective Practice

Dewey (1933: p. 275) insists that a teacher's knowledge "must be wider than the ground laid out in a textbook or in any fixed plan for teaching a lesson. It must cover collateral points, so that the teacher can take advantage of unexpected questions or unanticipated incidents." Here, Dewey makes an important distinction between routine action and reflective action. He explains that routine action is regularly guided by authority, impulse, and tradition. In every educational context there are established and maintained expectations for what teaching and learning mean and how they are practiced. These routines work well to sustain a specific perspective and restrain the exploration of other perspectives. Dewey describes reflective action, however, as consistent, active, and mindful consideration of the strengths and areas for potential growth of any belief or action—actively choosing how to move forward rather than simply following an established routine.

Educational researchers and theorists have made it clear that reflective action is not a series of steps to be followed (Dewey, 1933; Fecho, 2011; Garcia & O'Donnell-Allen, 2015; Palmer 2017; Schön, 1983; Zeichner & Liston, 2014). It is described as a way of being in which the professional remains committed to the process of purposeful learning and responsive practice. Schön (1983) illustrates the importance of practitioners engaging in reflection-on-action and reflection-in-action. Reflection-on-action can occur before or after teaching, whereas reflection-in-action occurs simultaneously with the act of teaching. This kind of reflective practice empowers teachers to examine unexpected conflicts critically and develop flexible, adaptive, and responsive instruction (Dewey, 1933).

Schön (1983) describes the importance of and processes involved in reflective practice. He names the very real challenges that arise when professionals shift from relying on technique-centric problem-solving to what he describes as problem-*setting*—framing and reframing problems within their broader and specific contexts. Parker Palmer (2017: p. 10) clarifies that the premise of his entire book *The Courage to Teach* is that "good teaching cannot be reduced to technique; good teaching comes from the identity and integrity of the teacher." This is part of the reflective practitioner's work, shifting from answering challenges by repeatedly selecting from the same toolbox to considering mindfully the value and application of their collected tools. Schön (1983: p. 50) explains:

> There is some puzzling, or troubling, or interesting phenomenon with which the individual is trying to deal. As he tries to make sense of it, he also reflects on the understandings which have been implicit in his action, understandings which he surfaces, criticizes, restructures, and embodies in further action.

As teachers encounter challenges, some choose to keep walking with the routine that is clearly outlined and externally awarded while others choose to name, critique, and join the journey of lifelong learning. Still others meander between these two paths. Maria chose to engage her reflective practice both in her classroom—before and after her post-observation meeting with her administrator—and in her communication with members of her communities of practice. Those reflective actions were supported by her teacher agency and parts of her landscape of practice.

Landscapes of Practice

This work—the vocation of teaching—is not easy. It requires intention and willingness to remain engaged in practice. It requires engaged educators who "recognize that each classroom is different, that strategies must constantly be changed, invented, reconceptualized to address each new teaching experience" (hooks, 1994: pp. 10–11). Fecho (2011: p. 1) describes this as a dialogical stance, "interrogating your own practice to better understand what is there and what is not there. It means seeing that practice is being forever in flux and under constant revision." He encourages educators to work within this tension instead of proceeding through our routines as if there is no tension, and to use the difficulties uncovered to inform our ongoing learning as educators. As Paige A. Ray notes in Chapter 6, when teachers choose to leverage the tensions between theory and practice to create and adapt responsively, both teachers and students are freed to learn. Engaged and responsive educators recognize that while their teaching repertoires represent experience, strength, and insight, the body of knowledge for teaching is bigger than what can be found in any one teacher, school, or prescribed curriculum. They recognize that they are part of the body of knowledge that Wenger-Trayner & Wenger-Trayner (2015: p. 13) describe as "a community of people who contribute to the continued vitality, application, and evolution of the practice." The teaching vocation is not easy, but it can be sustainable when we are members of professional communities of practice.

Wenger and various colleagues (Lave & Wenger, 1991; Wenger, 1998; Wenger, McDermott, & Snyder, 2002) have proposed communities of practice as a model of learning in which the process of learning and creating is the focus, not a predetermined outcome. They describe a community of practice as a group of individuals who share a concern or passion for something they do, self-select in and out of the group, and participate at different levels of engagement depending on their knowledge, abilities, and commitment to interacting with others. Participation in communities of practice refers to "being active participants in the practices of social communities and constructing identities in relation to these communities" (Wenger, 1998: p. 4). Wells (1999: p. 123) adds, "learning is an integral aspect of participation in practices that have some other object in view." Engaged teachers participate in multiple communities of practice, depending on their embodied practices and contexts. This makes sense; just as the body of knowledge cannot be located in one teacher, school, or prescribed curriculum, one community of practice is unable to hold the entire body. Wenger-Trayner & Wenger-Trayner (2015: p. 13) posit that for professional occupations the body of knowledge might "best be understood as a 'landscape of practice' consisting of a complex system of communities of practice and the boundaries between them." This framework for learning broadens our understanding of some of the spaces engaged educators travel within and between to support their individual and community practice.

Palmer (2004) describes the importance, for teachers, of growing in our awareness and presence of our self in solitude and in community. He explains that these parts of our lives are integral for one another, and notes that attending to our "hidden wholeness" allows us to embrace and begin to address the inequities, challenges, and flaws in our own lives and the lives of others in our immediate and broader social contexts. When teachers listen in both solitude and community, they are able to do the necessary inner work to thrive in their vocation and life. They are able to discover practices that help them on the journey toward what Palmer calls an "undivided life." They are able to do the work of exploring what Palmer (2017: p. 5) terms the "inner landscape of the teaching self":

> To chart that landscape fully, three important paths must be taken—intellectual, emotional, and spiritual—and none can be ignored …
>
> By *intellectual* I mean the way we think about teaching and learning—the form and content of our concepts of how people know and learn, of the nature of our students and our subjects. By *emotional* I mean the way we and our students feel as we teach and learn—feelings that can either enlarge or diminish the exchange between us. By *spiritual* I mean the diverse ways we answer the heart's longing to be connected with the largeness of life—a longing that animates love and work, especially the work called teaching.

This inner work is required for the health and mindful growth of the individual as well as the landscape of practice in which they walk. Returning to Maria, her participation in this work across her landscape of practice recursively supported her agency and reflective practice. She chose to walk the path that requires lifelong learning, even though she's been teaching—and learning—for 32 years.

While Maria's experience is unique to her, it is similar to those of many educators across diverse contexts. My hope in writing this chapter is that it encourages more educators to make the choices that will empower them to be their whole selves in the incredible vocation we call teaching. We can read the theories and research about reflective practice, teacher agency, and landscapes of practice, but stories of real, flawed, and striving teachers bring these ideas to life. So, in the next section, I offer my humble attempt to follow Palmer's lead and chart the development of the inner landscape of my own teacher self and how the three strands of teacher agency, reflective practice, and landscapes of practice have been present on the intellectual, emotional, and spiritual paths of this lifelong learning pilgrimage. I organize this journey by sharing some of my firsts as an educator.

A Personal Journey Toward Sustainable Teaching

Before my senior year of high school, my idea of teaching was based on the cutting and coloring projects my mom would have me do to help her prepare materials for her kindergarteners. I thought teaching could be fun because I loved kids and enjoyed coloring and creating learning activities. My senior year's community service project first opened my eyes to a deeper aspect of what loving and teaching others meant. I volunteered in a school that taught only students with moderate to severe learning differences—students who were unable to learn in their various districts' public schools. I suddenly realized that I had never previously seen, let alone known, students or adults with these differences. I wondered why. When I asked my teachers, they said, "Because they can't learn and act like you can." So, for my senior research project, I decided to study and better understand people with one of these differences that I saw and worked with in my volunteering context: people with Down Syndrome. It was through this project that I remember taking my first steps as an educator. However, for 18-year-old Sunshine, the intellectual, emotional, and spiritual paths described by Palmer (2017) were not separate and perhaps not perceptible. All I knew was that I believed that all people could learn, that we learn better together, and that differences should not (but unfortunately did) lead to exclusion. Thus, I set my mind to become a teacher who would make sure all of her learners were known and supported alongside their peers.

In my first semester as an education major, I was faced with the reality that I was not the smartest or most mature first-year student. I struggled to attend to the responsibilities that came with the freedom of a college education. This became abundantly clear when my education field experience reflective journal assignment was due. I started strong for the first two weeks, when I was observing in the back of a room and could record things as they happened. However, in week three the teacher invited me to work with students. My attention shifted to the students and away from my journal assignment. Ten weeks passed before I realized I had forgotten about this requirement. I remember getting out four different writing utensils and changing my handwriting to give the impression that these ten weeks of reflection had not been written in one sitting. I recorded weekly reports of things I remembered happening alongside an identified connection to something assigned in course readings. These were focused on the techniques and strategies the teacher used to keep the students on-task. While making these connections helped me identify similarities and differences between what we were reading and real classrooms and teachers, the reflections were limited and technique-centric. I earned an "A" and unfortunately drew the conclusion that reflection was helpful only for *observing* teachers, not for *teaching* teachers.

Thankfully, my first student teaching placement provided me with a classroom mentor who modeled for me that teaching teachers must also be observing teachers—not just teachers, but *teacher learners* forever. Teacher learners observe their students and their own practices on a daily basis to inform their own learning. When things went well, my mentor would ask me why I thought they had gone well and what I thought had helped them go well. When things didn't go as planned, instead of telling me what she had observed, she regularly asked me questions, supporting my growth both reflectively and responsively. She provided me with strategies to observe my students carefully and use those observations to inform my planning, teaching, and assessment routines.

To be honest, I struggled with this work. I remember complaining once to my mentor, "Now my whole lesson plan for tomorrow is messed up." She turned her head with a huge grin and chuckled, "Welcome to teaching." Throughout my time in her classroom, we laughed and even cried together as we faced challenges and worked collaboratively to respond to them with care. It was through this experience that I learned that reflection requires responsive action if it is to make any difference—for the student and for the teacher. While I had never heard of Schön or his description of reflective practice, I began to practice reflection-in-action and reflection-on-action, albeit clunkily at first. I learned the importance of planning and the willingness to adjust those plans when needed. I'd love to claim that I effortlessly sustained this mindset and work for the rest of my career, but I required a few more lessons—all of them more painful than the introductory one.

It was in my first student teaching placement where I first began to perceive the power of a community of practice. The connections my mentor had across her region (collaborating school districts) were clear throughout our conversations, in the workshops we attended and others she led, and in school, district, and regional meetings. When my mentor had a question about something, she'd reach out to some or all of these people and then share with me what she'd learned from them. My mentor had been teaching for 16 years, yet she demonstrated lifelong learning as both an individual teacher and one immersed in a school community. The concept of a professional community of practice was not yet a published idea and certainly not discussed in my teacher education program. However, this very real aspect of her professional practice was evident to me; I distinctly recognized that teaching is never a solo act. Teachers need their students and, as Tiana Tucker notes in Chapter 7, they also need their communities of practice.

In my first teaching position, I was connected to a Critical Friends Group and was reminded of all the lessons my student teaching mentor had taught me about reflection. I was surprised that not everyone in the group believed in the power of reflection and responsive action. Some colleagues seemed reluctant to attend, and admitted that they participated only to meet a requirement for professional development hours. Others, however, clearly demonstrated through what they said and in their practices that they were not done learning and were eager to learn more through reflective practices, both critical and collaborative. I wondered what the difference was between these two groups of teachers. At first glance, I made the inaccurate assumption that the reluctant group had become teachers principally because they wanted long summer holidays; they were teachers who clocked in and clocked out with the school bells. However, through one-to-one and small-group conversations, I gradually learned that most of them were among the first to arrive and the last to leave. Moreover, their students loved them and their colleagues respected them. This led me to ask one of them, Bob,[1] why he disliked the Critical Friends Group. He responded carefully and deliberately: "Sunshine, my students are my real teachers. When something doesn't work, my students help me figure it out. No critical friend knows me and my practice like my students."

Later that year, I hit a major wall in my progress with a group of students. I asked Bob if he'd be willing to observe me and reflect back what I was unable to see from my own reflection. After his first visit he came to my room at the end of the day and asked, "Do you listen to your students?" I pushed my chair back and stared in silence with a sick feeling in my belly. I was a special education teacher; *of course* I listened to my students. But I had to answer honestly: "No." I had fallen into the routine of creating and implementing a plan, trusting that the students would stay onboard, even if I was heading in an unhelpful direction. Throughout the rest of that semester, Bob and I talked weekly about things we were discovering by listening to our students. While we shared only one student, our dialogue supported our individual and collaborative practices. Once again, I was learning about the power of reflective practice while being part of a community of practice.

One year later, while preparing for a move to another state and a shift from teaching special education in high school to teaching special education in elementary school, I was both nervous and excited to discover what was ahead of me on this journey. During my last week teaching at the high school, Bob popped his head into my room and said, "Remember, listening to your students matters at all ages." We chuckled together. I wish I had written it down. I wish I had remembered. I had found a good rhythm again observing, listening, and responding to my high school students. But the tools and understandings I had developed with those students would prove insufficient—or would not work in the same way—once I started teaching kindergarteners and first-graders. Unfortunately, I was so focused on all of the other changes in my work that my *observing teacher* faded into the background as I struggled to establish and build co-teaching relationships.

Two more years passed, during which I served as a consultant teacher and resource room teacher. One day, our administrator raised the possibility of bringing students from our district with moderate to severe disabilities back to our building. I jumped at the chance and worked with our team to make it happen. The summer before they arrived, I met frequently with the children, their families, their previous teachers, their therapy providers, and other team members. Together we created plans that included these students in my 12:1:1 special education classroom (12 students, 1 teacher, 1 aide), which was connected with one of our general education teacher's classrooms. We mapped the year's curriculum, aligned the students' IEP goals and objectives, and planned for how I would need to adapt or modify the curriculum for them. We planned for times when all our students would be together and when we would work with them in small groups with our related services professionals. We felt prepared.

Preparation was key. The big picture and our goals were clear. However, our plans for attaining those goals began to crumble on the first day because our students arrived with varying levels of willingness and ability to follow those plans. By the third day, after I had transitioned my students to PE, I closed my door and began to weep. I did not feel prepared for this work. All our summer preparation felt like it was being thrown into the garbage. My principal was making her rounds, checking on all the teachers, and she opened my door. There was no hiding my tears when she entered the classroom. She sat in one of the student's chairs and leaned toward me: "What happened?" I began to babble about my failures and frustrations. Her concerned face broke into a smile. She asked, "What did you do this week to get to know your students? And what did you do this week that allowed them to get to know you?" She shared that the only objective for the first week is simply to establish a strong relationship with each student so that we can work with them openly and honestly throughout the rest of the year. She then asked me to tell her what I knew about my students, name by name. Much to my surprise, I could tell her a lot about each of them. She grinned again and said, "See, Sunshine, we can even learn a great deal from our failures. It's just more enjoyable to learn from our successes." She encouraged me to use the rest of the week to increase my knowledge of the students and my understanding of myself as a teacher.

Soon, I began to understand the freedom that comes with knowing one's students, and I began to identify as an observing teacher and teacher learner. While I still had not read anything by Schön, I began to practice framing and reframing the problems I was facing. I began the work he describes as problem-setting—applying the skills of inquiry, analysis, and mindfully responding to the setting in which I encountered challenges.

I believe that my administrator's observations and my own willingness to recognize my failures were key to understanding that I could accept and develop a new stance as a reflective educator. My principal's decision to serve me in this way—to hold up a mirror that I couldn't even find, let alone muster the strength to grasp, lift, and scrutinize—provided me with the space I needed to explore what Palmer (2017) characterizes as the teacher's identity and integrity, which inform good teaching. Within this practice, I discovered a sense of agency that supported my advocacy work in the district to expand our inclusive practices. My reflective practice evolved and was no longer focused solely on my own teaching; it also encompassed procedures and decisions that were made in the Committee of Special Education that would have impacts on students for years to come. My passion for inclusive and equitable teaching and learning practices gained momentum when I refused to allow the curriculum to bind and silence me as a member of the education body of knowledge. I felt free, once again, to observe, listen, and respond to my students and colleagues in ways that didn't threaten my sense of self.

Dewey (1933) identifies three attitudes that sustain reflective action: open-mindedness, responsibility, and wholeheartedness. He describes teachers who are open-minded as individuals who actively seek diverse perspectives and consider why they are doing what they are doing. Open-mindedness, a sense of responsibility, and careful consideration of the potential consequences of our actions all inform teachers' abilities to interrogate our practices. This interrogative work requires what Dewey terms wholeheartedness. Similar to what Palmer (2017) describes as the identity and integrity of the teacher, wholehearted teachers are committed to their own learning as well as the learning of all students. They are able to draw from their open-mindedness and responsibility to observe, name, and learn from their successes and, more importantly, from their mistakes. Fecho's (2011) challenge to work within the boundaries of the tensions and difficulties we encounter so that we may strengthen our ability to embrace the truth wobbling in our beliefs can lead us to develop further as reflective educators. Recently, I have especially appreciated Garcia and O'Donnell-Allen's (2015) expansion of Fecho's notion of wobble. With their Pose, Wobble, Flow (P/W/F) framework, they encourage educators to embrace the wobble as a necessary part of growth. Using these yoga terms as a guiding metaphor, reflective educators can recognize that the aim is not to perfect practice but to strengthen it continually. Many scholars have stressed this point (Dewey, 1933; Fecho, 2011; Garcia & O'Donnell-Allen, 2015; Palmer 2017; Schön, 1983; Zeichner & Liston, 2014) and it is something I strive to keep in mind every semester.

My commitment to reflective practice has been vital to sustaining myself through 15 years as a teacher educator. In some ways it would be easier simply to follow previous syllabi or find textbooks that provide all the presentations and test banks. But I would no longer be what I have come to identify as an educator: one who is free to free others through lifelong learning. I agree with Dewey (1933: p. 17) that reflection "emancipates us from merely impulsive and routine activity ... it enables us to know what we are about when we act." A dear mentor and friend once responded to my exhausted quip during lunch that I was done with lifelong learning with words I now share every semester with my students: "Sunshine, we are all lifelong learners, whether we know it or not. It's what we are learning that makes the difference." She was spot on here. We learn through all our actions and inactions. So why not actively participate in what we are learning? What I learn as a teacher will be different from what you learn because we are different individuals with different lived experiences with different teacher identities and different contexts. But taking the time to choose to engage in this reflective practice will sustain your work, your vocation, just as it sustains mine.

Together, as members of educational landscapes of practice, we must choose to remain engaged in reflective practice. We must choose to interrogate with care external realities like mandated curriculum as well as our own developed and comfortable plans and routines. We must observe, listen, and respond to our students, and remain willing to learn from and for them. Remaining engaged in reflective practice will sustain work that changes regularly. As individuals, we will all have different approaches to when, where, and how we reflect in and on our practice. However, I believe that the why behind our reflective practices is linked to our shared commitment to be free individuals working to promote—and free others for—lifelong learning.

Note

1 Name has been changed.

References

Ahearn, L. M. (2001). Language and agency. *Annual Review of Anthropology*, 30, 109–137.
Davies, B. (2003). *Shards of glass*. Hampton Press.
Davies, B. (2010). The implications for qualitative research methodology of the struggle between the individualized subject of phenomenology and the emergent multiplicities of the poststructuralist subject: The problem of agency. *Reconceptualizing Educational Research Methodology*, 1(1), 54–68.
Dewey, J. (1933). *How we think: A restatement of the relation of reflective thinking to the educative process*. Heath.
Fecho, B. (2011). *Teaching for the students: Habits of heart, mind, and practice in the engaged classroom*. Teachers College Press.
Finn, P. (2009). *Literacy with an attitude: Educating working-class children in their own self-interest* (2nd ed.). SUNY Press.
Freire, P. (1970). *Pedagogy of the oppressed*. Seabury.
Freire, P. (1973). *Education for critical consciousness*. Continuum.
Garcia, A. & O'Donnell-Allen, C. (2015). *Pose, wobble, flow: A culturally proactive approach to literacy instruction*. Teachers College Press.
hooks, b. (1994). *Teaching to transgress*. Routledge.
Johnston, P. (2004). *Choice words: How our language affects children's learning*. Stenhouse.
Lave, J. & Wenger, E. (1991) *Situated learning: Legitimate peripheral participation*. Harvard University Press.
Palmer, P. (2004). *A hidden wholeness*. Jossey-Bass.
Palmer, P. (2017). *The courage to teach* (3rd ed.). Jossey-Bass.
Schön, D. A. (1983). *The reflective practitioner: How professionals think in action*. Basic Books.
Wells, G. (1999). *Dialogic inquiry: Toward a sociocultural practice and theory of education*. Cambridge University Press.
Wenger, E. (1998). *Communities of practice: Learning, meaning, and identity*. Cambridge University Press.
Wenger, E., McDermott, R., & Snyder, W. M. (2002). *Cultivating communities of practice*. Harvard Business School Press.
Wenger-Trayner, E. & Wenger-Trayner, B. (2015). Learning in a landscape of practice: A framework. In E. Wenger-Trayner, M. Fenton-O'Creevy, S. Hutchinson, C. Kubiak, & B. Wenger-Trayner (Eds.), *Learning in landscapes of practice: Boundaries, identity, and knowledgeability in practice-based learning* (pp. 13–29). Routledge.
Zeichner, K.M. & Liston, D. P. (2014). *Reflective teaching: An introduction*. Routledge.

6

MINDING THE GAP

Seeing, valuing, and using the theory–practice tension in the classroom

Paige A. Ray

Toward the beginning of my teacher education program, I spent nine hours in a summer-long philosophy of education course. I loved it. I loved learning about the long, evolving theories of why and how we teach. I went to work on writing my personal teaching philosophy—the culminating course assignment—with verve and passion. My teacher was highly complimentary and I was floating in the ether of idealism. Mine was a post-baccalaureate certification program. I was hired that year on a provisional certificate, did my student-teaching in my own classroom, and, fearing I would lose my lunch from nerves and shock, hovered nauseously near the trash can during each passing period. I do not remember the content of my teaching that year, and I am fairly certain the students and I did more surviving than learning. The philosophy of teaching paper I had written during the previous summer—which had skillfully incorporated important theories from decades of studies and earned me a high score—did little to prepare me for the faces of 30 squirrely high-school freshman in a public communications class with a hodge-podge curriculum. I laugh now at the glaring gap between the elusive but sparkling theory I rolled around in all summer and the very concrete desks, chairs, and warm bodies of the classroom I entered that fall.

From Education Programs to the Classroom: Feeling the Gap

In my first few years of teaching, I suffered under the heavy weight of theories that made me believe a classroom is something to be managed. In a way, it is. The classroom must have some order. Students of all ages appreciate clear expectations, routine, and a sense of balance. But whether I favored a behaviorist approach, democratic classroom, or student-driven learning, management theory taught me to perceive the classroom as a place of manipulation, that my authority involved setting up a system that pushed the masses through the turnstile of learning and achievement. In my first

DOI: 10.4324/9781003124429-6

four years of teaching, I experimented with various approaches which all failed when I met the real Joe, or Jamie, or Demetrius.

Joe came from a broken home that was unsettled and uncertain. He moved in halfway through October and was gone by the end of January. He was not moved by discipline and a stern teacher; he was not motivated by grades; nor was he inspired by his own learning journey. Jamie was a bright student from a middle-class background. She had her own priorities and was not interested in a classroom constitution of rules or exit slips. She went glibly through the motions of her work and ignored me when I asked her to stop talking. She had parents on the school board and a promising tuition scholarship in her future. Demetrius wanted to learn, but as an intense introvert he saw no benefit in participating in the learning community I was trying to cultivate in the classroom.

While Skinner (1954), Kohn (1993), Glasser (1998), and others have offered helpful philosophical paradigms of leading students toward learning, none of these prepared me for the experience of knowing Joe's distinct human pain and dignity, Jamie's relative apathy, and Demetrius's unique learning style. None of these theories prepared me to see the individuals who came to my classroom. Likewise, the emphasis on classroom management as a system clouded my conception of real authority for years. What each of my students needed in order to consider joining a learning community was someone to trust.

My own story correlates with the daily experience of thousands of in-service and pre-service teachers and the simple illustration of the theory–practice tension related to what most educators call classroom management. We know that classrooms do not run by themselves. In even the best classrooms, teachers say, "Okay, everyone, let's come back together here." In a non-threatening way, some teachers count down—"Three, two, one"—to get students' attention. Others hold up a hand and, as students start to notice, they hold up their hands too, coming to attention one by one. These interventions are not meant to diffuse angry, high-temperature outbursts; they are simply maintenance strategies that ordinary teachers use every day to facilitate moving ahead with the next activity. They are examples of practices, of practice.

The tension between theory and practice—one might call it the non-reciprocal relationship—becomes apparent in the classroom management courses that many pre-service teachers take during their teaching degree. Some of these courses (i.e., some education professors) take a behavioristic approach to classroom management: to reduce or eliminate this kind of behavior, take these steps; in that scenario, take those steps. Doubtless, behavioral approaches work well for some of the situations that arise in classrooms. That is, at some points, behavioral theory works well in practice. Without irony, I say—and most agree—that Skinner was right.

But let me offer two other understandings of classroom management, both of which situate the discussion in a wider context. First, what if we conceived of the classroom day almost entirely in terms of more or less student engagement? During every moment of the teaching day students are more engaged or less engaged in their learning activities. In fact, Schlechty's (2011) proposed levels of student engagement (see Figure 6.1) give us a scale by which to gauge student responses and participation. Imagine a monitor tracking and graphing this engagement. We know, of course, that

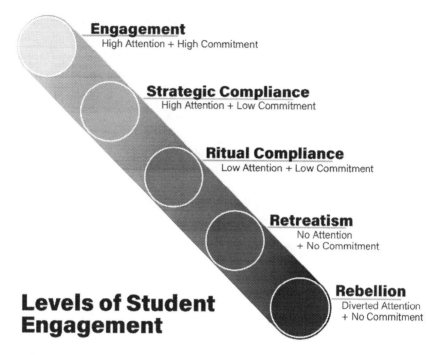

FIGURE 6.1 Schlechty's five levels of engagement

the level fluctuates in relation to such factors as reading ability, nutrition (especially blood sugar), sleep, happiness at home, and so on. But all those important environmental factors notwithstanding, we know that the classroom teacher's ability to plan creative learning activities is the most important determining factor in engagement. I will come back to engagement in a moment, after exploring my other, non-behavioristic approach to classroom management.

What if we framed all that goes on between the teacher and the students in a classroom in terms of the teacher's authority? By *authority* I do not mean that the teacher becomes an authoritarian and rules the room with an iron fist. Rather, I mean that the students in the classroom desire to join their teacher on the learning journey because, having witnessed that their teacher cares about them and has the necessary expertise to teach, they trust their teacher. In the same way that concert-goers who have paid $200 to hear a singer want to authorize that singer to sing, these students have authorized their teacher to teach. In this picture, the teacher has authority because the students have given her authority, or what political scientists call *consent*. Imagine that the monitor is now tracking consent throughout the school day. Everything the teacher did and every word she said would increase, maintain, or diminish the degree to which students gave her their ongoing consent to carry out her teaching program. We could graph each student's consent levels for every moment of the day. Per this framework, the sort of trust that translates into teacher authority is not an issue of "management." Rather, students grant authority to the teacher who is able to look past student behavior to the real issue, disarming anger or frustration and redirecting emotional energy to the collective work of learning together.

I have introduced three frameworks with which to think about classroom management: behavior, engagement, and teacher authority. By definition, the first of these focuses on what students do—their behaviors—noting especially what teachers need to do when those behaviors distract from the classroom program. If you like, behaviorism is a description of how things work (or a body of theory) that teachers can apply when necessary. Engagement and authority are also descriptions of frameworks, or theories, each of them focused on a particular aspect of classroom life.

Led into an analysis of the roots and kinds of classroom authority, in-service and pre-service teachers invariably respond with something like, "This is so much more complex than what the classroom management books say. This makes sense." I have not studied engagement as much as I have studied authority, but I suspect the education professor who frames classroom management in engagement terms likely hears similar responses. Among other commonalities, I believe the authority frame and the engagement frame share two important characteristics: they both focus on the classroom ethos in which student and teacher do their work together; and they both keep the whole teacher's program in view. I'll get bold here and claim that, compared to behaviorism, these are superior ways to frame classroom management because, as theories, they take more into account.

I wrote earlier that I wanted to offer this argument about approaches to classroom management to illustrate a notable tension between theory and practice. If the pre-service teacher learns only a behavioral approach to classroom management, then in her practice-teaching placements and eventually in her own classroom she will have more problems with student behaviors than if she had a more broad-based approach. She will experience the theory–practice tension. She may even experience what some call the breakdown between theory and practice. At some point, in frustration, she may exclaim, "This isn't working!" In those circumstances, I would argue that she has provided evidence that, to put it simply, some theories are better than others. Some theories are better than others at offering us descriptions of what is going on. In this particular case, either engagement theory or an understanding of teacher authority offers teachers more insights than behaviorism into how students behave.

Of course, the gaps between theory and practice we experience in the classroom are not limited to issues of management and authority. They also appear when implementing best instructional practices, designing lesson plans, building assessments, and anticipating student responses. For example, most practitioners recognize the benefits of accessing students' prior knowledge. This is a baseline theory that informs good instruction. But even this time-tested method meets unexpected challenges related to the unique demographics of each classroom. Accessing the prior knowledge of students in a white-collar suburb of a booming metropolis looks quite different from accessing the prior knowledge of rural students with low-level literacy. When I moved from a competitive suburban district to a district in which over half the student population qualified for the state's free or reduced-price lunch program, accessing my students' educational exposure and life experience required moment-by-moment adjustment in instruction. And in any sociocultural setting, the psychological and emotional mood of students when they enter the classroom demands that teachers adjust the ways they carry out even the simplest housekeeping and instructional tasks. The teacher learns when theory meets real time that engaging students at 9:00 am differs from engaging them after lunch, or before the big pep assembly, or after hours of state-mandated testing.

It is also important to note that though the tension is most prominent in the early years of teaching, the disjuncture between theory and practice does not necessarily dissipate with time. In this, my 15th year of teaching, the world is responding to the novel coronavirus pandemic, and educators and students around the globe are turning to online modes of learning. The students I currently serve represent a rural demographic and have limited means. I have been encouraged to teach as much as possible through "asynchronous, text-based materials"—that is, sending long emails of instruction.

There is a theory at play here, albeit not a formal one; it is a theoretical response to crisis and rapid change. The hope is that simple digital modes, such as email, will give students equal access to all instruction and equal opportunity to succeed, regardless of varying household bandwidths, unreliable internet access, and limited technology. But as I have implemented this text-based approach, I have found that students are feeling alienated from learning as they know it. Though the instruction is fully articulated in emails and online documents, they struggle. The learning environment they are familiar with involves my physical presence as a sign of comfort and normalcy, the sound of my voice and rhythm of my delivery as key components of instruction, and my movement in the space of the classroom, which helps them stay focused and engaged. Additionally, this population, which includes many first-generation college students, faces the complicating factor of low literacy. Text-based instruction may be reliable, but it is inflexible and impersonal. It cannot gauge cognition and adjust as necessary. In response, I have enriched my text-based delivery with video and one-on-one virtual meetings as necessary. The students are reaching out to thank me for the video resources—for the familiarity and reassurance they provide as well as the added visual and aural instruction. My own recognition of and response to the tension between the recommended intervention and the real needs of my students has played a key role in their learning success.

Given such gaps between theory and practice, it is little wonder that many teachers roll their eyes at the naiveté of isolated theory once they enter the world of practice. It is a response that new teachers either feel themselves or more likely witness in the cavalier dismissals of their veteran colleagues who have long eschewed the idealism they associate with theory. And in truth, that long-ago summer philosophy of education course would have served me better had I been made to write through and beyond my theory, all the way to practice—to write and think and imagine the abstract hope of my personal philosophy taking shape in the time and space of an actual classroom with actual teenagers.

So what does this excursion show us about reciprocity? Teachers give time and energy to understanding how to build a productive classroom. In fact, the initial teaching degree often includes courses focused on classroom management and best instructional practices. Justifiably, teachers want to know what they will get in return for the time and energy they give to studying theory. Sadly, sometimes they don't get much. But what if the time and effort they give to theory—to understanding how classrooms work—paid big dividends? What if we could teach them to see value in the gaps between learning theory and implementing it in practice? They might conclude that there is nothing as practical as good theory.

As one who now instructs pre-service teachers, I have to ask myself how to address this tension. I do not think the answer is to abandon philosophy of teaching courses. Likewise, it is not very productive or helpful to respond glibly when I watch my English Education students present unit plans on the teaching of writing and literature—letting them know that a million unpredictable classroom management issues will impede the effectiveness of their objective-driven, assessment-linked, airtight lesson plans. Rather, preparing my students to enjoy the benefits of the theory–practice tension involves prepping them for the reality check of the classroom even while engaging meaningful theory. In what remains of this chapter, I want to investigate how we (whether new or veteran practitioners, and as voices and participants in teacher education programs) should coach aspiring teachers to use the tension between theory and practice to refine and increase their effectiveness in the classroom.

Standing in the Gaps

Although it sometimes develops in a vacuum of abstraction, we know that theory is essential. According to Mason and Waywood (1996: p. 1056), "What is common in the use of the word 'theory' is the human enterprise of making sense, in providing answers to people's questions about why, how, what. How that sense-making arises is itself the subject of theorizing." Good pedagogical theory, both the kind that we learn from the experts and the kind we hope for and form on our own, informs teacher behavior in the classroom and arms teachers with sense-making mindfulness. The teacher who is well versed in the evolving theories of pedagogy and methodology is equipped with language and understanding that frame her interpretation of real-time experience in the classroom.

Many have witnessed the teaching of instructors who have no exposure to or concern with theories about diverse learning styles, the making of learning communities, effective authority in the classroom, or the benefits of differentiated instruction. Some such instructors find themselves in a classroom without the benefit of traditional and rich teacher training. Some have been in practice so long that they have forgotten the ideals and theories that once gave them energy for creatively engaging students. And still others have not been granted the necessary time or impetus to process the daily rhythms of their classes through the developing lens of instructional theory.

Closing the gaps between the contemplation of theory and the doing of teaching grants teachers the license to ask learning questions. When the car does not start, we speculate or theorize, "Is it the battery? How old is the alternator?" When patients do not respond to the first treatment, physicians engage their prior knowledge, consult the medical texts, rise for a moment into the world of isolated theory, and return with a new treatment plan. By what methods can we prepare prospective teachers to remember, revisit, and implement theory—theory that is all the better for being challenged by the gritty reality of practice?

Arguably, the tension that arises between theory and practice is key because that tension is the space all good teachers must inhabit. She is present in the classroom navigating the varying needs of real warm-bodied students, but yearly, semesterly, daily, minute-ly she zooms out to remember the driving trajectory. The teacher who does not exist with at least a little sense of peace in the space of this tension is the teacher who loses the task/vision balance. An effective classroom ethos develops out of the teacher's willingness to hold that space. And holding that space involves the ability to keep a sustained vision for herself and her students alongside the details of classroom practices *and* render an abstract instructional arc accessible through manageable steps.

Steve Klabnik (2012), a prominent voice in the field of computer programming and programming education, explains the value of the person who inhabits the inevitable space between theory and practice, between the ideal and the real. He identifies this daring person as an artist, a creator, and grants that

> there's a certain art to explaining the core of Theory in the words of someone who Practices, and there's a certain art to combining the essences of Practice and presenting it to those who Theorize. Building this bridge is an act of creation, of building, an opening of space.
>
> *(Klabnik 2012)*

Klabnik (2012) concludes that such a person ultimately becomes "a conduit."

While the voice of a conduit is helpful for connecting all sorts of thinkers and doers in all sorts of disciplines, for our purposes, the critical space the conduit opens is the territory of the classroom. The effective teacher, then, inhabits the space between theory and practice for the express and productive purpose of bridging those two worlds. She remains open to what she has learned about the best ideas for classroom management, inclusion, fostering community, differentiating instruction, designing assessment, and scaffolding excellent units. And she allows the often frustrating disjuncture between these theories she's absorbed and the real time/space in which she stands, with spitballs flying, to foster creativity in her pedagogy. If the teacher bridges well, she has not resolved all of the incongruencies between theory and practice, but she does allow the tension to foster creativity in her practice.

I want to argue, as others have, that teaching is most truly an art. However, for a moment, let's think about it as a science. Scientists theorize about the natural world—they hypothesize about the concrete in a separate, pure abstraction. The practice of science, though, calls them to determine the application of their theories in the laboratory with actual cells and real pond-water specimens under the pristine light of the microscope. Science calls for a meeting of hypothesis and application. Through this paradigm, we can certainly acknowledge the classroom as the theorizing pedagogue's laboratory. However, this is an inadequate analogy. Scientists observe; they faithfully report any disconnect or inaccuracy between theory and the factual phenomena they encounter in nature. They cannot manipulate the natural world; in fact, they are careful not to do so. Nor, in the work of honest observation, do scientists stretch theory to meet nature. In the name of intellectual integrity, they cannot alter or adjust.

By contrast, because she is called not only to observe but to facilitate and direct, the creative teacher, the building teacher, the artist-teacher does have the freedom to alter and adjust. She brings theory and hypothesis to the environment of her classroom, and she gauges whether the theory is correct, whether it has accounted for all the dynamics of teaching in real time and the natural impulses of children. Finding any dissonance, finding junctures where the "nature" of classroom application does not perfectly meet theory, she maneuvers. Manipulation is the happy work and freedom of an expert who can assess the discrepancies between the ideal and the real, and who can then dirty her hands and manipulate the media by which she applies that theory so that it successfully meets the classroom.

Thus, conceiving of teaching only as a science fails to acknowledge the possible, reciprocal relationship between theory and practice through which the teacher refines her application of good theory. The work of an artist, or builder, as Klabnik (2012) suggests, better reflects the critical awareness, agility, and creativity that give life to theory in the classroom.

Tension as a Feedback Loop

I did not realize it during that first, terrifying year, when I was standing in front of a squirrely group of freshmen, but the tension between theory and practice has been the most productive tension in my vocation as a teacher. And while the dissonance between my best pedagogical theories and my practice frequently presents itself as frustration, that frustration is a necessary ingredient in forming great teaching because it demands the teacher's attention—it forces reflection. As Carrie R. Giboney Wall suggests in Chapter 11, this dissonance can be a key catalyst for our best work. Notably, in order for tension and dissonance to prompt positive change, the shock of the disconnect between theory and practice should not hit when the young teacher is spending her first year in her own classroom. Teacher education programs must head off the demoralizing effects of this tension and instead prepare pre-service teachers to expect it and put it to good use.

Many aspiring teachers move through their major courses floating on clouds of happy idealism (as I did), imagining that the theories they prize—those that capture all their energy for cultivating productive learning communities, for deep and organic relationships in the classroom, and for unit plans that spin out in perfect rhythms of content delivery and successful assessment—will play out perfectly when plucked out of the world of ivory tower abstraction. Other pre-service teachers live for real moments in real classrooms when they will hold conversations with real students. In that case, who needs theory?

What teacher education programs must teach is that the theories addressed in foundation courses have inherent value in and of themselves, and then *greater* value for how they will morph and materialize when embedded in the space/time of the classroom—in reality, those theories will half work and half fail. This half success of theory, though, gives the engaged teacher the space and motivation to make the classroom her own. The best educators delight in both theory and practice, and actually find pleasure, challenge, and freedom when the two do not perfectly align.

Thus, the most appropriate posture of teachers is not so much resolve (in the direction of either theory or practice) but readiness—expecting the rather unpredictable interactions between the two. In this way, significant portions of teacher education programming should aim to form a certain flexible disposition in pre- and in-service teachers. The young teacher will surface from the frustrating tension between theory and practice in her own classroom when she perceives her role not as theorizer only, nor as practitioner only, but as a mediator between the two. If the pre-service teacher knows that the tension will be inevitable and recognizes it as beneficial for influencing how she navigates moments in the classroom, then she can learn theories well and hold them loosely. This is a much more productive stance in the classroom than believing that theory will play out perfectly.

Specifically, pre-service instruction would do well to shape the pre-service teacher's perception of theory and practice as bodies in continual dialogue. These two bodies of knowledge and experience interact and inform one another because they meet in the space of the classroom and in the hands of the mediating teacher. In this way, language that dichotomizes the roles of researcher as theorist and teacher as practitioner misses the mark. The teacher is actually the place where the two roles meet and interact. In "Theory and Practice: The Mediating Discourse," Bjorn Gustavsen (2001: p. 18; original emphasis) discusses the necessary role of the one who mediates between theory and practice:

> While a theory can certainly influence, or inform, practice and vice versa, there is no question of a *direct* relationship. The link is a discursive one where ideas, notions, and elements from theory can be considered in the development of practice but with no claims to being automatically applicable. The relationship between theory and practice can be seen as a relationship between three different but interdependent discourses—a discourse on theory, a discourse on practice and a mediating discourse on how to link them.

Gustavsen's depiction of discourse is helpful in that the gap between theory and practice invites a necessary discourse, but it remains incomplete in its portrayal of the dialogue it promotes. The best pre-service programs train teachers to see the relationship between theory and practice not simply as discursive, but as recursive—not a

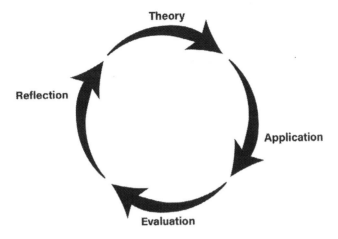

FIGURE 6.2 The recursive relationship between theory and practice

back and forth, but a circular feedback loop. The teacher who successfully mediates between theory and practice enacts a circular pattern like that in Figure 6.2: first she studies theory; then she applies it in the classroom, evaluates the tension, reflects on the disconnect; and finally she revisits theory again to adjust her application.

The teacher who is ready to mediate in this circular fashion works flexibly and expectantly and innovates where needed, creating an environment guided by theory with a posture that can negotiate practice. Essentially, the teacher's flexible movement between study, implementation, evaluation, reflection, and adaptation models the learning patterns she hopes to see in her students, achieving a satisfying model of metacognition.

Segal (1998) suggests that the agile posture of the teacher inside this circular feedback system does more than shape her actions—it actually informs and forms her sense of identity in the classroom. He explores "the role contingency plays in shaping classroom practice and, in particular, the ways in which stress, anxiety, fear and uncertainty contribute to the shaping of the character of the teacher in the classroom" (Segal, 1998: p. 200). In his article, Segal proposes that the contingencies of the classroom do not merely disconnect theory from practice, but rather push the teacher to the threshold of her productivity in marrying theory and practice—it is in the face of unanticipated contingencies that the reflective and reflexive teacher reads the feedback loop and adjusts so that theory can meet and inform practice, and vice versa. He argues,

> in order for teachers to develop a congruity between their espoused beliefs and their everyday practices, they need to develop an appreciation of the ways in which their practices are formed by how they respond to the stresses and anxieties of the classroom.
>
> *(Segal, 1998: p. 200)*

Closing the Gaps

This vision of resolving tension implies two necessary disciplines that answer the two apparent gaps addressed in this chapter. We have discussed at length the gap between the teacher's own vision of the ideal and her actual experience—all of the contingencies for which she cannot plan. We have discovered that though responsive behavior is often seen as a negative concept, in the classroom the skilled and reflexive reactions of creating, thinking, and resolving theory–practice tension are actually the teacher's best skills—negotiating the dynamics between control and response, between planning what will happen and abandoning those plans. In order to address this gap directly, teacher education programs have a duty to teach pre-service teachers how to view the tension between theory and practice. Teaching pre- and in-service teachers that the interchange is not one-way, that practice can and should also speak to theory, empowers them to respond creatively and even optimistically to "theory-gone-wrong." The new teacher is somewhat protected from disillusionment and does not become jaded at the disconnect. This posture allows teachers to stay soft and agile as they stand in the gap.

The vision of resolving theory–practice tension also reveals a significant gap between universities' teacher education programs and the classrooms of K-12 teachers. And while most teacher education programs ingrain in students the disciplines of thinking in terms of objectives, lesson-plan structure, and assessments, the discipline of reflection can be renewed through the model of recursivity. The recursive feedback between theory and practice that K-12 practitioners should be observing, mediating, and learning from must also serve as a larger model for the ideal interaction between teachers in schools and professors in teacher education programs.

Successful implementation of this model rejects the fallacy that relegates theory to teacher training and practice to teacher in-service because the professional teacher is in an ongoing dialogue with both. Thus, the model dictates that education professors must visit school classrooms to watch, listen to, and have conversations with teachers. Some already do, of course, often because their appointment includes observing and meeting with pre-service teachers during their practice-teaching placements. Interestingly, though, many education professors try to avoid school visits and hope their teacher education program will hire recently retired teachers to serve as field supervisors so that they do not have to drive around the district. But all professors—especially those inclined toward more theoretical aspects of education—need to show how and witness whether their work connects to classroom teaching.

Likewise, though school districts emphasize professional development through workshops and departmental collaboration, an often-overlooked form of developing as a professional is this cycle of entering the classroom with renewed, fresh theory in hand, and then reflecting on what did not play out as expected. Many teachers find that the mid-career jolt of theory has the power to reawaken their sense of the vocation of teaching. They have taught for a few years and, through thousands of hours of classroom practice, they have clarified their questions. They go back to university to complete their next degree, to finish an advanced qualification, or to qualify for another endorsement on their teaching license. Some step out of teaching to do so, although most continue their classroom work. Either way, such teachers often discover that, having brought the questions that arose out of the crucible of their classroom experience, they have genuine fun in these advanced studies. While they may have found their original teaching degree overly theory-heavy, they now find that they can satisfy their hunger for some time to think—for some more theory—to bring balance to the practice-heavy work they do in their classrooms. Such teachers find that the typical calculation (the financial bump that accompanies graduate degrees) is the wrong calculation—that economic terms are the wrong terms. They typically encounter a different calculation altogether—that theory and practice can inform and enrich each other. And, in truth, a re-entry into the world of theory need not imply a new degree. An increase in dialogue between academics and practitioners can exist in the form of rich, ongoing professional learning communities and workshop settings.

Thinking, then, of our circular model as a physical enactment that involves real bodies moving between institutions—bringing more education professors into the physical classroom, and inviting K-12 practitioners into the academy for conversations about theory—gives us a meaningful model for fashioning a consistent discipline. When educators on either side—those focused more on theory and those engaged more in practice—understand the relationship between theory and practice properly, they will indeed be able to achieve a healthy reciprocity.

Tension as a Discipline

While more interchange between those in the academy and those in the K-12 sphere will help close the disconnect between bodies of theory and daily practice and will reshape our view of it as looped in a necessary dialogue, I do not think education programs can eradicate the tension teachers meet in the classroom. And, as this chapter suggests, we would do ourselves a disservice to eliminate it. That said, my own pre-service education program could have prepared me better for the very active, rewarding role of negotiating between the two, of reading the feedback loop.

Gustavsen's (2001) previously cited discussion of theory–practice tension comes not from an education text, but from a larger, ongoing conversation on action research. Scholars in that field define action research not as a method but as a paradigm—one that speaks with unique relevance to the work of teachers. In *Teacher Action Research*, Pine (2009) describes this paradigm as an exact model of what I have been striving toward in this chapter. In fact, he seems to say that the disciplinary posture of action research is the most apt description of the teacher's daily and career-long work. Action research, he explains,

> assumes that teachers are the agents and source of educational reform and not the objects of reform. Action research empowers teachers to own professional knowledge because teachers—through the process of action inquiry—conceptualize and create knowledge, interact around knowledge, transform knowledge, and apply knowledge.
>
> (Pine, 2009: p. 30)

Moreover, we see that this paradigm allows for the truest view of unanticipated, real-time classroom dynamics. Pine (2009: p. 30) assures us that action research "assumes practice is embedded in the science of the unique, recognizing that human events are idiosyncratic; they vary with time, place, cultural circumstances, the ecology of the moment, serendipity, obliquities, and unforeseen circumstances." We can offer a resounding affirmation that the human events of the classroom are idiosyncratic. Recognizing those idiosyncrasies as ideal and necessary circumstances for her own growth frees the teacher for the action that Pine lauds.

In my first year of teaching, standing in front of 30 squirrely freshmen, I needed someone to tell me—and maybe convince me—that I should expect dissonance between the theories I had encountered in my foundational education courses and the unforeseen circumstances of my classroom, and that such dissonance actually creates the necessary space to do some of the best theory-informed, responsive teaching. So whether we employ Klabnik's language of teacher-as-conduit, or Pine and Gustavsen's action-research paradigm, or my own conception of the teacher as mediating artist, our conversations in courses and practicums need to recast the vision and prepare the expectations for aspiring teachers who are ready to encounter one of the most promising reciprocities the classroom has to offer.

References

Glasser, W. (1998). *Choice theory*. HarperCollins.

Gustavsen, B. (2001). Theory and practice: The mediating discourse. In P. Reason & H. Bradbury (Eds.), *Handbook of action research* (pp. 17–26). Sage.

Klabnik, S. (2012). Theory and practice. *Writing*, November 6. https://steveklabnik.com/writing/theory-and-practice.

Kohn, A. (1993). *Punished by rewards: The trouble with gold stars, incentive plans, A's, praise, and other bribes*. Houghton Mifflin.

Mason J. & Waywood, A. (1996). The role of theory in mathematics education and research. In A. J. Bishop, K. Clements, C. Keitel, J. Kilpatrick, & C. Laborde (Eds.), *International handbook of mathematics education*, volume 4 (pp. 1055–1091). Springer.

Pine, G. (2009). *Teacher action research: Building knowledge democracies*. Sage.

Schlechty, P. C. (2011). *Engaging students: The next level of working on the work*. Jossey-Bass.

Segal, S. (1998). The role of contingency and tension in the relationship between theory and practice in the classroom. *Journal of Curriculum Studies*, 30(2), 199–206.

Skinner, B. F. (1954). The science of learning and the art of teaching. *Harvard Educational Review*, 24, 86–97.

7
COLLEAGUES

Tiana Tucker

Every teacher would love to have perfect colleagues. No teacher does. Still, teachers with their eyes and ears open can gain immeasurably from their colleagues. What do teachers get by paying attention to their teaching colleagues? What do they get by intentionally asking questions, requesting help, and engaging in deep listening? Teachers who ask and listen benefit from the wealth of experience and the surplus of ideas their building colleagues represent.

Teaching can be a surprisingly isolating profession (Aisenberg & Oplatka, 2019; Stone-Johnson, 2016). Teachers often enter the profession thinking they will have myriad colleagues ready to offer resources, time, support, and a vision similar to their own for student learning and school improvement. They often find that their colleagues are busy with their own classrooms, their own students, and their own sets of pressures. Even willing building mentors with the best intentions can fall short in offering support or extra resources to their beginning teacher colleagues.

Beginning teachers are ready to work in teams and departments; they want to function as colleagues. However, upon entering the profession, many teachers find that time with colleagues, while precious, remains in short supply. Even protected time for planning and collaborating can easily be eaten up by the pressing details of running classrooms. Because time and energy are limited, teachers at any stage in their profession who want to improve in their teaching practices with the help of their colleagues must be intentional about connecting with and learning from their peers. The kind of collegiality by which teachers gain from each other has two aspects, the first of which I call *mindsets*. By that term, I mean the cognitive frames within which we view our colleagues and the attitudes we have toward them. The second aspect of the collegiality that fosters professional growth consists of our *actions*. Without wanting to sound either manipulative or mechanical about relationships, one might think of these actions as approaches or even as strategies. In the remainder of this chapter, I address these two aspects of collegiality in turn,

DOI: 10.4324/9781003124429-7

beginning with the ways we view our colleagues—our mindsets. Indeed, mindsets are the usual starting point for teachers who desire continuous improvement and view their own school staff as one of the sources of that improvement.

Mindsets

In what follows, I highlight five characteristic thinking patterns or mindsets related to our relationships with colleagues: continuously improving; keeping an open eye; learning from mistakes; sharing responsibility; and investing time. In the second main section of the chapter, I will discuss some of the ways in which teachers can realize—make real—these mindsets. However, as noted above, the kind of collegiality that fosters professional growth does not start with strategies or methods. It starts with a frame of mind or mindset.

Continuously Improving

A commitment to self-improvement and the improvement of others is a cornerstone of professional reciprocity. But wise teachers add a health-giving caveat to this commitment: they have a clear understanding that they will never achieve perfection. In teaching, there is no pinnacle where we can stop improving in our own practice or supporting the practices of other educators. Teachers who enter the profession aiming to reach perfection will likely end up selling themselves and their students short. I will return to this matter shortly when dealing with learning from mistakes as an essential part of the necessary mindset for our own professional growth and the growth of the colleagues with whom we work.

With a *no-such-thing-as-perfection-in-teaching* caveat firmly in place, we are now able to consider the first element of this mindset: supporting colleagues in their professional growth and having them support our growth require that we aim at constant improvement. Underwriting that aim, of course, is our desire to support the success of all the students in our school and to strengthen the overall quality of our school. We aim at constant improvement, not to gain more recognition for ourselves but for this larger cause.

Keeping an Open Eye

Keeping an open eye for opportunities is the second key element in this mindset of continuous improvement. Teachers with an open eye find a wealth of information and resources when they look for specifics to apply in their classrooms. If teachers have content, assignments, or practices they want to implement or strengthen, they can find examples of support all over the building. What are other teachers doing well in writing, math, or literacy instruction that I can ask about or replicate in my own classes? What were my colleague's students doing that seemed to engage them so thoroughly when I peeked in this morning? What questions have you been using in your morning meetings? Keeping my eyes open for the promising, reproducible practices—

with or without my own spin on them and not as a means simply of keeping up—can have a transformative effect on my teaching practices and my students' learning.

If students are not making gains in reading fluency, for example, and teachers have reflected on this area of improvement, there are likely examples of fluent classrooms in the building to pay attention to and ask specific questions about. The following brief account from Jerod, a fourth-grade teacher, illustrates this point:

> After reflection, I know I am struggling with writing instruction as my students' production is low and their scores are not improving. After carefully looking around, I noticed a wall of writing samples from a fifth-grade teacher down the hall. What do I want to know about the processes used in that classroom in which these are the results? What specific strategies are implemented in a room where students produce that kind of writing? After I find out, I must find someone who can help me plan and implement said strategies. Who can watch me do it and give me feedback? Or after implementation, who can help hold me accountable to trying something different and talk to me about what I tried?

Without this ongoing form of professional development (Tucker, 2015), there is an implementation gap between what teachers *should do* (according to what educators have agreed are best practices) and what *actually happens* in the classroom environment. One way to address this implementation gap is for teachers to keep an open eye for ideas and support in their own school building.

Learning from Mistakes

Teachers who want to give professional development gifts to their colleagues and receive others in return need to remember the old adage about learning from our mistakes. More specifically, such teachers should consider initiating a process by which the school becomes a learning lab for both students and teachers.

In his excellent book on piano pedagogy, *The Perfect Wrong Note*, William Westney (2003) develops what we might call a philosophy of mistakes. His assumption throughout the book is that the piano student did not intend to play the wrong note; she meant to play it correctly, but something else happened. In his view, rather than speaking sternly to the student, the piano teacher should work with her to get under or behind the mistake and find out what happened. His chapter "Big Juicy Mistakes" is especially useful for school teachers who want to work with their students to open up the question of how we will treat mistakes and learn from our mistakes in class. Indeed, this is assessment *for* learning or assessment *as* learning at its best.

My question here is whether we should apply Westney's argument to *our* work and *our* mistakes in addition to our students' work and their mistakes. If we create a learning-lab structure and participate in learning-lab activities—especially collegial observations and debriefings—we can get under and behind some of our mistakes. And we can likely put some of our mistakes behind us. In this learning-lab model, we look with our colleagues at units, assignments, experiments, and lessons. We pay attention to what went well and what didn't go quite so well in our colleagues' classrooms, and they watch for the same things in our classrooms. (Jay Mathisen addresses this in Chapter 8, too.)

Examples abound for the ways colleagues can learn from and teach each other. What are the pros and cons of individual science projects versus whole-class projects? Can we really keep salmon fry alive in the classroom in order to finish the project? When using the "Daily 5" framework (read to self; work on writing; read to someone else; listen to reading; word work), how did classes that started early in the school year fare compared to those that waited until later in the school year?

Finding out what teachers have done—or tried to do—in their classrooms and then discussing what could be strengthened the next time has the power to transform our professional practice. Many teachers have taught the same or neighboring grade (s) for many years, and with that repetition comes familiarity and instructional experience with similar content. These teacher colleagues can offer wise advice that only experience can provide, along the lines of: "I've taught this unit five times, and three of them worked better because of X." In most schools, this kind of information is powerful and readily available to teachers who are willing to use the experience of others to build their own practice. In short, let us work with our administrators and colleagues to develop a philosophy of mistakes (a.k.a. a philosophy of professional learning) and let us implement the practices that will best bring that philosophy to life.

Shared Responsibility

Teachers need to understand their role as members of school staffs. Yes, we are independent professionals, responsible for executing an instructional program in our own classrooms. As Sunshine Sullivan argues in Chapter 5, we need to work authentically; our classroom program needs to arise out of the deepest places in our teacher selves. That said, as Dana Antayá-Moore and Joanne Neal note in Chapter 12, we do this while the political, economic, and curricular winds within which schools must operate continue to blow and seemingly change direction all too frequently. Thus, we work *in*dependently but we also work *inter*dependently. We are interconnected, and in some sense we need to align our work with that of our colleagues.

Within a vertically and horizontally aligned system of K-12 education, we cannot avoid the responsibility we have to other teachers to help them develop their skills. Why do I make this point? Teachers are part of a system in which educators on all sides (and the larger public) are counting on us to do a good job in our classes with our students, in part because someone else will be teaching our students the following year … and someone else the year after that. And, ultimately, our students will graduate and enter the workplace or higher education. Viewing through this multi-year lens, it is clear that we share responsibility for our students' education with colleagues who have already taught those students in the past as well as colleagues who will teach them in the future. We all have a responsibility to do the best job we can. In my view, that includes helping our colleagues grow professionally so they can do their best job. As someone who has served as a vice principal, a principal, and a human resources director, I know that formal or legal responsibility for teachers' professional development is largely shared between the teachers themselves and their administrators. However, in my doctoral research into teachers' professional development (completed in 2015), I discovered that some of the best professional development happens when teachers help their fellow teachers. When we think about fulfilling our responsibilities to students, we need to view our own building colleagues as allies and supporters ... and as our teachers.

In one of the schools where I served as principal, the teachers and I expected the primary schools that fed our school to shoulder their educational responsibility by preparing their students for the transition to us. In turn, we accepted responsibility to prepare our students for the school they would attend when they left us. In other words, we took the long view. And when we did, we saw how it worked to our advantage to build up all teachers for the sake of our students. You can see the reciprocity here, inasmuch as what we got from the teachers who taught our students before we met them had an impact on our work and even on the work of the teachers who would meet them when they left us. In the long view, we all share responsibility for improving our practice in the best interests of our students.

Time Investment

Without a doubt there is a cost to helping another teacher within an already limited working day. Public school teachers are governed by their collective bargaining agreements and they have student responsibilities throughout the day. Minutes before school, minutes after school, and preparation minutes are all precious. So, offering to spend time with a colleague has a personal cost; and asking a colleague for some of their time corresponds to asking them to make a personal sacrifice on your behalf. Yet, this time is not lost; it is an investment. If we think of helping each other become the best teachers we can be for our students, school, and district, the reciprocity of sharing time strengthens the whole system.

If teachers consider the time they invest in others as support for building a better school, school system, and even society, the cost—or what we might more accurately call *the subjective cost*—diminishes. But the cost diminishes for another, more personal reason, too. Teachers who work with a colleague to help that colleague improve their practice also improve their own practice (again, as Jay Mathisen describes in Chapter 8). When teachers reflect on an observation or deconstruct a lesson or some curriculum materials in this way, *both* teachers learn. Yes, it may be said that only one gives her time. But she learns as well. This is why I recommend that such collaboration be clear and focused. Teaching observations, reflection, discussion, data analysis, planning, and researching are all forms of collaboration by which colleagues can exchange gifts. These kinds of collaborative relationships are truly reciprocal.

In the following main section, I suggest five practical strategies that teachers can use to grow through their collegial interactions.

Strategies that Promote Collegial Exchange

Teachers' calendars are full of to-do lists that include grading, planning and preparing instruction, parent conferences, standardized test administration, and tracking student progress. With limited time and energy, teachers may wonder how they can possibly engage in the kinds of collegial work and collaborative professional development I described in the first half of this chapter. Here, I offer four strategies teachers can use to improve their practice alongside their colleagues. As I noted in the introduction to the chapter, I use the word "strategies" somewhat cautiously because I do not wish to reduce collegiality and collaboration to techniques or something mechanical. The practices I describe here require a humble posture and arise out of a collegial mindset.

Asking Questions

Because of sheer busyness and the fact that they primarily work alone during the school day, many teachers have few opportunities to observe their colleagues' teaching practices. However, teachers who are willing to ask questions of other teachers in their building will likely gain much that can inform their own practices. Teachers can ask their colleagues questions about which selections to use in a novel study, how to teach fractions using manipulatives, which field trips go best with a particular social studies unit, and which science experiments students find most engaging. Teachers with the humility to ask and the skills to word their questions unambiguously learn a plethora of creative and stimulating ways to improve their own practice from their colleagues.

Another dimension of asking questions warrants mention here. Teachers who reflect and ask questions of themselves are better positioned to ask questions of their colleagues. This assertion relates to my concern about reducing the approaches I recommend here to mere techniques; we are discussing teaching, one of the most complicated processes on earth, not how to put a new battery in a computer mouse. Both colleagues in such conversations need to dig past simple questions of teaching methods and on to deeper questions of how our students might demonstrate their proficiency and how best they might acquire the understanding we desire for them.

One of the questions teachers can ask their colleagues is: will you come to my room and observe a live class or watch a lesson video? If you recall my discussion of developing a philosophy of mistakes—that is, a philosophy of learning—being vulnerable and asking colleagues to observe our teaching should not threaten us. In fact, we and our colleagues should work together to build a school culture where we consider such collaboration and learning natural. Still, it is humbling to be observed, humbling to find ourselves almost in a student role. Perhaps we ought to do it more often, if only to remind ourselves of what it is like to be a learner. Having another set of teacher eyes on our teaching implies a kind of accountability. Asking a peer to come in and look for specific things, then discussing what they observed in a post-class or end-of-day conversation, is critical to moving forward in our own development as teachers. Such conversations encourage metacognition for both the teaching teacher and the observer, leading to new understanding and thereby adjustments in practice (Costa & Garmston, 2002).

Commit to Core Content

Teachers sometimes feel constrained by the curriculum prescribed for the grade and subjects they teach. As much as they might like to go their own way, most teachers know that if they sign a contract (and accept the auto-deposit in their bank account every month), the adult thing to do is to follow the specified curriculum. As a school district human resources director, I am quite keen for teachers to teach what the district pays them to teach. But I want to take a moment to suggest a way to frame the prescribed curriculum without the language of responsibility or duty. A gift is buried in the prescribed curriculum. It is this: when you and your colleagues follow the curriculum, you become resources for each other. Irrespective of whether you teach in a school that is big enough to have subject-area or grade-level teams, you will be able to find colleagues who will support you in your work and whom you can support in turn. Teacher colleagues support us in the same way as textbooks offer us the gift of work already done (as Ken Badley and Dana Antayá-Moore argue in Chapter 4).

Teachers at all grade levels and in all content areas can serve as resources, especially when they have common learning goals. Remaining committed to core content as well as core outcomes provides not only a clear baseline or benchmark for all students but also a clear baseline for teachers to share a common language, curricular materials, and best instructional practices. Additionally, teaching colleagues who use shared curricular materials typically follow a pacing and assessment schedule that provides three important things: accountability; a schedule from which to plan and teach; and assessment data by which teams can evaluate the effectiveness of their instruction. Teachers can share their successes and learn from their mistakes—even the big, juicy ones—in order to find shared strategies to re-teach and fill in the learning gaps.

At this point, I wish to highlight an irony lurking in a tension between professional independence and collegial interdependence. When teachers set and share common curricular goals and instructional targets, they create academic freedom for themselves with reference to other content and units. When teachers commit to the core contents and work collegially to help their students master those contents, they still retain the freedom to create think-tanks, laboratories, world parliaments, writers' workshops, or whatever else they might want in their other classes. They can spend their salaries with a clear conscience and go home at the end of the day feeling like they taught from the deepest core of their being. However, when teachers commit to the core and consistent teaching practices within the team, some teachers may feel that these practices stifle their professional discretion, independence, and creativity. There is a constant push and pull between the way teachers view best practice as independent teachers; there is strength that comes from teaching consistently within a team and using agreed standards.

Novice and Veteran

Teachers learn early on that experience, materials, and resources are all key to improving practice. Elizabeth, a first-year teacher in her forties, has none of these commodities to trade with her veteran teaching partner. Although Elizabeth's life with-it-ness is not in short supply, the learning curve for a beginning teacher is much the same as it would be were she 20 years younger. Although she has much life experience and general confidence, she has low teacher self-efficacy (Bandura, 1977; 1997). As a result, she needs considerable support from her colleagues. She gains wisdom, materials, and resources from her one science department colleague's years of experience. At the same time, she wonders what she can possibly give to him in return in their experienced–inexperienced teacher relationship. Finding a shared time to converse about practice, labs, lessons, and grading while also asking about pedagogy will support Elizabeth. Likewise, questions she poses to her colleague encourage him to reflect upon his own practice. Any time Elizabeth seems to take from him is valuable. She wants to offer ideas in return. As her colleague presents his classroom experience to her, any new resources Elizabeth finds and shares have the potential to enhance his current repertoire or even replace materials that are no longer effective ... should he be willing to accept Elizabeth's fresh ideas.

This example demonstrates how veteran teachers can mitigate any sense of sacrificing time to help a novice teacher. They receive too, by gaining fresh ideas and learning about new approaches to old subjects, so helping a new teacher can create a space within which they can reflect and appraise their own practices in the field.

Vertical Colleagues

There is a wealth of knowledge, skills, and experience in the K-12 teaching force. When teachers meet with colleagues from whom they receive their students and to whom they send them, they help align the system in which they work. Developing relationships with colleagues who teach students in previous and subsequent grades can have powerful effects on teacher practice.

Maximizing student learning in a given school year implies that students achieve at least one year's growth each year. In order to have clear direction from the start of each school year, teacher collaboration with the previous grade-level teacher becomes key to starting strong with content and skills. Additionally, clearly knowing the scaffolded expectations for what students should know and have the ability to do across grade levels helps teachers complete the loop for students. Schools' traditional teacher teams and learning communities are often focused on same-subject or grade-level horizontal groupings. Only rarely is time built into school or district schedules to encourage a vertical community in which teachers study content, assessments, samples of student work, and the overall demands of previous and subsequent grades. Teachers should see these *vertical* colleagues, these educators from other grade levels, as partners in their work alongside those of their own grade level—their *horizontal* colleagues.

Rather than providing only isolated experiences for students and teachers, vertical meetings encourage strong collaboration within a school and K-12 system for student achievement. To the point of this book, vertical collaboration allows teachers to apprehend more clearly the gifts they receive each year from their colleagues at lower grade levels. Moreover, as a corollary, this gives them a deeper understanding of the gifts they should pass on to colleagues who will teach their students in subsequent years.

Conclusion

Teachers enter this noble profession to serve students. Most teachers enjoy the challenges that teaching presents. And, as several other contributors to this book note, most teachers, knowing that they cannot skirt around the challenges of teaching, go straight through them and grow through them.

In this chapter I have focused on the teacher-to-teacher relationship, and I have noted repeatedly the importance of collegial collaboration and cooperation in professional development. Together, as colleagues who want to improve continually while knowing we will never reach perfection, we keep an open eye, we make mistakes and learn from them, we share responsibility and our time, and we grow in our professional practice. When we adopt a posture of humility and then engage in collaborative strategies such as asking questions, seeking and welcoming feedback, committing to core content, and trusting our colleagues—both novice and veteran, and from previous and subsequent grade levels—we grow in our practice.

I hope that this chapter has provided ample evidence that you are not alone in the teaching profession. Our students are better when we seek out the abundant expertise and collegial relationships in our schools. We are better together. We give gifts to each other. And we receive gifts from each other.

References

Aisenberg, K. & Oplatka, I. (2019). From professional isolation to effective leadership: Preschool teacher-directors' strategies of shared leadership and pedagogy. *Teachers and Teaching: Theory and Practice*, 25(8), 994–1013.

Bandura, A. (1977) Self-efficacy: Toward a unifying theory of behavioral change. *Psychological Review*, 84(2), 191–215.

Bandura, A. (1997). *Self-efficacy: The exercise of control*. Freeman.

Costa, A. L. & Garmston, R. J. (2002). *Cognitive coaching: A foundation for renaissance schools* (2nd ed.). Christopher Gordon.

Stone-Johnson, C. (2016). Intensification and isolation: Alienated teaching and collaborative professional relationships in the accountability context. *Journal of Educational Change*, 17, 29–49.

Tucker, T. J. (2015). Bridging the research-to-practice gap: factors affecting teachers' efficacy about instruction. Unpublished doctoral dissertation, George Fox University.

Westney, W. (2003). *The Perfect Wrong Note*. Amadeus Press.

8
THE POWER OF GIFTS FROM SUPERVISORS WHO SHARE

Jay Mathisen

What gifts do teachers receive from relationships and engagement with their supervisors? Asking a teacher that question might lead to a wide range of answers. We might imagine some teachers pausing and needing time to scratch their heads as they try to articulate an answer at all. Others might respond very quickly with a list of things they appreciate or like about their supervisor. But things we may admire about our supervisors may be quite different from the gifts we receive from them as teachers. Those with a quick wit might welcome the question, as the possibilities for comedic and sarcastic responses seem to be endless: "My supervisor offers me … a headache/time to catch up on my emails during interminable staff meetings/a wonderful example of why I chose to teach instead of becoming an administrator," and so forth.

As you will have read in previous chapters in this volume, relationships with other people in schools, including students (Chapters 2 and 3) and colleagues (Chapter 7), offer rich gifts to those who teach. The reciprocities or gifts we receive from the relational and human work of teaching may be more readily identified when we explore our relationships with such people. However, teachers are often offered gifts by their supervisors that they cannot get from any of the other people they encounter. We will explore three such gifts in this chapter.

For certain, teachers who have been in the profession for a number of years have likely had several outstanding supervisors. Some might even say that they have worked for a great principal or headmistress. It is my hope that all teachers have had such an experience or two. Those who remain unconvinced that they have ever worked for a good or great supervisor might have to exercise a degree of imagination to picture one. However, they should rest assured that such school leaders do exist; indeed, some might say that their ranks are growing even as the complexities of leading schools increase (Bottoms & Egelson, 2012).

In cases where teachers acknowledge that they have served under a good or great supervisor, it may be quite straightforward to explain why one likes one's supervisor.

DOI: 10.4324/9781003124429-8

Framing that list of "things I like about my boss" as gifts they have offered to teachers is a bit more interesting. As I roll through my mental log of previous supervisors' good points, I quickly remember that one had a great sense of humor. Another was exceptionally skilled as a communicator—both as a listener and as a disseminator of information. How can I forget the one who first made me think that I might someday want to be a principal myself, as I admired the passion for student success and the drive that she brought to work each day? But the question remains: are these positive attributes necessarily gifts I received that brought meaning to the work of teaching and fueled me as a professional to do that work?

What follows is a discussion of three gifts that we receive from our supervisors. To some extent, these gifts are available regardless of the strengths and weaknesses of a given supervisor. Certainly, though, the best supervisors offer them in greater quantity and to greater degrees. Such leaders tend to set these gifts out in the open for us to see and access easily. The not-so-great supervisors may not offer the gifts to the same extent, or their gifts may be hidden and require some work on our part to find and develop them. In fact, teachers may need to instigate or initiate in order to begin the cycle of reciprocity with their supervisor. The reciprocities in such cases might be challenging to identify, as the gifts in question may be hidden and may require us to search for them creatively. However, I believe that all teachers are offered gifts in their work and relationships with their supervisors that are not entirely dependent on the quality of the supervisor.

Getting Better ... and Getting Better at Getting Better

As every teacher knows, and as others have already made clear in previous chapters in this book, teaching is highly complex work. Through repeated teaching of curriculum materials and sheer accumulation of classroom time, teachers typically experience a degree of improvement (Papay & Kraft, 2015). Still, sustained and meaningful improvement in any complex human endeavor requires feedback, reflection, and almost a laboratory approach to trying new things. Supervisors can have a significant impact on how teachers get better, and on how teachers get better at getting better. Improvement in one's teaching is not solely dependent on the words and actions of a supervisor, but when that supervisor and their teachers approach improvement in the craft of teaching together, those teachers can receive significant gifts related to their professional improvement.

Daniel Pink's (2009) book *Drive* notes mastery as one of three elements that bring meaning to complex work, such as teaching. Reaching new levels of mastery and getting better add fuel to the tank of any teacher. Recognizing that one is better at teaching than one used to be is empowering. Realizing further that one's growth as a teacher is having a positive impact on the growth of learners is even more enriching. It is a gift. Most supervisors—from the great to the not-so-great—contribute to that gift as they interact with teachers.

My early experiences as a 20-something high school teacher offered me little in the way of a supervisor who had an impact on my ability to improve as a teacher. Though

I liked several of the principals who supervised me in the first seven or eight years of my teaching career, I can't say that I remember any of them helping me get significantly better at my day job. Yes, some of them did occasionally wander into my classroom and observe the teaching and learning that was going on. I remember the nervousness I experienced when my boss walked into the classroom I was sharing with dozens of high school students. At the time, I would not have considered anything about that visit from my principal as a gift, as I began to sweat profusely and hoped for all I was worth that the students would not misbehave in a way that would make it obvious that I had a lot to learn about this teaching thing.

One or two of those supervisors would offer some words of wisdom and advice after visiting my classroom. However, I often felt like they and I were jumping through a hoop together, rather than sincerely thinking and talking about how my teaching could improve in ways that would lead to improvements and progress in my students' learning. Yet, even in those somewhat prescribed and perfunctory situations, I can vividly remember understanding that I could get better—that my teaching was a work in progress and that my students needed me to improve. Coming to understand that I could and should improve was a gift my supervisors gave me that I would not have received on the sole foundation of my own reflection on my teaching and my experiences with students.

Since those early years of teaching, I have had the opportunity to learn much about how teachers can improve in their craft, and about the role a supervisor may play in that improvement process. As a teacher who became an administrator and is now a university Education Department leader and professor, I have been able to view the improvement of teaching from a range of vantage points and in a variety of contexts. In fact, improving teaching is one of the things I think about most—I hope always to be learning more about it in my work.

Chief among what I have learned is that the most meaningful gift a supervisor can offer to a teacher related to improvement is not actually a direct contribution to that improvement itself. Let me explain what I mean. To say that a supervisor's most meaningful contribution to a teacher's improvement can be contained in a required system of classroom observations and reports is shortsighted and a bit hopeless. Rather, it is in setting the conditions for teachers to improve at improving—get better at getting better—that a supervisor offers the greatest gift to the teacher who desires mastery and growth in their teaching. As Michael Fullan (2000) notes, a principal of a school should influence teacher growth through individual classroom observations and evaluation form completion. However, when that same school leader works with teachers to set up a system that encourages teachers to improve—a system that goes beyond the individual supervisor's own observations and communications with teachers—then that leader has truly offered a sustainable gift that can be replicated.

Kevin Feldman, a friend of mine, was the first person from whom I learned about setting up a system that allows teachers to get better at getting better. Kevin is a former teacher, school district administrator, researcher, and educational consultant who digs in with schools and school districts to help teachers improve their teaching and to help supervisors and teachers develop and improve the systems that facilitate that improvement. He helped me set up a system he calls "scrub-ins" in a high school in which I served as principal. After a conversation with a surgeon on a flight from San Francisco to Seattle, Kevin grew excited about the language and concept of "scrubbing-in." In the medical operating room, surgeons will often wash their hands before observing and assisting colleagues in performing surgery. This practice is often referred to as "scrubbing-in." When Kevin explained to the surgeon sitting next to him that we don't have a parallel system in schools, the surgeon replied with a question: "In that case, how do you learn how to do hard things?"

Kevin encourages teachers and supervisors to set up systems that offer teachers the ability and opportunities to observe and assist their colleagues as they teach in classrooms, then debrief about that teaching later (Feldman, 2017). Some refer to a similar practice as setting up a system of classroom "walk-throughs." Whatever the term, teachers get better when they observe other teachers at work—when they scrub in and watch and think with colleagues while the students are involved. Some teams of teachers find success in the more structured lesson-study approach to this work, which facilitates collective lesson planning, observations, and reflections by the team (Willems & Van den Bossche, 2019).

As a school principal who worked with teachers to set up a system where teachers were able to observe their colleagues and reflect together on a lesson, I quickly learned that the greatest growth and improvement happened when I was not talking. The most important role I could play as a supervisor was to work with teachers to make that scrub-ins system better. In other words, I needed to focus on helping teachers get better at getting better. It was my job to ensure that substitute teachers could rove around the school and cover classrooms so teachers could do this deep laboratory learning. Further, I needed to provide time and structure so teachers working with each other in this way could focus on the "look-fors"—or points of emphasis—that they had agreed to experiment with, so they could track the data they had agreed were relevant, and so they could support each other's efforts to improve their teaching. Finally, providing sufficient time to monitor that data, celebrate improvements, and learn from failures was key. Again, most of the learning and growth had little to do with any words that I said; rather, they were connected to the leadership moves I made to honor teachers as the agents of their own growth.

I believe that teachers are quite capable of improving and strengthening their practice. Further, I am certain that when teachers are able to work with other teachers, and scrub-in to the classroom, improvement is nearly certain. As a teacher, I receive an amazing gift from my supervisor and system when I am able to focus with colleagues on growing professionally with the goal of improvement in full view. The dual gifts of getting better and getting better at getting better are deep and rich when shared between supervisors and teachers.

Community with a Cause

Tammy Doty is a principal of a school with 500 students in kindergarten through fifth grade. She has shaped her school around the central theme of kindness.

Teachers who share in the work at the school Tammy leads are offered the reciprocity—the gift—of being partners in a community of professionals with a cause greater than any single individual or student learning target. That gift is rich in rewards for any teacher who hopes to make a difference beyond test scores and attendance rates. For teachers who work with Tammy, kindness resonates as a cause the school community can rally around and champion.

It is not hard to see in today's headlines that we could all use a little more kindness in our work contexts. Tammy's school transforms kindness into a theme that is woven throughout her school's curriculum content, instructional practices, administrative systems and structures, and communication and language. In other words, teaching kindness is a cause that brings her school community together. The walls are decorated with slogans and art that shine a light on kindness. Students proudly wear t-shirts that proclaim, "Kindness Matters." They often identify their own actions and the actions of their peers as either kind or needing higher levels of kindness.

Two features of this school and Tammy's approach to school leadership bear mentioning. First, notice the driving purpose or cause: kindness. Second, notice the strong sense of community, a feeling of being a family or a team, in pursuit of that cause. When a school is led by a supervisor who purposefully nurtures a sense of community, teachers enjoy the who of their work as well as the what of their work. I am reminded of one example of how Tammy created, fostered, and worked to sustain this sense of community in her school that typifies her attention and focus on community. As the global Covid-19 pandemic struck the United States in the early spring of 2020, many schools around the world closed their doors to students. Supervisors and teachers had to adjust to teaching digitally and in other ways that did not look at all like the classrooms full of students they had taught just weeks prior. While the logistics of leading and teaching in schools seemed overwhelming in the first weeks and months of the pandemic, Tammy purposefully attended to the sense of community. The challenge of learning the school's new video-conferencing system that teachers and students would be using for lessons was daunting and troubling to many. So Tammy enthusiastically organized an evening event for teachers and their families using that video-conferencing system. A scavenger hunt called for teachers and family members—all sheltering in their individual homes—to scramble for items that Tammy asked them to find, and she awarded prizes to those who could find the most items. Of course, alongside their teachers, children participated from their respective homes, and both teachers and students became more familiar with features of video-conferencing to which we have all since become accustomed—mute buttons, chat boxes, camera access, changing screen views, and the like.

Tammy approached the challenge of learning new teaching technology as an opportunity to build community among her team. Or was it the other way around? For Tammy, it is hard to know, because community and cause are interwoven throughout all she does. For her teachers, these gifts are life-giving. Veteran teachers recognize the gifts when they join Tammy's school from elsewhere. The long years of a professional career can be draining when the work is so complex. When a supervisor offers community with a cause to teachers, the work and the teamwork offer new meaning and purpose.

As far as I am aware, perhaps the strongest example of community with a cause is the high school (grades nine through twelve) that H. D. Weddell led as principal. He wanted each and every one of the 1700 students who attended the school to feel as if it was truly *their* school. The students came from a wide variety of socio-economic contexts and represented a variety of other demographic categories. However, every student found a home in the school that H. D. and his teachers operated. School culture was the beginning and end of the collective focus for H. D. and the teachers with whom he worked. Together, they established and nurtured a school culture where all students were accepted and honored.

Over the years, that community with a cause and a strong sense of belonging for every student became the glue that bonded teachers and leaders together. Challenges came, as they inevitably do for school communities, but tragedies became opportunities for teachers, students, and supervisors to reaffirm their commitment to care for each other. Successes were held up as evidence of a school culture in which each person could achieve more as part of the larger community than they would have achieved on their own. Teachers who worked alongside H. D. to build, foster, and sustain that culture of belonging found deep meaning in building relationships with students and they recognized they needed those relationships to thrive. The powerful stories and reports from students who appreciated the role that the school's culture played in their lives are the stuff of Hallmark movies. For the teachers, it was clear that their community with a cause was a gift that they received because of the work and vision they shared collectively with H. D.

Building community with a cause makes showing up to work more enjoyable. Being part of a team that enjoys each other is a gift that a supervisor can give. Workplace culture and climate are key elements that skilled leaders and supervisors understand and value. A team that enjoys each other is more likely to dig in collectively to solve the big challenges that all organizations, including schools, face (Society for Human Resource Management, 2016). However, liking one's colleagues is only one aspect of the gift that teachers may receive from their supervisors and colleagues. When team members who enjoy each other believe in the purpose or the cause of their team, professional educators realize a powerful concept in leadership. Focusing that strong sense of community on a central story that defines a cause unleashes the best in teachers who want to do more than teach skills to students (Ellwein & McCoy, 2019).

Supervisors who understand the power of a simple cause—even one that is challenging to measure or chart—can help teachers breathe life and meaning into their work. Don't get me wrong, Tammy knows her students' reading scores as well as any school principal does; and H. D. knew the graduation rates at his school. Teachers in both of these schools work hard to help students learn mathematics in ways that help them pass the grade-level benchmarks on the state exams. However, complex improvement planning and monitoring have never been confused with the role of a simple, shared, and enduring cause in a community.

Teachers in Tammy's school received her invitations to join a community of professionals committed to bringing kindness to students and each other. Teachers who partnered with H. D. knew they were part of a family with a mission to make students feel like school was their place. When students learn those lessons, and teachers see the evidence of that learning, the school community draws closer together and the power of the cause grows stronger. Teaching becomes human in the best sense. What a gift!

Collective Agency

Bill Rhoades is one of the brightest thinkers I know on all things education. Whether the topic is teaching and learning, leadership, or large trends in the field, he is usually in the know. We tended to use our Saturday morning runs as opportunities to talk through those work-related questions. We really should have been paid during those runs ... because we were working for sure!

Bill had completed dozens of marathons in his serious running years, including Boston nearly ten times, and he was going to punish me (again) one particular Saturday morning. Lurching along next to him, I knew I was out of my league. Due to the fact that Bill is crazy smart, and the fact that I couldn't breathe well enough to speak, he did most of the talking. As we headed over a snowy path in the mountains of Oregon, he disclosed that he had seen the recently posted—and improved—test scores of the high school where I was serving as principal. I puffed up with pride as much as I could, further taxing my struggling lungs, and choked out a few sentences on the adroit leadership moves I had made to achieve those numbers. Bill listened quietly and waited for me to finish trying to impress him. His reply was to ask who was on my leadership team. I wondered if he hadn't heard what I had just told him about my wizardry, but grudgingly explained that the school had an assistant principal who worked closely with me (probably close enough to be blinded by my brilliance). I explained that the improvement in scores had really been due to a group of awesome teachers working hard with the vision I had set before them. Again, I placed a heavy emphasis on my role.

Next, Bill asked if a group of teachers met regularly with their supervisors to chart the path forward and monitor the steps they took along the way. I paused as the realization dawned that I had run straight into a trap: there was no team to share in the visioning, planning, and monitoring that we all considered the school's most important work. As I reflected on my lack of team leadership, I understood that I was guilty of withholding a gift from my teachers. Whether they were veterans or new to the profession, many were willing and able to share in guiding and leading the school. By excluding them from the vision-setting and direction-planning, I was robbing them of the gift of agency that would have added levels of ownership and meaning to their work as teachers.

Collective agency is unwrapped when teachers are included in the leadership thinking in ways that enhance the whole of the improvement process and increase their levels of commitment to the journey (Trammell, 2016). We have likely all been in "shared leadership" meetings in which teachers are asked for (shallow) feedback on the school's mission statement. In many schools, this is often the sum total of shared leadership. Collective agency cannot spring from such stony ground.

Rather, the gift of this type of agency for teachers is opened authentically as they continually design the school's work and lead the process from ideation to implementation to ongoing reflection and adjustment. (This process is analogous to the recursive relationship between theory and practice that Paige A. Ray described in Chapter 6.)

Providing collective agency to teachers often means that they end up with greater voice and choice in both the direction and the efforts that everyone in the school makes to give students the best possible education. Each time a supervisor sets a goal and articulates action steps to achieve that goal without recognizing that teacher voice and choice are foundational to that process, that supervisor likely misses some of the best ideas on the table—ideas that will never be attempted. When supervisors do that, the gift of collective agency is withheld from teachers. I am not talking here about the type of "shared leadership" that pretends to offer agency to teachers under the guise of a dizzying number of committees that produce to-do lists that exhaust teachers. I am not suggesting giving teachers group work to accomplish. Rather, I am talking about creating settings where teachers feel they are leading alongside their supervisors; in such settings teachers gain a sense of ownership in the school's successes and failures.

Some teachers prefer to be left to their own classrooms and to teach as the school bells ask them to, doing their work without much connection to the broader vision for and improvement of the school in which they work. (I will go out on a limb and suggest it is unlikely that any such teachers who view teaching as a solo performance are reading this book.) However, I believe that most teachers desire to be a part of the school-level thinking work in the schools where they teach. The kind of collective agency characterized by true sharing of the leadership work of a school is a gift that supervisors can give teachers.

While the ideas driving a school will likely be better when a supervisor harnesses collective genius (Hill, Brandeau, Truelove & Lineback, 2014), the reciprocity of sharing leadership that offers collective agency to teachers also raises the level of ownership and buy-in that teachers have in the work of the school. This increased level of ownership adds fuel, and even joy, to the teachers' tanks—fuel they need to power through the rough patches that always arise in teaching. This kind of ownership sweetens the flavor of the drinks we hold as we toast the successes of the school's mission and vision.

Conclusion: A Note on Synergies and Nudging Supervisors

To summarize, the three main gifts that supervisors can give to their teachers are:

- getting better ... and getting better at getting better;
- community with a cause; and
- collective agency.

These gifts overlap and strengthen each other, so if there is even a sliver of one in your school, there is a chance of nurturing it and even uncovering one or both of the other two. The three gifts complement each other. The presence of just one generates hope that the other two can be developed and become rich gifts that energize us as teachers.

As a young boy growing up decades ago, I often spent time in the weeks before Christmas with a department store catalogue. It was full of glossy color photos of a wide array of items for sale. Of course, the toy section was my favorite, and its pages were well worn by the time the holidays finally arrived. I pored over those pages and dreamed about unwrapping my gifts on Christmas morning. I would picture playing with them, and consider how my life would be extraordinarily different if I could have them. One day, I took it upon myself to approach my parents and show them the catalogue of potential gifts. I lobbied hard for those gifts, explaining all the good I could do in the world if only I were able gain access to them. Did my mother and father know anyone who might be able to provide one or more of those gifts in the days to come? It seemed a reasonable question, albeit not a particularly subtle one. Sometimes my nudging would work; other times it would not. Yet it was always worth the effort of trying.

It is the same with teachers and their supervisors. In my view, it helps to nudge your supervisor by suggesting ways you might contribute to their efforts to foster and provide the three gifts noted in this chapter. Supervisors who don't currently provide any of these gifts may, through your nudging, catch the vision and set about giving them to their teaching staff. It is always worth the effort of trying.

References

Bottoms, G. & Egelson, P. (2012). *Progress over a decade in preparing more effective school principals*. Southern Regional Education Board.

Ellwein, D. & McCoy, D. L. (2019). *The revolution: It's time to empower change in our schools*. Dave Burgess Consulting.

Feldman, K. (2017). Actionable feedback for teachers: The missing element in school improvement. www.macombfsi.net/uploads/1/5/4/4/1544586/actionable_feedback_for_teachers__a_missing_element_in_school_improvemen....pdf.

Fullan, M. (2000). The role of the principal in school reform. Occasional Paper Series 2000(6). https://educate.bankstreet.edu/cgi/viewcontent.cgi?article=1254&context=occasional-paper-series.

Hill, L. A., Brandeau, G., Truelove, E., & Lineback, K. (2014). Collective genius. *Harvard Business Review*, June. https://hbr.org/2014/06/collective-genius.

Papay, J. P. & Kraft, M. A. (2015). Productivity returns to experience in the teacher labor market: Methodological challenges and new evidence on long-term career improvement. *Journal of Public Economics*, 130(10), 105–119.

Pink, D. H. (2009). *Drive: The surprising truth about what motivates us*. Riverhead.

Society for Human Resource Management. (2016). *Employee job satisfaction and engagement: Revitalizing a changing workforce*. www.shrm.org/hr-today/trends-and-forecasting/research-and-surveys/Documents/2016-Employee-Job-Satisfaction-and-Engagement-Report.pdf.

Trammell, J. M. (2016). The relationship between distributed leadership and the affective commitment in public and private schools. Doctoral dissertation, Carson Newman University.

Willems, I. & Van den Bossche, P. (2019). Lesson study effectiveness for teachers' professional learning: A best evidence synthesis. *International Journal for Lesson and Learning Studies*, 8(4), 257–271.

9
A LONG AND REWARDING APPRENTICESHIP
The sustaining inspiration of our mentors

Andrew Mullen

Each year in one of my elementary methods courses, I share with prospective teachers two sets of three-to-five-sentence "compositions" on birds and wildflowers I completed as a first-grader. "A woodpecker eats insects," begins one. "He lives in a hole in a tree. He is a winter bird." The extra-wide-ruled school paper—still deeply engraved with each carefully spaced, painfully wrought individual letter—is now faded. The original crayon freehand illustration of a red-headed woodpecker in its natural habitat, however, is in no worse shape for the intervening years.

I have used this same folder in class to make a variety of instructional points on different occasions—everything from the need to embed initial literacy instruction in meaningful content and the reciprocal roles of text and image to a consideration of the sometimes cyclical nature of fashions in curriculum to the question of what makes instruction stick (days or even many years later). The pages implicitly remind my students of the potentially lasting influence for good and ill of every teacher who steps into the classroom. As much as anyone, Mildred Brown taught my 30-some fellow first-graders and me to read and write. In the process, in my own case, this plain and unpretentious dairy-farmer's wife helped to lay the foundation for two avocational interests—birding and botany—that have endured for 55 subsequent years.

For present purposes, these carefully saved notes on natural history underscore, first of all, the relative impact of our earliest years in school. As a six-year-old immigrant from a Canadian province where kindergartens had not yet been incorporated into the public school system, I was imprinted by Mrs. Brown's instruction perhaps even more deeply than my fellow students, who had already had a year's experience in school. In any case, Mrs. Brown may well have had a more fundamental influence than any better-known graduate-school professor I might initially identify as a mentor. Volumes of tributes to great teachers have a tendency to emphasize the inspiration and modeling provided to the writers in their secondary or post-secondary years. Those educators at the elementary level who arguably enabled

DOI: 10.4324/9781003124429-9

such later learning are too often forgotten, or at best their artistry and craft are underappreciated. What Philip Jackson (1986: p. 51), the instructor for my first doctoral-level course, suggests about subject matter may apply equally to those who instruct us—and to our instructors in the early grades in particular:

> What we do know about the retention of what is learned in school is, alas, not very encouraging. Research tells us that the bulk of it disappears from memory almost before the ink on the pupil's report card is dry. Yet some of it obviously endures. And even the portion that is forgotten leaves a residue of some sort that has a way of changing the person in whose mind it was temporarily housed. These changes are … seldom fully fathomed by the person experiencing them. But they are real nonetheless.

The archival evidence from Mrs. Brown's classroom is indicative of the underestimated, lasting, and even in my own case, less than "fully fathomed" role of the models to whom we are exposed in our early years when we are most plastic.

The pages from Mrs. Brown's classroom in 1966–1967 not only point to the relative imprintability of the very young. They suggest in similar fashion the relative complexity of the mentoring or apprenticing process in becoming a teacher. In the recent literature of teacher education, the term "mentor," in both its noun and verb form, has acquired a fairly specific connotation. The experienced teacher charged with mentoring a new hire has a defined role and responsibilities, often with a similarly definite set of expectations for release time and compensation, and all to be completed within a defined period specified in the contract. Conscious and unconscious paradigms about the processes of teaching and learning, paradigms that may shape our future work as much or more as formal teacher education, begin to form much earlier and have no formal date of expiration. The pages from Mrs. Brown's classroom are (in my case) one concrete response to David Smith's (2018: p. 131) rhetorical question: "Whose stories animate our unconscious dreams about how teaching and learning are supposed to work?" As another mentor's own mentor—educational historian Larry Cuban (1993: p. 19)—notes in his effort to explain the relative constancy of actual classroom teaching amidst a century-long "hurricane" of national educational reform efforts, to be a public school student for 12 years is to have served "an apprenticeship as [we] watched [our] teachers teach," leading, for good and ill, to the "basic conservativism of the occupation."

Setting aside Mrs. Brown's influence on me as a person, she deeply impacted my understanding of the teaching-learning process and my conception of what a teacher is and ought to be. In no small way inspiring and sustaining my personal and professional energies through a long pilgrimage in the field of education, she has truly served—in the broadest sense of the term—as a mentor.

In related fashion, finally, the written work from Mrs. Brown's classroom may remind readers of the different roles we have all played throughout our academic journeys and the different levels or layers of understanding we have acquired about teaching from mentors at each stage—all well below the surface of the persona we now present to the world. As a student, teacher, and teacher of teachers—among other roles—I have sometimes thought of my professional development or my close colleagues in terms of those nesting Russian dolls—the *matryoshka*—to which tourists seem invariably drawn. That is, in the present case, I carry deep inside me a series of similar but initially hidden roles—and hidden influences. At each level of the professional journey I have presented a new face to the world, while not abandoning related identities and scripts about teaching and learning that I carry beneath. I cannot think about the layers of educational identities I carry without acknowledging the personal influences and role-specific mentors that shaped each stage. At my deepest recoverable, consciously available layer of understanding of education is the model of teaching my first-grade and other elementary teachers provided.

At each stage of my journey I have been blessed beyond measure by a range of professional mentors and role models. With age comes sufficient detachment that I can be grateful even for the occasional counter-model or counter-mentor who has helped to define more clearly my professional identity. More directly, though, it was my elementary and secondary teachers who made me want to be a teacher myself in the first place. Perhaps, for all of us in the field, part of the joy of teaching is the opportunity it presents to relive positive experiences and remind ourselves of the winsome models we have encountered at different steps of our pilgrimage. Given the length of our putative "apprenticeship" in the educational enterprise, we who teach (as opposed to those who become, say, lawyers or accountants) have a particularly extensive range of models and mentors on whom to draw. And, more than our classmates who presumably benefited at the same time but chose to pursue other professions, we have the distinct pleasure of being able to apply the rich store of memories and models we have been given far more directly in our day-to-day work.

While present purposes do not include an attempt to explore further the full range of mentoring and modeling on which teachers may draw, it may be helpful to acknowledge in passing the scope of resources educators have available. In addition to our own teachers and professors, those of us who supervise student teachers or are otherwise involved in K-12 classrooms have a constantly renewed array of inspiring models in the professional mentors we select for our teacher-candidates. Further, those of us with children in school are often inspired and renewed by *their* teachers. Direct acquaintances aside, many of us can testify to the virtual or indirect mentoring we have received from teachers' autobiographies or memoirs (e.g., Sylvia Ashton-Warner's *Teacher* or Eliot Wigginton's *Sometimes a Shining Moment*), biographical portraits (*Escalante, Small Victories, Among Schoolchildren*), and teacher-related films (*Dead Poets' Society, Freedom Writers*). Those of us immersed in educational history may draw further sustaining energy from historical role models, as explored indirectly in the author's dissertation (Mullen, 1996).

In the following pages, I consider the enduring influence of two models who have inspired me in particular roles and continue to offer strength. While identifying multiple ways in which they have served as a pattern for my own work, I chose one focusing ideal or set of ideals I associate with each and my attempts to live out those ideals in my own professional practice. Whether these individuals actually shaped my ideals, whether each was attractive to me because they represented ideals I had already begun to form, or whether it was some combination of the two is not altogether clear or necessarily even worth resolving. In any event, these men are two of many to whom I have turned, deliberately and less deliberately, throughout my teaching years and to whom I attribute, in part, a great deal of sustenance and joyful resilience.

Mr. Nelson

However, my first-grade teacher shaped my initial understanding of what an effective teaching-learning community might be, I associate my first conscious desire to become a teacher myself with Mr. John Nelson in fifth grade. Partly because of the vivid contrast he provided to a less fondly remembered teacher the year before, Mr. Nelson may have been my single most formative educational influence of all. Not surprisingly, upon first considering teaching elementary school, I consistently identified fifth grade as the year on which I wanted to focus my preparation. Nor is it surprising that I ended up at that grade level (or the grade below) for most of my roughly nine years of full-time teaching of elementary-age children.

Like my first-grade teacher, Mr. Nelson clearly loved the world of nature. It was soon apparent that he was equally curious about the vast range of human experience in other times and places. His classroom was a veritable museum. Standing at the door, one's eyes were attracted to a model solar system and the teacher's models of various explorers' ships that hung from the light fixtures. Stepping further into the room revealed the stuffed alligator on a shelf over his desk. A model bank he had meticulously crafted and painted ("First Nelson Bank," which contained the class's daily lunch money and other valuables) was glued to a nearby counter. A pictorial timeline of American history wrapped around the walls of the classroom. A lifelong friend to whom I recently mentioned Mr. Nelson's name immediately identified the intricate, hand-made model ships, followed by the daily games or logic puzzles I myself only dimly remember. He also recalled our mutual teacher's "calm and gentle spirit ... I don't think he ever raised his voice that whole year."

Mr. Nelson's creative energy was not contained by either the walls of the classroom or the school. Across the road, the year before I entered fifth grade, just in time to celebrate the world's first Earth Day, he had begun to create a nature trail. During my year in fifth grade he enlisted his own students as research assistants in preparing the written guide and posted signs for each designated point of interest. He made us want to go on exploring long after we left his classroom. His Kodak slides of traveling west with his four daughters made all of us aspire to visit Yosemite and Yellowstone and other national parks someday ourselves. Long before it became fashionable, he individualized instruction, offering a range of activities to different groups of students throughout the day.

For all the years I have consciously identified Mr. Nelson as a model, I do not recall ever sitting down and listing the qualities I wanted to emulate in my own teaching. Clearly there were many. The one aspect of his teaching to which I have returned again and again, however, is that of agency. The notion of teacher agency has been variously defined in the professional literature of educational policy, but in most cases the emphasis is on the individual teacher's judgment and locus of control, both in defining instructional purposes and in identifying the most effective means to accomplish such purposes. In corollary fashion, the term may carry a connotation of "resistance" to top-down mandates and/or standardized procedures (Priestley, Biesta, & Robinson, 2015; Achinstein & Ogawa, 2006). As used in the present context (and as Sullivan treats it at length in Chapter 5), the term incorporates something of Parker Palmer's (1997; 2000) emphasis on the teacher acting out of his or her deepest, most authentic, holistic self. It connotes as well a predisposition to proper contextualization: to adapting curriculum and instruction to the particular needs of a given place, to a given historical moment, to each unique classroom community, and to each never-to-be-replicated student.

While "agency" is not a term I would have used as a fifth-grade student, I did already have some incipient awareness of the creativity, the range of resources, the constant experimentation, and the day-to-day activities that differed from what my peers in other fifth-grade classes in the building were doing. There was, to begin with, the daily contrast with the fourth-grade teacher I made reference to above, in whose classroom every lesson seemed to come straight out of the textbook, or straight off the worksheet. Back in fourth grade, if you illicitly snuck a peek at the next page, you knew exactly what you would be assigned tomorrow. From fifth grade on, and continuing to the present, my fourth-grade teacher has served as an explicit counter-model. In contrast, I have consistently tried—consciously and unconsciously and across multiple roles—to live out the kind of professional teacher agency Mr. Nelson represented.

Different instructional contexts clearly offer varying levels of encouragement—or toleration—for teachers with a strong sense of agency. Another of my graduate-school professors characterized the individual teacher as the ultimate "curriculum-instructional gatekeeper" and suggested that teachers often have more freedom than either they or educational policy-makers at the state or national level may recognize (Thornton, 1991). Once the classroom door was closed, different teachers would inevitably have different approaches to the implementation of any particular educational mandate. But just how much freedom an individual or group of like-minded teachers may exercise depends in part on their particular historical and geographic context as well as on the nature of the individual school itself. At each stage of my work with elementary-age children, I was blessed with administrators and senior colleagues who actually valued autonomy and agency in the teachers they had selected. Even in a climate of increasing national, state, district, and school accountability, I was always assured that I could use the district- or school-adopted materials selectively as well as whatever other resources I thought would best meet the students' needs. As much as a focus on literacy and achieving higher test scores in reading/language arts were emphasized in the schools where I taught, there were few constraints on how individual teachers planned their days. Whether I taught math to my fourth-graders as a whole class or (as I did one year) in five separate groups was a choice that was left to me. It was also my decision to do more history and science, and to offer a more literature-based curriculum in language arts than either my immediate colleagues or my counterparts across the district were providing. I often look back on my work with K-12 students with regret and wish that I had done this or that; still, I do not fault myself for not exercising agency. As far as I can reconstruct, I took full advantage of the professional freedom I was given. And if anything I attempted with elementary-age children approached Mrs. Brown's natural history units in terms of meaningfulness and long-term memorability, I attribute that in part to my willingness to initiate, to express my own passions, and to tailor my curriculum and instruction to the perceived needs of the individuals under my tutelage. Looking back, I think that, on this score at least, Mr. Nelson might well be proud of his unrecognized protégé.

Of course, a strong sense of agency can be an ambiguous asset. A teacher who is too committed to relying on his or her own professional judgment may fail to give adequate support to a larger professional team—may fail to work in concert with broader networks of fellow professionals. There is no guarantee, moreover, that a teacher acting on his or her own individual professional judgment will necessarily offer a stronger curriculum or set of instructional approaches than those the district or school provides. And, as implied above, an overly autonomous candidate for the profession may never be accepted into the guild: not every hiring committee is looking for a strong sense of agency. Much as I attempt to cultivate a sense of their own professional agency in teacher-candidates, I remind myself that they may soon be interviewing with principals who want to hear that they will faithfully implement the state-adopted standards, coupled with fluent parroting of the current educational buzzwords.

For these reasons, I am cautious not to oversell the virtue of teacher agency or the overlapping ideal of professional autonomy. I share with teacher-candidates my own need to align coursework with institutional and the ever-changing, far more intrusive mandates from the state capital—and how their experience in my own classroom always represents some kind of pragmatic compromise between my ideals and prevailing policy and practice. In the end, though, I will always come down on the side of encouraging a rising generation of teachers to look within, and not merely at what others are doing in the classroom next door. I ask them, in light of what stands out from their own experience in K-12 classrooms, what they could do to make instruction memorable 10—or even 55—years later. I continue to challenge them to make choices from a wide range of resources and instructional plans, and not merely to adopt uncritically what the school has provided. I encourage them to create a curriculum that is potentially meaningful for a wider range of students than has sometimes been the case in the past. I ask them to find strength and ongoing motivation by aligning day-to-day activity as much as possible with their own avocations and ideological commitments.

Professor Whelan

Inspired not only by my teaching experience in the upper-elementary classroom but also by the surprisingly positive experience I had in the 15 months of earning a

Master of Arts in Teaching (MAT) and state certification, I eventually entered a doctoral program in education. There I focused on the history of curriculum and, specifically, the history of K-12 historical study itself. Throughout the program I partnered with full-time faculty in helping to prepare secondary teachers in the field of history and social science. Again, I am grateful for several helpful mentors. One in particular stands out, however, in shaping day-to-day interactions over the past 20 years with my own candidates for teaching.

I met Professor Whelan as one of two new doctoral students in a department welcoming that same September approximately 45 students working toward a Master's degree and initial certification in teaching history. For two days prior to the commencement of classes, it was my job to run interference while Professor Whelan met with each of the 45 Master's students. It was, to say the least, not the most efficient process, especially when the students who had already seen him insisted on checking in again before their peers had seen him even once. I ended up feeling like one of Jesus' disciples, trying to protect him by turning away the pleading children, only to be reprimanded by my new supervisor for not permitting any return visits. In a building full of luminaries, Professor Whelan's C.V. was by no means the longest. As long as I knew him, however, the lines of students outside his office were without compare. He was a professor whom even returning alumni waited in line to see.

Unlike any other tenured or tenure-track professor I knew involved in teacher education at this particular institution, Professor Whelan would spend an entire morning or afternoon with small groups of students visiting different kinds of schools. He observed and conversed with history teachers at length to help each new candidate who had chosen to join him on these expeditions find a suitable placement for his or her student teaching. As I was new to New York, as well as to graduate school, these visits were my orientation not just to Professor Whelan's wide professional networks but to the city itself. From him I also learned how to talk to the homeless on the sidewalk, and how not to look like a tourist on the subway.

The time he devoted to individual student advising, to field placements, to interaction in the classroom, and to commenting on each student essay enabled him to know each of his students on a different level than other professors—and, of course, generated even more work for himself because of subsequent requests for letters of recommendation or the even more time-consuming trouble-shooting in relation to situations that arose during student teaching. I remember his gentle rebuke when I complained or poked fun at some of the more troubled and naive 22-year-olds. He seemed to find the good and see the potential in each and every student, including a first-year doctoral candidate others might legitimately have dismissed for his arrogance or distractedness or difficulty in finding a clear professional pathway. It was the personal relationship I had with Professor Whelan that helped me hear his critiques of my writing or thinking, and encouraged me to pay particular attention to the books and articles he recommended and the tips he offered for surviving a doctoral program.

Throughout my career, I have observed a few remarkable individuals who apparently manage to have it all and to do it all. Professor Whelan was not one of those. On the one hand, prioritizing his work with individuals and devoting so much time to mentoring students were *not* detrimental to his teaching preparation. And his presence in the classroom and mastery of the rhetorical arts were unsurpassed. The quantity of his writing did suffer, however. Accordingly, his colleagues suggested that this particular institution might not be the best match for someone of his rather meager scholarly output. As a result, before he and I ever got to the stage of a formal dissertation proposal, Professor Whelan was gone. Nevertheless, his love of American history, love of Columbia University and its history, and love of the history of curriculum and instruction in that same eponymous subject left as deep a cognitive and intellectual impression as any of several distinguished graduate-school professors I studied under for longer periods. And his modeling of priorities, his relationality, and his concern for even the most idiosyncratic individual are even deeper engraved in me.

Professor Whelan did not gravitate toward educational jargon, the early adoption of buzzwords, or anything that might reek of pretension. But for want of a better word, I apply the term "person-centeredness"—or "personalism"—to the essence of what I saw and continue to see in Michael Whelan. The notion of personalism seems to have had limited use within the field of education. But more than "humanistic education," more than the educational "existentialism" of the 1960s or simply "student- or child-centeredness"—aspects of which certainly overlap my focusing concerns here—it seems to capture more fully the ideals I associate with Professor Whelan and the ideals that inform my own work as a teacher–educator. Outside the field of education, the notion of personalism, often associated with Karol Wojtyła (later John Paul II), may include an emphasis on the supreme worth of each individual, our uniqueness, and the value of providing choice in encouraging each person to develop his or her unique full potential (Inglis, 1959; Spinello, 2007).

Whatever label one might put on it, the ideals I associate with Professor Whelan inform all aspects of my work. To be a person-centered professor, to begin with, means prioritizing getting to know each individual insofar as each is willing to be known—making the effort throughout the academic year, not just on the first day, to understand each student's faith and family background, his or her sources of joy and pain, and (again, insofar as these may be communicated) each one's deepest hopes and fears. It means making time—during advising, on the sidewalk, before and after class. It means listening during class discussion—listening more patiently than is my nature and refusing to watch the clock—even when a student's comments might not initially seem particularly germane. It also means (a much more difficult task in my case) giving up imposing on students any overly narrow or unduly prescriptive notions about what a student—and especially a student pursuing the field of education—ought to be. Rather, having done my due diligence in exposing students to a wide range of models, resources, and philosophical ideals, I invite them to become their own best and unique selves, and try to respect their personal and professional choices along the journey, however different from my own they may be. For many years, I have spoken to teacher-candidates about developing or expressing more fully their "Emily-ness" or "Amanda-ness." That notion has appeared on course evaluations as much as or more than anything else I have done or emphasized in my classes. I am even more excited when I see beginning teachers, in turn, employing that same language or concept with their K-12 students.

The supervision of student teachers is the sphere in which my commitment to person-centeredness is maybe most intentional, perhaps even most manifest. I try to choose a range of mentors, consistent to the maximum feasible extent with the student teacher's temperament and ideals, but I consistently try to avoid cooperating teachers who may be over-controlling. As generous as I am with raising questions with student teachers and reflecting honestly about the learning and instructional challenges I see, I try to provide choices and explicitly disavow any one right way to serve students more effectively. While highlighting strategies other teachers—or their own peers—have used successfully, I work to avoid comparing individual student teachers with one another in any competitive or hierarchical manner.

In the design of other courses, my commitment to person-centeredness—and to following the example set by Professor Whelan—has contributed to each of the following: first, an emphasis on written assignments incorporating some level of autobiographical reflection, furthering the relationship between student and professor (and, in some courses, fostering relationships among students as they share their written work with one another); second, a growing emphasis on teaching students to listen to one another and setting assignments that involve listening to others, with a view to affirming more fully the personhood of others; and third, whenever possible, using first-person narrative books and articles (as opposed to disembodied ideas about teaching) that allow prospective teachers to see how veterans' teaching grows out of their personhood.

I happen to teach in a small liberal arts institution that has traditionally prized interactive teaching, community, and personal relationships as much as or more than scholarly output or number of committees chaired. Even in such an institution, however (and presumably much more so in a research university), there is always a temptation to discount the value of time or effort invested in the individual. I continually need to remind myself, for example, that time spent reading and responding to student work is not cutting into time for "more important matters"—that interacting with each student's paper is, in fact, a great privilege. For that reminder, and for the resulting joy I have often experienced even in my least favorite aspect of the job, I am grateful for the example of a graduate-school professor with person-centered priorities.

Those of us who value a sense of individual agency may be tempted to practice that ideal too robustly. As implied earlier, we constantly need to temper our sense of agency with a concomitant concern for the professional communities in which we operate. On the other hand, it is hard to see how we can ever be *too* concerned—as teachers or professors—with the human beings who sit directly in front of us. As C. S. Lewis (1980) might have said, paralleling the oft-quoted concluding words from the sermon he preached in Oxford in the early days of World War II, committees come and go, as do academic journals and academic publishers. Persons are the supreme investment. I remember Professor Whelan, and I have attempted to pattern my professional life after his primarily because he prioritized the person. To the extent that any of my students will ever reflect back and consider me a mentor, again, it will be a function of my ability to live out my theoretical commitment to person-centeredness.

Conclusion

In my work with teacher-candidates today, I do not talk explicitly about my fifth-grade teacher or even employ the term "agency." I have rarely mentioned Dr. Whelan by name and do not recall ever using the term "personalism" or even "person-centered teaching" with students. I do, however, ask them to delve deeply into their memories of teachers, pre-school through college, short-term Sunday School teachers and swimming instructors, as well as year-long grade-level or subject-area teachers. I ask them to honor their teachers' example—those they remember by name and those whose memory may have blurred over time. I challenge them to perpetuate the best of what they remember from their own teachers while cautioning them, again, that what worked for them in one situation might be less workable in another.

As a doctoral student, I worked as a research assistant for a different kind of mentor, Ellen Condliffe Lagemann, focusing on locating and reviewing sources for what was eventually published as *An Elusive Science: The Troubling History of Education Research* (Lagemann, 2000). The title is apt, encapsulating as it does the difficulty generations of would-be scholars have encountered in reducing the complexities and value-laden enterprise of teaching and learning to any kind of manageable science. The questions that teaching raises are never going to have definite answers. Lagemann ends her book almost as she began, echoing the words of Josiah Royce, a pioneer in the field of education, on the subject of whether there could ever be a "universally valid science of pedagogy ... capable of ... complete formulation and ... direct application to individual pupils and teachers" (Lagemann, 2000: p. ix). I happen to share much of Lagemann's perspective about the complexity of learning and teaching, about the questionable value of much of the received and published wisdom in the field, and about the need for a more contextualized and holistic understanding of educational scholarship and educational practice. Certainly, from the perspective of the individual practitioner, much of the teaching and learning process must always feel like an "elusive science." Twenty years after Lagemann's study, much about the calling—let alone the history of relevant scholarship—remains troubling. In such an uncertain profession, where scientific answers may never be available, one of our greatest resources will always be the ongoing inspiration and discerning application of our own teachers' and mentors' examples.

References

Achinstein, B. & Ogawa, R. T. (2006). (In)fidelity: What the resistance of new teachers reveals about professional principles and prescriptive educational policies. *Harvard Educational Review*, 76(1), 30–63.

Cuban, L. (1993). *How teachers taught: Constancy and change in American classrooms, 1880–1990* (2nd ed.). Teachers College Press.
Inglis, W. B. (1959). Personalism, analysis and education. *International Review of Education*, 5 (4), 383–399.
Jackson, P. W. (1986). *The practice of teaching*. Teachers College Press.
Lagemann, E. C. (2000). *An elusive science: The troubling history of education research*. University of Chicago Press.
Lewis, C. S. (1980). *The weight of glory and other addresses* (revised and expanded ed.). Collier/Macmillan.
Mullen, A. D. (1996). Clio's uncertain guardians: History education at Teachers College, Columbia University, 1906–1988. Doctoral dissertation, Columbia University.
Palmer, P. (1997). *The courage to teach: Exploring the inner landscape of a teacher's life*. Jossey-Bass.
Palmer, P. (2000). *Let your life speak: Listening for the voice of vocation*. Jossey-Bass.
Priestley, M., Biesta, G. J. J., & Robinson, S. (2015). Teacher agency: What is it and why does it matter? In R. Kneyber & J. Evers (Eds.), *Flip the system: Changing education from the bottom up* (pp. 134–148). Routledge.
Smith, D. I. (2018). *On Christian teaching: Practicing faith in the classroom*. Eerdmans.
Spinello, R. A. (2007). *The genius of John Paul II: The great pope's moral wisdom*. Sheed & Ward.
Thornton, S. J. (1991). Teacher as curricular-instructional gatekeeper in social studies. In J. P. Shaver (Ed.), *Handbook of research in social studies teaching and learning* (pp. 237–248). Macmillan.

10
FAMILIES

Michelle C. Hughes and Ken Badley

Throughout this book, we (the co-editors) and our colleagues have focused on what teaching gives back to teachers. In this chapter, we examine a teacher's experience with parents. Some teachers experience parents as unflinching supporters of their work while others feel an uncomfortable sting of judgment and misunderstanding. Some educators might wonder why we would write about what parents and families give to teachers. After all, some teachers have had very negative—even threatening—experiences with parents. Why would we devote a chapter of this book to individuals who are often a teacher's harshest critics? To start, we will frame parental involvement historically rather than with reference to teachers' positive or negative experiences. Following a brief history of educational provision, we will turn to those parents who seem to default toward criticism as well as those who offer endless support to teachers and schools.

Parental Involvement in Education: A Thumbnail History

Had we written this chapter before the year 1800, its thesis that parents can function as partners with educators or that they give back to teachers would have struck most readers as odd for one simple yet important reason: until the emergence of common schooling in the nineteenth century, parents historically had and took responsibility for their children's education. The notion that the state would somehow end up taking on that responsibility—or that parents would expect it to do so—is a relatively new idea, barely two centuries old.

Historically, many ancient cultures left no written records of how parents educated their children. However, several did, and these accounts, supplemented with oral traditions, give us at least some idea of ancient education in five settings: Athens, Sparta, Rome, Israel, and China. Parents' educational ideals in these five locations varied (Edmunds, Nickel, & Badley, 2014). Sparta wanted to produce soldiers, while

DOI: 10.4324/9781003124429-10

Athens and Rome wanted their young to learn oratory and receive what we might now call a classical education. Israel wanted its young to remember its origin story and to believe that God had given it special status among the nations. China wanted its young to develop moral integrity and to learn their duties toward family and society. Interestingly, though, there were significant variations within each of these five settings. Wealthy parents could hire tutors who came into the home, or they could send their children to a tutor who taught several pupils together. Poor parents could not afford to do either. In each of the settings, boys typically received education while girls did not. Thus, class and gender were major factors. Additionally, patterns of tutoring and teaching evolved over time in all five places. Therefore, to say "Athenian education" or "Chinese education" is to oversimplify; one should at least specify a century. We admit that this brief overview tends to generalize where more nuance is needed. Nevertheless, across the five settings we have mentioned, and throughout their respective ancient histories, parents initiated and directed their children's education.

This pattern of parental direction and control continued through the Middle Ages and into the Renaissance. However, in both Europe and Asia, a noteworthy difference from ancient education appears in the form of schools organized by religious groups. Synagogues, churches, monasteries, convents, and temples all founded schools to which parents could send their children. The decision to educate children by sending them to schools operated by religious organizations remained with parents; no one was required to attend. Yet one important difference from ancient Roman and Greek education emerges in all of these settings in the Middle Ages: some of these schools did not charge tuition and were available to the poor. A significant similarity persists from the ancient world, however: education remains largely for privileged boys.

To frame the question of this chapter properly, we need to jump forward to the nineteenth century, when state-funded school systems became the norm. We do not wish to repeat in detail what many have addressed elsewhere, but we will provide sufficient examples to illustrate a pattern, beginning in Germany, which founded its first Bureau of Education in 1809. By 1834, success in secondary exams overseen by this branch of government (although by then it was called the Ministry of Religion, Education, and Public Health) qualified students for admission to a university, thus bestowing a significant measure of legitimacy on state-operated schools. By 1890, the national government was calling on schools to prepare their students for practical careers in science, and to educate them in German history and language. The second directive grew out of the notion that schools could be used to reinforce national allegiance and unity. Therefore, in the course of rather less than a century, the German state stripped parents of their traditional responsibility for educating their own children and took on the role itself.

The development of universal, state-funded education in the United States and Canada followed a similar path to that of Germany. Indeed, in some cases, the German system served as a template. At the turn of the nineteenth century, there was no government provision of education in either the United States or the

British colonies that eventually became Canada. However, shortly thereafter, a number of educators in New York and Massachusetts began founding schools, sometimes after touring schools in Germany. These founders envisioned and called for free education, arguing that it should be available to all. By mid-century, local and state governments began to heed this call for universal, free education. The motives of those calling for state-funded schools varied: while some focused explicitly on moral training, others envisioned general education, and yet others argued that a flourishing democracy required an educated populace. Implicitly—and often explicitly—some viewed public education as a means of socializing non-Protestant immigrants into society. As had happened in Germany, by the turn of the twentieth century, governments in the United States and Canada—and those of many other nations—assumed responsibility for organizing schools.

This brief, thumbnail sketch of the history of educational provision allows us to frame the issue of parental and family involvement as an organic question, on the assumption that most or all of our readers have worked in classrooms and met parents who seemed determined to criticize how their children's schools and teachers were doing their work. Likewise, many of our readers will have met—or, more accurately, not met—parents and families who seemed to have no interest in their children's education.

In the remainder of this chapter, we will highlight the many ways in which parents can support a teacher's work in schools. Of particular significance, wherever parents fall on the "supportive-to-critical" continuum, their desire to be involved is a natural and contemporary expression of a historical pattern. Given three millennia of educational history, we should be more surprised by those parents who choose to have no involvement in their children's schooling.

Parents: Advocates or Adversaries?

We have established that a school is traditionally a venue that hosts students, yet what happens when families question a teacher's judgment or think they know more than teachers about teaching? In this section, we will highlight some of the uncomfortable and often difficult conversations that occur between families and educators. We will also explore what happens when families ask teachers and principals questions such as: "How can we help? How can our family serve your school community? What do you need, what can we can do, or what can we give?" Specifically, we shine a light on several examples of families and schools working as partners to cultivate unexpected exchanges and foster community, paying it forward for all concerned.

Throughout her career, Michelle C. Hughes has seen parents stepping up and asking a teacher or principal, "How can I help? What do you need?" These parents model a humble commitment to service. They make a conscious decision to serve, validating a servant leader's desire to practice what they preach and help others (Greenleaf, 1998). Whether it's serving on a parent council, leading a fundraising committee, or acting as a booster selling team t-shirts, hot dogs, or sodas at sporting events, parents donate their time, money, and energy in the interests of students and the whole school community. Such parents and families typically donate money for their own children but they may also support scholarships for other students.

Many parents see the bigger picture and are concerned with the success of the whole school community. During difficult seasons, they often show up in amazing ways to support schools. Michelle C. Hughes has first-hand experience of the types of tragedies that can rock a local school community, as two students and a pair of parents all died unexpectedly over a four-month period. Each of these heartbreaking events had a profound effect on numerous schools, students, teachers, and families across the school district and the wider community. However, teachers, students, and families came together through the shared experience of grief. They felt collectively numb during this shocking, unexpected, and tragic season, yet they worked together to support the grieving families. Teachers and parents attended the memorial services, and parents made meals and decorated schools and classrooms with flowers and touching messages. Each tragic and heartbreaking loss was recognized with collected donations, signs of support, dinner drop-offs, and candlelit vigils.

In such best-case scenarios, parents and families become partners and champions for and with schools, teachers, and students (Bono, 2020). School communities that welcome in parents often see an enthusiastic willingness to serve alongside the teachers; hence, a partnership forms that has a ripple effect on the whole community. It is important to note that teachers and educational leaders who prioritize service typically model professional attitudes, humility, and courage (Von Fisher & De Jong, 2017).

Researchers have consistently concluded that a parent's or guardian's involvement in a child's school contributes to that child's academic performance. Historically, we know that parental involvement generally decreases as students move to higher grades. Research into the middle-school years, in particular, has revealed a need for parental involvement and its positive effects on school engagement for students. One study recommended that schools promote parental involvement and keep parents informed about school activities (Mo & Singh, 2008). An additional recommendation included seeking parental input for educational decisions in formal and informal ways. A later study noted an important correlation between parental communication, parents' high expectations, and parenting style and academic achievement (Shute, Hansen, Underwood, & Razzouk, 2011). Hence, the quality of the parent–child or guardian–child relationship influences school engagement, grades, and achievement—and highlights the significance of parent–student and teacher–student relationships. Here, it is important to note that adolescents in low-income urban environments may have additional achievement and engagement challenges (Murray, 2009), so the historical pattern of privilege, mentioned above, evidently persists.

One educational researcher spent several years visiting and examining what she called "How It's Being Done" schools that demonstrated success through a focus on student achievement data (Chenoweth, 2009). She concluded that teacher collaboration, formative instruction, relationship-building, and a focus on data-driven instruction led to high levels of student achievement. Ironically, her research revealed that many parents and families feel uncomfortable at schools; as a result, she encouraged teachers and schools to foster the parent–teacher–school relationship through family nights, regular communication, and more opportunities for parental access and connection.

A more recent model, Harlem Village Academies, provides an example of branding that promotes a particular school and team mentality. Deborah Kenny (2012), founder and CEO, designed Harlem Village Academies with a vision to respect and support teachers and validate individuals to foster a positive culture. Parent involvement is both expected and required in order for a child to enroll at Harlem Village Academies or schools that practice similar models, such as the Harlem Children's Zone Schools or KIPP Academies. These schools traditionally serve underprivileged populations and recognize the value and rewards of parental engagement.

Many school leaders also appreciate the link between parental involvement and student success. One school leader advocates for school communities explicitly devoting time to ensure that all parents, teachers, and students understand school initiatives (McCoy & Edwards, 2016). He proposes using digital tools for messaging and carefully crafting user-friendly, non-intimidating communications to parents and families. He also advocates for outlining the rationale for each new initiative and seeking ways for parents to engage with and experience such initiatives, even suggesting increased use of social media and other digital tools to showcase the school's efforts and progress. Another educator (Brannon, 2010) also encouraged both student teachers and new teachers to advocate for parental support and respect by growing in partnership with them. She suggested regular communications regarding assignments and behavior expectations as well as specific invitations to volunteer in the interests of cultivating relationships and trust.

We cannot ignore the reality that many teachers need to do a better job of communicating about the kinds of help they need in and for their classrooms—and even with particular students. One aspect of this is technology. From their meta-analysis of research into the connections between media use and academic achievement, Schmidt and Vanderwater (2008) question the widely held view that more time online leads to lower achievement. They point out, for example, that online gaming increases certain visual capacities, and that time spent watching educational television correlates positively with academic achievement (although entertainment television does not). Their work serves as a warning to educators that we may need to re-examine some of our assumptions about the support we need on the home front. We sometimes hear educators expressing frustration over parents' desire to control the school environment even though they seem to have little or no control over the home environment. Schmidt and Vanderwater (2008) note that what happens on the home front is often more complex than we assume, so perhaps we should give it more thoughtful consideration. For instance, can educators proactively engage and communicate with parents about students' online time at home? What steps could families take to support and reinforce academic learning at home? Decades ago, technology critic Neil Postman (1985) pointed out that electronic media serves as an alternative curriculum and attention-grabber with which schools cannot compete. This remains an issue for educators today. Long before the arrival of the internet, Postman argued that there are long-term negative effects of time spent in front of screens. His main concern was that our brains need to translate symbols when reading, but no such translation is necessary when viewing images. Consequently, for as long as education continues to rely on reading, students who watch a lot of television will be disadvantaged. Others have made similar arguments, both from philosophical perspectives (Ellul, 1985) and on the basis of empirical research (Hancox, Milne, & Poulton, 2005). Therefore, we suggest considering how we, as teachers, can better engage parents and students in conversations about the use of technology at home.

We noted in the introduction to this chapter that most K–12 educators have met disgruntled parents who seem intent on criticizing teachers and schools, become angry, play the blame game, and may even initiate a phone campaign with other parents before registering an official complaint with the school. Most of these parents are uninterested in helping or supporting schools and teachers. We also mentioned that some parents abdicate all responsibility for their children's education. And many others have tunnel vision and desire only what's best for *their* child or children, with little or no regard for other students. However, because our purpose in this book is to remind ourselves and our readers what teaching gives back to us, our intention with this chapter is to focus on what parents, guardians, and families give back to us. Hence, we decided to say no more on the issue of parents and families who criticize or even undermine a teacher's work. Such criticism is but one of many factors that can lead to teacher demoralization and burnout, and there is no shortage of popular volumes and academic research for those who wish to explore the subject further. We especially recommend Santoro's (2011; 2018) work. Now, though, let us return to the more positive aspects of dealing with students' families.

Parent Councils

Most private schools have had parent councils since their founding, often for the simple reason that parents initiated the formation of the school. Then, in the 1990s, partly in response to the widespread consolidation of local school boards into larger districts, a movement began to create parent advisory councils. For example, schools in several Chinese provinces and all of Canada's provinces were encouraged—or sometimes required—to operate in accordance with advice from parent councils. The authority of these councils varies from school to school and jurisdiction to jurisdiction, but they tend to have a kind of soft oversight function. Obviously, when elected school boards give ultimate authority to central office administrators who directly oversee the schools in their district, the existence of parent councils may prove problematic if the administrators start to receive advice from the central or district office that contradicts the advice they receive from the parent council. We must also acknowledge that advisory councils sometimes attract complainers who may mistake partnership for power or may think securing a seat on the council will give them a forum in which to air their grievances.

That said, several researchers have noted that parent advisory councils bequeath significant benefits to schools and teachers, along with the aforementioned headaches. For example, following research in rural China, Wei and Ni (2020) suggested that parents felt more connected to schools with functioning councils, even if they did not serve on the council themselves. On the other hand, a study of six schools with parent councils in Saskatchewan, Canada, found no significant effect on parents' sense of their own involvement in school decision-making (Stelmach, 2016). Without plunging further into the research on the efficacy of parent councils, we believe that they usually have a positive impact on school and student success. Although some parent council members may experience disappointment when they discover they are not authorized to remove a particular teacher or change a particular curricular decision, others enjoy fundraising, planning school and community events, and recruiting parent volunteers to help in classrooms.

It is important to note that most teachers share parents' concerns for their children. Both parents and teachers want students to be able to read, write, and think critically and creatively with the goal of graduation and developing a strong sense of civic responsibility. Depending on who you talk to, you may encounter surprised responses when an individual realizes that most parents and most teachers want precisely the same thing: for children to succeed academically and in life. Sadly, some parents operate under the false impression that teachers view students as an inconvenience—almost a barrier to their short workdays and long holidays. Meanwhile, some teachers operate under the misapprehension that each parent wants teachers to cater solely to their own child's needs. From our experience as teachers, as professors of education, and, yes, as parents, we know that a minority of parents and a minority of teachers live with these false impressions, but we also know that most teachers want what is best for all students. Recent educational frameworks such as Universal Design for Learning (UDL; 2014) and a focus on assets-based instruction support this approach. UDL offers a set of principles and structure to optimize learning opportunities and ensure that all learners can access and participate in learning experiences. Assets-based instruction focuses on each student's strengths and funds of knowledge, and recognizes culture and diversity as student assets. As previously mentioned, we can testify that most parents recognize that their child is not the only child in any given classroom. The majority of parents want to support the teacher, the school curriculum, and the current academic program and do not seek to interfere. Such parents recognize and honor the teacher as a trained professional.

As long ago as the mid-1970s, Dan Lortie (1975) coined the phrase "the apprenticeship of observation" to explain why some student teachers learn less in their teacher education programs than those who are teaching them want them to learn. He argued that everyone who enters teacher training has already spent thousands of hours observing classrooms and that this has largely shaped their thinking about teaching long before they begin higher education. Extrapolating from Lortie's argument, every parent has similarly spent thousands of hours in classrooms, and these experiences have shaped their views, too. Because of this, parents come to their own children's education pre-formed, so we should not be surprised when a parent's expectations of their child's teachers align with their own pre-formation. All parents, ourselves included, bring our own stories, our own educational histories, and our personal views on education to the classroom. We have all had teachers who were more or less kind, more or less expert, more or less creative, more or less fair. All parents—as former students who have had long apprenticeships of observation—can recognize phrases, patterns, and practices we favored when we were students, and we will have our antennae raised for any behaviors that irritated us years before we sent our own children into a classroom. For this reason, Lortie's point explains—if not justifies—the posture some parents take toward a teacher's work. Ken Badley, despite his familiarity with Lortie's work, has often wondered quietly during a parent conference, "Do you also think you know how to weld because you once watched someone install a trailer hitch?" That silent retort, despite the temporary satisfaction it might give, misses an element of what we, as teachers, should take from Lortie's work: parents actually *do* have thousands of hours of classroom experience and valuable perspectives that teachers and schools would be well advised to embrace.

Lortie focused his study on pre-service teachers' self-assessments of their pedagogical knowledge and skills, not on their level of care for their students. With reference to parents, if we add to the apprenticeship of observation the undeniable reality that our students are *our* children too, then we recognize that they essentially belong to the future and we all share responsibility for them. Grasping this idea may help us all better understand the urgency and fervor with which some parents present their cases or their complaints. Furthermore, many teachers appreciate the thank-you notes, gifts of coffee mugs, and words of gratitude with an enlarged and grateful perspective. Imagine someone who has spent 12,000 hours watching people do the kind of work we do. Now imagine that they come to parents' night specifically to inform us, "My daughter told me I have to come and meet you because she absolutely loves your class." Such comments come from people who, based on Lortie's account, have a fairly detailed conception of what ought to be going on in our classrooms, so any teacher who receives one should consider it a true validation of their work.

Mindsets: Partnership with Perspective

Every teacher and every parent lives with a perception of the kind of relationship they have with their counterpart in the educational task. This perception, while relatively fixed, could change incrementally over time, or even dramatically on a given day, depending on what the other party does or says. Furthermore, teachers and parents have a general perception of the other party: "Parents are all like this"; "Schools and teachers are all like that." You do not need to check scholarly research to test this claim. Simply typing "don't like my child's teacher" into Google yielded 75,000,000 hits at the time of writing, while "don't like my student's parents" yielded 28,000,000.

In our view, parents' and teachers' mindsets have a significant impact on parent–school connections. Of course, there are weaknesses and flaws; educators and parents are flawed human beings. But, on both sides, we need to understand that vignettes, single events, and one-off failures do not negate the successes and dedication of all involved. Perhaps we should all take a page out of Carol Dweck's (2007) research on fixed versus growth mindset. Rather than keeping a fixed or static mindset, teachers and parents alike should seek to stretch our minds to thrive together, alongside one another, as we educate and care for our children both at school and at home.

We have focused throughout this chapter on what parents and families give back to teachers, yet we must admit that everything is not perfect. For instance, teachers and families often have different ideas about involvement (Latunde, 2019). As mentioned throughout this book, teaching is hard and courageous work, but being a parent is even harder and takes even greater courage.

After wrestling with the question of what parents give to teachers, we wonder, "What if we, as educators, were able to see each parent as a former student who cares deeply for their child, wants what is best for that child, and is trying their best?" If we take these ideas into account, can we, as teachers, be the greater champions for every child? We are reminded once again of Latunde's (2019) framework of hospitality with a focus on relationships, community, and inclusivity. Considering this countercultural idea that parents need to build trust and relationships with teachers suggests that a focus on hospitality is worth the effort in schools. Poet Morgan Harper Nichols (2018) validates this type of connection when reminding readers that we should always act with empathy:

> Let me hold the door for you.
> I may have never walked
> A mile in your shoes,
> But I can see that
> Your soles are worn
> And your strength is torn
> Under the weight of a story
> I have never lived before.
> So let me hold the door for you.
> After all you've walked through
> It's the least I can do.

Can we partner with parents and families? Can we own and acknowledge that we are on the same team? Can we show up in the bleachers, classroom, and cafeteria to cheer for each other with the shared goal of student success? The journey of educating students alongside parents is not easy and is rarely smooth, yet we can choose to collaborate and move forward together with perspective, empathy, and humility.

References

Bono, A. (2020). School culture is a way of being: 18 elements to keep in the forefront to create a strong, sustained, celebrated school culture, *Association of Middle Level Education*, 8 (2), 5–8.

Brannon, D. (2010). Helping student teachers face their fears. *Middle Ground*, 14(1), 22.
Chenoweth, K. (2009). *How it's being done: Urgent lesson from unexpected schools.* Harvard Education Press.
Dweck, C. (2007). *Mindset: The new psychology of success.* Ballentine.
Edmunds, A., Nickel, J., & Badley, K. (2014) *Educational foundations in Canada.* Oxford University Press.
Ellul, J. (1985). *The humiliation of the word.* Eerdmans.
Greenleaf, R. K. (1998). *The power of servant leadership: Essays.* Berrett-Koehler.
Hancox, R. J., Milne, B. J., & Poulton, R. (2005). Association of television viewing during childhood with poor educational achievement. *Archives of Pediatric and Adolescent Medicine*, 159(7), 614–618.
Harper Nichols, M. (2018). Empathy [artwork]. https://mastermlinduniverse.net/2018/12/30/empathy-inspiration/.
Kenny, D. (2012) *Born to rise: A story of children and teachers reaching their highest potential.* HarperCollins.
Latunde, Y. (2019). Towards more inclusive schools: An application of hospitality in parental involvement. *International Christian Community of Teacher Educators Journal*, 14(2). https://digitalcommons.georgefox.edu/icctej/vol14/iss2/5.
Lortie, D. (1975). *Schoolteacher: A sociological study.* University of Chicago Press.
McCoy, D. L. & Edwards, N. (2016). Four questions to consider when communicating with parents. *Association of Middle Level Education.* www.amle.org/youre-doing-what-keeping-parents-informed-about-new-initiatives-2/.
Meyer, A., Rose, D. H., & Gordon, D. (2014). *Universal design for learning theory and practice.* CAST Professional Publishing.
Mo, Y. & Singh, K. (2008). Parents' relationships and involvement: Effects on students' school engagement and performance. *Research in Middle Level Education*, 31(10), 1–11.
Murray, C. (2009). Parent and teacher relationships as predictors of school engagement and functioning among low-income urban youth. *Journal of Early Adolescence*, 29(3), 376–404.
Postman, N. (1985). *Amusing ourselves to death: Public discourse in the age of show business.* Viking.
Santoro, D. (2011). Good teaching in difficult times: Demoralization in the pursuit of good work. *American Journal of Education*, 118(1), 1–23.
Santoro, D. (2018). *Demoralized: Why teachers leave the profession they love and how they can stay.* Harvard University Press.
Schmidt, M. E. & Vanderwater, E. (2008). Media and attention, cognition, and school achievement. *Future of Children*, 18(1), 63–85.
Shute, V. J., Hansen, E. G., Underwood, J. S., & Razzouk, R. (2011). A review of the relationship between parental involvement and secondary school students' academic achievement. *Education Research International.* https://doi.org/10.1155/2011/915326.
Stelmach, B. (2016). Parents' participation on school councils analysed through Arnstein's ladder of participation. *School Leadership and Management*, 36(3), 271–291.
Von Fisher, P. & De Jong, D. (2017). The relationship between teacher perception of principal servant leadership behavior and teacher job satisfaction. *Servant Leadership Theory and Practice*, 4(20), 53–84.
Wei, F. & Ni, Y. (2020). Parent councils, parent involvement, and parent satisfaction: Evidence from rural schools in China. *Educational Management, Administration, and Leadership*, October 28. doi:10.1177/1741143220968166.

11
JOYFUL RESILIENCE THROUGH DISSONANCE, DOUBT, AND DISILLUSIONMENT

Carrie R. Giboney Wall

My first year of teaching was almost my last. As a recent graduate in need of employment, I took the first teaching job offered to me. Being a novice teacher, I was unprepared for the difficulties I faced at a middle school nestled in an impoverished neighborhood and comprised of students with a plethora of physical, academic, and social-emotional challenges. Though half my teaching load was in my content area of math, the other half was elective courses outside my area of expertise, taught in a classroom crammed with over 40 students each period. I struggled with classroom management, and a large number of my students were failing due to familial hardship, excessive absences, failed assessments, unsubmitted homework, and (if I am honest) my own inexperience as an educator. Question after question besieged my mind about how I could teach, engage, support, and motivate students to facilitate deeper learning for all. In the absence of mentors and colleagues who would share resources, support, and camaraderie, I floundered in isolation. Helpless to ease my students' burdens, I despaired as I watched them wrestle with food insecurity, overcrowded living conditions, and physical abuse as well as familial mental illness, substance abuse, and incarceration. Tears flowed frequently, self-doubt permeated my efforts, and feelings of failure remained ever present as I questioned my call to the teaching profession. Though I always thought I would be a good teacher, I began to dread each day of work and I often considered quitting.

It is human nature to want to flee from pain, discomfort, and suffering. We pop pills, engage in avoidance behavior, and distract ourselves from distressing realities in an attempt to numb the pain or ignore its adverse impact. Most teachers are no different, seeking to avoid conflict and to resolve dissonance the moment it occurs. Our work is replete with tension or clashes between what we *thought* or *wanted* teaching to be and the reality of what it actually *is*. Like a cacophonous musical chord, the dissonance is often uncomfortable, unsettling, and even painful. Festinger (1957: p. 95) defined dissonance as "two items of information that psychologically do not fit

DOI: 10.4324/9781003124429-11

together." It festers within our emotions. It rankles our cognition. It gnaws away at our self-efficacy and identity. It is fueled by the contexts in which we teach.

Dissonance can seep into every aspect of the educational process, igniting doubt and disillusionment. We experience *emotional dissonance* when facing the harsh reality that numerous external factors beyond our control (such as poverty, trauma, or familial hardship) negatively impact student learning and that we can do little to change such circumstances. We experience *cognitive dissonance* when our best efforts to promote learning are not met with student success and we wonder what pedagogical strategies or management techniques we can employ to meet the plethora of student needs. We experience *identity dissonance* when our visions of personal effectiveness and aspirations to make a difference are crushed by the reality of our human limitations to effect change for every student, causing us to wonder if we have selected the right vocational path. We experience *contextual dissonance* when our convictions about what is best for our students clash with institutional, bureaucratic, and political contexts that limit or constrain our academic freedom. To be sure, teaching is a multifaceted, dilemma-ridden, holistic journey abounding with questions that have complicated answers.

So, what are we to do as educators? Throw in the towel? Run in the other direction? Pursue another profession? Is there anything good to be gained from dissonance within teaching? Rather than fleeing from it, is it possible to make peace with dissonance and even befriend it as an opportunity to stretch and grow as an educator? A body of research gives a resounding "yes" to these questions. Though dissonance in teaching is inevitable, uncomfortable, and sometimes anxiety-provoking, Galman (2009) claims that cognitive disequilibrium is an important catalyst for transformational change and healthy educator development, and, therefore, something to welcome and work through, rather than avoid and work around. Teachers can harness the various forms of naturally occurring dissonance in their practice in order to challenge their assumptions about students and teaching, promote deep learning, and ignite transformational change.

In order to understand the generative nature of dissonance in teaching, this chapter begins by briefly reviewing the literature on dissonance in education. This is followed by explanations of four forms of naturally occurring dissonance within teaching, each infused with quotations and examples from five female elementary teachers. These teachers—Shantelle, Tima, Leigh, Barb, and Sue[1]—articulate the dissonance, self-doubts, and disillusionment they experienced as they wrestled with what it means to be a teacher and how to meet teaching's many demands. Their quotes are extracted from questionnaire and interview data collected by the author over a nine-year period in a longitudinal investigation examining initial pre-service teacher conceptions about teaching and learning and how those conceptions changed throughout the participants' teacher preparation program and into their in-service teaching (Wall, 2016; 2018). It is my hope that these teachers' candid accounts of their struggles will resonate with readers, who will consequently find comfort in the shared journey. In addition to acknowledging the doubt and disillusionment teaching ignites, each section offers strategies that educators may use to harness dissonance and promote healthy educator development.

Literature on Dissonance

The concept of cognitive dissonance originated with Festinger (1957), who theorized that it is a conflict between two or more concepts, beliefs, or actions that are not consistent with one another. This clash often causes psychological stress and discomfort, and motivates the person to resolve the tension and thereby reduce their distress (Festinger, 1957; 1962). Researchers have investigated the role of dissonance within education, documenting its benefits for growth and learning. From a cognitive constructivist perspective, Piaget (1952) posited that learning occurs through three interrelated processes: organization, adaptation, and equilibration. He theorized that individuals construct personal meaning and understanding when they experience cognitive disequilibrium by encountering information that does not align with their existing schemas, adapting their cognitive structures to fit the new information, and restoring equilibrium or balance among cognitive elements.

Expanding on Piaget's concept of cognitive disequilibrium, in the field of science Strike and Posner (1992) examined the process of conceptual change, defining it as a transformative restructuring of an existing conception or belief. They posited that for conceptual change to take place learners must experience cognitive dissonance within their current understandings to be "forced" to consider other explanations that are plausible, intelligible, and fruitful. Without cognitive dissonance, they contended, people maintain the status quo in their conceptual structures. Though initially taking an overly cognitive approach, Strike and Posner later embraced a more holistic view, suggesting that emotion and social elements also impact conceptual change.

Some scholars have documented the benefits of cognitive disequilibrium or dissonance within teacher education as a way of prodding pre-service teachers to confront traditional notions of teacher-centered, transmissive instruction based on prior schooling experiences (Bryan, 2003; Leavy, McSorley, & Bote, 2007; Pajares, 1992) and consider more innovative, student-centered, knowledge-construction theories (Britzman, 1991; Bryan, 2003; Furlong & Maynard, 1995; Hollingsworth, 1989). Hollingsworth (1989) and Weinstein (1990) found success in placing pre-service teachers with cooperating teachers who did not share their educational views as a way of promoting disequilibrium and eventual intellectual growth. Hill (2000) and McFalls and Cobb-Roberts (2001) found cognitive disequilibrium and tolerance for ambiguities to be central to intellectual growth in their education courses. Other teacher educators found success in carefully scaffolding (Vygotsky, 1978) dissonant learning experiences, designing reflective assignments, igniting classroom discourse, selecting dilemma-ridden readings, and posing questions that incrementally challenge pre-service teacher conceptions and trigger cognitive dissonance in a supportive context. Such pedagogical strategies enable pre-service teachers to experience cognitive dissatisfaction with their current conceptions and allow supportive teacher educators to introduce new research-based pedagogical methodologies that are plausible, intelligible, and fruitful in creating deep learning (Strike & Posner, 1992).

Taking a more integrative, reflective approach, Korthagen (2004; 2017) claimed that educator dissonance is often the result of a clash between the external, professional aspects of teaching (such as teacher competencies, behaviors, and school environment) and the teacher's inner core qualities (such as their mission, identity, and beliefs). Korthagen proposed that, because core qualities are the driving force behind teacher competencies and behavior, educators should work through dissonance from the inside out, through core reflection. His Onion Model (Korthagen, 2004) posits that an effective teacher seeks alignment between his or her onion layers, working toward "coherence between [his or] her core qualities, ideals, sense of identity, beliefs, competencies, behavior and the characteristics of the environment, e.g. a classroom or school" (Korthagen, 2017: p. 397). Rosenberg (1977) also examined the tension between one's *internal* conceptions, emotions, and beliefs and the *external* realities of one's environment, coining the term "contextual dissonance" to describe incompatibility between the two, and "contextual consonance" to describe harmony between them. In an educational context, the former can describe the incompatibility between a teacher's educational beliefs and the prevailing norms of his or her school, and the latter can describe harmony between them. In her investigation of the tension between teachers' *individual* idealistic conceptions of being a teacher and *institutional* realities concerning the bureaucratic and politicized terrain of schools, Galman (2009) posited that dissonance triggered by these two discordant realities can be powerful and generative, playing a catalytic role in healthy teacher identity development. She continued by stating that though removing the dissonance may result in greater inner peace, doing so may be detrimental to one's ability to reflect, change, and develop. Researchers on dissonance in education tend to agree that, though initially uncomfortable or even anxiety-inducing, it can catalyze teachers' deeper core reflection, which in turn can fuel the development of new pedagogical competencies, promoting greater student learning.

So, how do we, as educators, go about embracing the growth that dissonance has to offer? The following pages examine four areas of dissonance: emotional dissonance, cognitive dissonance, identity dissonance, and contextual dissonance. Each discussion is situated in the lived experiences of five female elementary teachers who have navigated dissonance in its various forms over a nine-year journey from pre-service teacher to in-service teacher and have moved forward resiliently. Their quoted comments allow us to "enter into the situation and thoughts of the people represented" (Patton, 1990: p. 430) and provide rich descriptions of how teachers work through (not around) dissonance to gain greater clarity and joy in their teaching.

Emotional Dissonance

Teaching is an emotionally taxing profession "in which feelings and motivation play an essential role" (Korthagen, 2017: p. 391). Students' home lives, backgrounds, and other factors *outside* the classroom profoundly (and sometimes detrimentally) impact life and learning *inside* the classroom. The five elementary teachers who feature in this chapter told stories of students who "wormed their way into nearly every thought and moment" of their lives. They spoke passionately about student hardships that were "unfair" and "heartbreaking" and of situations that caused them to "cry all the way home." Tima reflected, "Those day-in, day-out things that happen at home largely impact the kids. I know you're told that, but until you see it with your own eyes, you just don't know." Shantelle explained:

> You often have to spend a lot of time in the classroom making up for what happened outside the classroom. So many factors affect students' lives—prior teachers, home life, availability of resources, parental help (or lack thereof), etc. These factors are all critical in determining how a student might perform in an academic setting, and as a teacher it's incredibly challenging to navigate those immense extenuating circumstances. You do what you can to compensate for those hours spent outside the class, and try not to let it get you down.

This emotional dissonance is experienced by many teachers who find that students' personal challenges and trauma *beyond* the walls of the classroom seem to seep into life *within* those walls. Discouragement takes hold as teachers are forced to confront their human limitations and inability to move students beyond the reach of difficult external factors to the extent they initially believed they could. Gill and Hardin (2015: p. 232) observed, "Emotions shape beliefs and are shaped by beliefs ... To ignore affective constructs such as emotions is to present an incomplete and even faulty understanding of teachers' beliefs."

Situating emotional dissonance in our broader teaching journey, reflecting back on our growing competence as educators, and considering ways in which we successfully wrestled through dissonant moments in the past are good starting points on the path toward greater emotional consonance and peace. If teachers adopt a growth mindset focusing on student improvement over achievement and progress over proficiency, they may be more likely to choose perseverance over despair and resilience over resignation when they next face emotional turmoil. Additionally, as Tucker noted in Chapter 7, fostering a strong relational network with colleagues can be a source of support and encouragement during times of emotional dissonance, compassion fatigue, and discouragement.

Cognitive Dissonance

Dissonance is ignited not only by the challenge of meeting students' emotional needs but also by the challenge of meeting their varied learning needs. Because students are culturally, linguistically, and cognitively diverse, teachers experience dissonance regarding which pedagogical strategies and supports might best facilitate their learning. Though differentiating instruction is essential in helping students meet their learning objectives and advance their understanding, it is difficult and fraught with challenges. Shantelle described her cognitive dissonance:

> I have a hard time making sure everything is applicable and meaningful for every student. I feel like, for the most part, I can reach the majority, but what about the kids on the fringes who can't keep up with the class? They need

help and I want to give it to them. I go home and think about individual kids ... like, what do you do? I feel like every issue in teaching gives way to new issues and I haven't resolved any of them. There's a lot of stuff to think about. I can't imagine doing anything else, but there are days when I just don't want to do it.

Facing a similar quandary, Sue inquired, "How do I individualize instruction for each child, challenging those who need challenging while giving the support and aid to those who are struggling?" Tima asked, "Obviously they [English learners] need extra help, but where do we fit it in? How do we make this better? How do we make this work?" Leigh confessed, "I've had a couple of really tough kids the last couple of years and I just keep wondering how I can best serve them. It's really hard." These teachers' cognitive dissonance sounds all too familiar. Though we wish to promote learning among all students, our internal wrestling and questions remain. How do we successfully differentiate instruction for all students? How do we meet every child's needs?

When wrestling with these dilemmas, it is important not to run away too quickly. Though dissonance is often uncomfortable, it is a "motivating state" that prods people into action (Festinger, 1962: p. 3). Strike and Posner (1992) claimed that cognitive dissatisfaction with our current conceptions prompts teachers to be more open to new or different pedagogical methodologies if such strategies are plausible, intelligible, and fruitful in creating deep learning. Without it, we may never consider the need for change and therefore can be in danger of stagnation. Galman (2009) posited that all teachers and learners need some degree of dissonance to prompt them to grapple with new ideas and take the cognitive leaps and risks that are necessary for reflective and transformative learning.

Reflecting on our current teaching, articulating gaps in student learning, considering other pedagogical best practices, and implementing new approaches (instead of perpetuating the status quo) can help teachers productively address cognitive dissonance and promote greater student learning. In her 15-year longitudinal study, Levin (2003) observed that cognitive dissonance can simultaneously be resolved *internally* (through thinking, reflection, and metacognition) and *externally* (through reading, attending workshops, and conversations with others). Professional development and learning can be nurtured further through endeavors such as action research, partnering with other teachers, adding a new skill, continued personal education, and soliciting advice from mentors. Cognitive dissonance and dissatisfaction can be catalysts for teacher professional and pedagogical growth, which, in turn, can enrich student learning and academic success.

Identity Dissonance

As noted in previous chapters, the learning-to-teach journey is a voyage of self-discovery and identity formation; most of us entered the profession because we wanted to change the world and improve lives. Thousands of hours' experience in K-12 classrooms as learners ourselves helped construct our conceptions of what it means to teach—what Lortie (1975) called "the apprenticeship of observation" (see Chapter 10). However, because those conceptions of teaching are based on observations of the performance side of classroom teaching, they are often idealistic (Furlong & Maynard, 1995) or at least underdeveloped. For example, Barb entered her teacher preparation program with the assumption that teaching was simple and easily accomplished. She explained:

> My view of a teacher was what I saw as a student—their job ended when I left. I had no idea how much there was outside of showing up in the morning, delivering your lesson, and loving those kids, and when the bell rings, you can pick up your coffee mug and go home and maybe grade some papers in the evening while you're watching *American Idol*. I had no idea that it was so much more!

Shantelle also held idealistic notions of the impact she would have as a teacher:

> At the beginning [of my teacher preparation program], I watched all the teacher movies, read all the books, and I was like, "Aaah, I'm going to be that *Chicken Soup for the Soul* teacher and do awesome." My grand illusion of being a teacher is that they [the students] would all be perfect. I would help them learn and they would all grow up to be astronauts, doctors, or lawyers, and I would, you know, go home by five.

Many of us entered our teacher preparation programs with similarly naive conceptions constructed from our obscured, student-oriented perspectives (Lortie, 1975). However, it did not take long for those understandings to be challenged as we experienced the complex, multifaceted, and demanding true nature of teaching. Confronted with challenges to student learning and instructional tasks that had once been invisible to us, the private work of teachers was slowly demystified like "the lights turning on in Space Mountain [at Disneyland]" (Leigh).

As the realistic complexities of teaching came into clearer focus, so did our identity dissonance. Our expectations of what a teacher is, constructed over a lifetime in schools, clashed with our ability to enact that role. Our aspirations about the impact our teacher-selves can have on *all* students conflicted with our actual, finite success. Initial deep-seated visions of personal effectiveness and an ability to "save the world" were crushed by the realities of life in and out of classrooms, resulting in diminished idealism and discouragement. As Leigh explained, "You initially have this conception that I am going to have an impact on every single child in the classroom. It's hard to wrestle with the fact that not every kid is going to grow by leaps and bounds." Shantelle shared a similar struggle in embracing and embodying a realistic and authentic teacher identity:

> Before, I thought the success of my students was going to be directly related to how hard I worked. However, I've learned if I stay at school until nine at

night, my students aren't going to have that much more success. It's just a hard profession because you don't feel like you're making a difference some of the time. You come in with this feeling that I am going to save the world. Like, if I just work hard, I can make a difference. You have this very idealistic idea of what you'll do.

Leigh summarized this tension by reflecting, "While I'm certainly still passionate about my job, it [teaching] can sometimes be flat-out hard!" Wrestling with our own human limitations while facing the dissonant fires of reality, we teachers sometimes wonder, "Can I really do this?" or even "Do I want to do this?"

If these sentiments resonate with you, you are not alone. Ticknor (2014: p. 290) described the teacher identity formation process as "slippery, messy, contradictory, and full of tension," while Ó Gallchóir, O'Flaherty, and Hinchion (2018: p. 140) observed that it has "no definitive endpoint or end-product." So, if identity dissonance along the teaching journey is inevitable (Galman, 2009), what should we do about it and how can we harness it for personal and professional growth? Galman (2009: p. 477) suggests that, though identity dissonance can be unsettling or even anxiety-provoking, it can also ignite positive change and serve as "a catalyst not only for identity development, but also to the understanding of the complexity of teachers' work and identity."

A common response when working through identity dissonance is to address the exterior, observable elements of our teaching practice, such as our classroom environment, student conduct, management strategies, lesson planning, curriculum, and/or instructional competencies. Our thinking is that if our external environment is more harmonious, then our inner core will be, too. However, Korthagen (2017) disputes this "outside-in" approach, instead urging teachers to reflect systematically on their teaching practice from the "inside out." His Onion Model (Korthagen, 2004) posits that identity dissonance originates from a disconnect between one's *inner* core, which encompasses mission (What is my ideal?), identity (Who am I?), and beliefs (What do I believe?), and one's *outer* layers, which include competencies (What am I good at?), behavior (What do I do?), and teaching environment (What am I dealing with?). He concludes that the more teachers' core qualities are aligned with their professional behaviors, "the more positive emotions will evolve and the more effective the teacher will be" (Korthagen, 2004: p. 397). Though Korthagen warns that the core reflective process must be sustained over time and is not a one-shot approach or a quick fix, he asserts that the chief benefit of professional learning originates not from an externally imposed, uniform solution for all but from who the teacher is and what they believe and value.

Contextual Dissonance

Even if we take Korthagen's advice and align our personal self with our professional practice, dissonance can still exist. Contextual dissonance (Rosenberg, 1977) results when pedagogical strategies teachers deem best for student learning clash with an institutional context that limits or prohibits them. It appears when teachers' vision of self-as-teacher and expectations about their teaching role are incongruent with the institutional, bureaucratic, and political realities of curricular mandates, high-stakes testing pressure, and/or administrative philosophical differences within their school. This incompatibility between a teacher's educational beliefs and the prevailing norms of the school often causes feelings of abandonment, anxiety, or isolation (Ó Gallchóir et al., 2018), as other contributors to this book have noted.

Contextual dissonance is often experienced by pre-service teachers as they are forced to reconcile the preconceptions they have about teaching based on prior learning experiences with the realities of teaching in the present. For example, pre-service teachers often believe educators have endless freedom to make instructional decisions and that their work is self-directed and autonomous (Wall, 2016). As they progress through their teacher preparation programs, they are often frustrated by limitations to their academic freedom imposed by scripted curriculum, state standards, high-stakes testing, cooperating teachers, administration, grade-level teams, parents, and school schedules.

Though Sue initially assumed, "I can be in my own classroom and do whatever I want," it did not take long for her to express her frustration regarding "how controlled it [teaching] could be by outside forces." She wondered, "Is it really possible to teach the way *I* want to teach?" Tima experienced contextual dissonance between her desire to inculcate a love for reading within her students and her school's push to "get through" the curriculum. She lamented, "It's amazing how stuck on curriculum administration is, but I feel like I need to do other things with my struggling kids and that they are missing out on the wonderful parts of literacy."

In her first months of teaching, Barb expressed similar dismay at the constraints on her academic freedom:

> I really thought teachers were more autonomous and could do what they wanted to do. I had no idea how many people's breath would be on your neck the whole time! If I'm doing well with my class, don't hover. If my game is fine, leave me alone!

She later articulated her contextual dissonance between what she deemed best for students and the constraints of her school context:

> How am I going to do what I believe in and what I think is important? I feel like I'm juggling two separate things that don't want to be in the air at the same time. I keep telling myself that they're not opposite and they can go together, but that is the cognitive dissonance ... I would leave my fieldwork a lot of times wondering, "Is this what I really want to do? Is this what I really believe in?"

Though Shantelle preferred incorporating experiential, project-based learning and child-centered pedagogies aligned with her beliefs, she taught at a charter school that required her to utilize a formulaic curriculum, give daily quizzes, and omit labs from her science curriculum. The magnitude of her contextual dissonance was high when she was told she should hold off on all science labs until May—after state testing was over. She shared, "I was blown away! I was like, 'Have you ever met a child?' My principal had to repeat it three times. I just did the labs anyway and didn't tell. I turned in my lesson plans after the fact." Though she began her teaching journey with heightened idealism regarding her ability to make a difference in the lives of students, this waned not only as she wrestled with the demands of the profession but also as she experienced administrative pressure's power to diminish her efforts. She explained:

> Before I started teaching, I was fairly unaware of the bureaucracy, red tape, and amount of influence outside administration, agencies, and governing bodies have over what happens inside my classroom. I thought, for some reason, that teaching was a bit above all that, and that those industrial problems wouldn't be as big a factor in my classroom and personal pedagogy. But they are. They really are. This has been a huge revelation, and one I still have a hard time dealing with when conceptualizing teaching overall.

If this sounds familiar, you are in good company. As teachers, we sometimes feel stifled by our lack of teacher agency and our inability to have an authentic voice in our own pedagogical decisions, given the many limitations and restrictions.

So, what are our options if we are experiencing contextual dissonance within our school? One option would be to consider whether our current teaching context is a good fit for us and well aligned with our educational philosophy. After all, it seems we should enjoy a certain level of contextual consonance—or compatibility—in order to thrive and persevere in our school environment. Maybe teacher applicants should be more judicious about whether a school's educational approach aligns with their personal preferred pedagogies before signing a contract. Perhaps if Shantelle had worked at a school that was more philosophically congruent, she would have been more satisfied teaching at that school.

Rather than bemoaning our teaching context and/or seeking to leave our school (though this might be the only viable option in some cases), an alternative is to stay and lean into contextual dissonance, realizing that dissonance almost always permeates teaching and that it is a naturally occurring aspect of the journey. Those of us who are teacher educators should be careful not to valorize the teaching profession, but rather be appropriately forthcoming about its challenges (Levin, He, & Allen, 2013) and the political and bureaucratic nature of teachers' work. Although we, as teachers, must work collaboratively within environments brimming with pedagogical, political, and institutional complexities, we can also become teacher leaders and change agents who ask tough questions, expose injustices, cast new visions, and engage in productive change. By converting our awareness of needed change into action, we can stimulate continual, meaningful improvement and innovation within our educational contexts, providing equitable and meaningful learning experiences for all students.

Although contextual dissonance is unsettling and aggravating at times, wrestling through it (instead of trying to go around it) can result in a more carefully crafted, authentic teacher identity that we can realistically embody within the current political and bureaucratic climate. Moreover, contextual dissonance can be a catalyst to strengthening personal agency to be part of the solution and to advocate effectively for purposeful change.

Befriending Dissonance along the Teaching Journey

So, how did I fight the fires of dissonance during my first year of teaching? Although several factors bear on my answer, a move out-of-state provided an opportunity to begin afresh and give teaching a second chance. My second job, teaching math at the high school level, was a better contextual fit for me. Reasonable class sizes of 30–35 students per period afforded me greater success at classroom management, differentiating instruction, and meeting students' varied personal and academic needs. Helpful and friendly colleagues who shared resources and pedagogical strategies allowed me to address my cognitive dissonance as to how to support all students. Nurturing these friendships reduced my sense of isolation and provided a community of colleagues with whom to process emotional dissonance and discouragement. In addition to benefiting from this new school context and supportive colleagues, I engaged in "inside-out" reflection (Korthagen, 2017) to address the disconnect between my outer layers of math teaching competency, affinity for high school students, management strategies, and need for collegial support with my inner core mission, values, beliefs about teaching, and identity as a developing educator. By working through, rather than around, the dissonance, I came to a place of greater peace and joy in my teaching.

Teaching is a deeply personal journey that profoundly impacts every aspect of the teacher self, eliciting an array of conflicting emotions—from satisfaction to disillusionment, consonance to dissonance, clarity to confusion, hope to despair. As such, dissonance is inevitable and can seep into all aspects of the teaching process, igniting emotions, fanning or snuffing out self-efficacy, and honing identity and sense of self. The task for educators is not to eliminate the source of dissonance, nor to overextend their capacity for conflict, but rather to harness the various forms of naturally occurring dissonance to promote transformative learning and healthy educator development. By situating momentary dissonance in our broader teaching journey and reflecting on the ways we successfully wrestled through dissonant moments in the past, we are more likely to choose perseverance over despair and resilience over resignation when facing new emotional or cognitive turmoil. After all, the goal is not to eradicate the dissonance but rather to befriend it and embrace the fine-tuning, deep learning, and transformative growth that can follow.

Note

1 All names have been changed.

References

Britzman, D. P. (1991). *Practice makes practice: A critical study of learning to teach*. State University of New York Press.

Bryan, L. A. (2003). Nestedness of beliefs: Examining a prospective elementary teacher's belief system about science teaching and learning. *Journal of Research in Science Teaching*, 40(9), 835–868.

Festinger, L. (1957). *Theory of cognitive dissonance*. Stanford University Press.

Festinger, L. (1962). Cognitive dissonance. *Scientific American*, 207(4), 93–102.

Furlong, J. & T. Maynard. (1995). *Mentoring student teachers: The growth of professional knowledge*. Routledge.

Galman, S. (2009). Doth the lady protest too much? Pre-service teachers and the experience of dissonance as a catalyst for development. *Teaching and Teacher Education*, 25, 468–481.

Gill, M. G. & Hardin, C. (2015). A "hot" mess: Unpacking the relation between teachers' beliefs and emotions. In H. Fives & M. G. Gill (Eds.), *International handbook of research on teachers' beliefs* (pp. 230–245). Routledge.

Hill, L. (2000). What does it take to change minds? Intellectual development of preservice teachers. *Journal of Teacher Education*, 51(1), 50–65.

Hollingsworth, S. (1989). Prior beliefs and cognitive change in learning to teach. *American Educational Research Journal*, 26(2), 160–189.

Korthagen, F. A. J. (2004). In search of the essence of a good teacher: Towards a more holistic approach in teacher education. *Teaching and Teacher Education*, 20, 77–97.

Korthagen, F. A. J. (2017). Inconvenient truths about teacher learning: Towards professional development 3.0. *Teachers and Teaching*, 23(4), 387–405.

Leavy, A. M., McSorley, F. A., & Bote, L. A. (2007). An examination of what metaphor construction reveals about the evolution of preservice teachers' beliefs about teaching and learning. *Teaching and Teacher Education*, 23(7), 1217–1233.

Levin, B. (2003). *Case studies of teacher development: An in-depth look at how thinking about pedagogy develops over time*. Lawrence Erlbaum Associates.

Levin, B., He, Y., & Allen, M. H. (2013). Teacher beliefs in action: A cross-sectional, longitudinal follow-up study of teachers' personal practical theories. *The Teacher Educator*, 48, 201–217.

Lortie, D.C. (1975). *Schoolteacher: A sociological study*. University of Chicago Press.

McFalls, E. L. & Cobb-Roberts, D. (2001). Reducing resistance to diversity through cognitive dissonance instruction: Implications for teacher education. *Journal of Teacher Education*, 52(2), 164–172.

Ó Gallchóir, C., O'Flaherty, J., & Hinchion, C. (2018). Identity development: What I notice about myself as a teacher. *European Journal of Teacher Education*, 41(2), 138–156.

Pajares, M. (1992). Teachers' beliefs and educational research: Cleaning up a messy construct. *Review of Educational Research*, 62(3), 307–332.

Patton, M. Q. (1990). *Qualitative evaluation and research methods* (2nd ed.). Sage.

Piaget, J. (1952). *The origins of intelligence in children*. International Universities Press.

Rosenberg, M. (1977). Contextual dissonance effects: Nature and causes. *Psychiatry*, 40, 205–217.

Strike, K. A. & Posner, G. J. (1992). A revisionist theory of conceptual change. In R. A. Duschl & R. J. Hamilton (Eds.), *Philosophy of science, cognitive psychology, and educational theory and practice* (pp. 147–176). State University of New York Press.

Ticknor, A. S. (2014). Negotiating professional identities in teacher education: A closer look at the language of one preservice teacher. *New Educator*, 10(4), 289–305.

Vygotsky, L. S. (1978). *Mind in society: The development of higher psychological processes*. Harvard University Press.

Wall, C. (2016). From student to teacher: Changes in preservice teacher educational beliefs throughout the learning-to-teach journey. *Teacher Development*, 20(3), 364–379.

Wall, C. (2018). Development through dissonance: A longitudinal investigation of changes in teachers' educational beliefs. *Teacher Education Quarterly*, 45(3), 29–51.

Weinstein, C. S. (1990). Prospective elementary teachers' beliefs about teaching: Implications for teacher education. *Teaching and Teacher Education*, 6(3), 279–290.

12
NAVIGATING POLITICAL, ECONOMIC, AND CURRICULUM CONSTRAINTS WITH JOYFUL DEFIANCE

Dana Antayá-Moore and Joanne Neal

In 350 BCE, Aristotle penned his landmark treatise, *Politics*, which summarized his views on the central enigma that has historically dogged the field of curriculum studies:

> That education should be regulated by law and should be an affair of state is not to be denied, but what should be the character of this public education, and how young persons should be educated, are questions which remain to be considered. As things are, there is disagreement about the subjects. For mankind are by no means agreed about the things to be taught, whether we look to virtue or the best life. Neither is it clear whether education is more concerned with intellectual or moral virtue. The existing practice is perplexing; no one knows on what principle we should proceed—should the useful in life, or should virtue, or should the higher knowledge, be the aim or our training; all three opinions have been entertained. Again, about the means there is no agreement; for different persons, starting with different ideas about the nature of virtue, naturally disagree about the practice of it.
>
> *(Aristotle, 1999: Book 8, part 2)*

Some 22 centuries after Aristotle, Herbert Spencer addressed the same question within the context of the Victorian era and social Darwinism (Gutek, 2010):

> Before there can be a rational curriculum, we must settle which things it most concerns us to know—we must determine the relative values of knowledges. These are the general ideas with which we must set out in discussing a curriculum: life is divided into several kinds of activity of successively decreasing importance; the worth of each order of facts as regulating these several kinds of activity, intrinsically, quasi-intrinsically, and conventionally; and their regulative influences estimated both as knowledge and discipline. What knowledge is of most worth?
>
> *(Spencer, 1860)*

DOI: 10.4324/9781003124429-12

While Aristotle and Spencer had differing approaches to the central question of what should be included in a given curriculum, the common theme of values permeates their arguments. In short, they posited that what is contained within a given curriculum holds high value in the minds and hearts of its authors. That values should persist to this day as the cornerstone of debate surrounding curriculum is hardly surprising.

Any given curriculum designed for public education is a reflection of the hopes and aspirations of the society that develops it. Viewed this way, curriculum acts as a bridge between the present and the future. It is an act of both forecast and faith as it seeks to prepare the next generation for the worlds of work and citizenship, while simultaneously attempting to shape the future that generation will inhabit. Curriculum for public education is typically legislated by provincial or state governments that usually attend to voices in the public square. Questions of values intersect at this point with the realms of politics and finance. Like a braid, these three strands of values, politics, and finance are interwoven when decisions are made about curricular matters. This braid is essentially encased in beliefs about the nature of reality (ontology), the nature of goodness (axiology), and the nature of knowledge (epistemology) in relation to education. These three areas of belief typically form the crux of educational philosophy, not only as educational philosophy might be taught in an education program but as teachers act out of their respective philosophies in classrooms day to day.

Educational philosophy encapsulates what an individual or group of individuals believes to be pedagogically and ethically valid (real, good, and true) about teaching and learning, stemming from a broader worldview or philosophy of life. As such, educational philosophy provides the parameters and direction for preferred educational action. A more evolved and mature educational philosophy represents a constellation of critically examined beliefs about such matters as the purpose of education, curriculum, assessment and reporting of student progress, instruction and the role of the teacher, learning and the role of the learner, the role of parents and guardians, organization of the school (e.g., students are organized by grade levels), and curricular resources. As a developed entity, an educational philosophy should be internally coherent: that is to say, beliefs about the purpose of education logically mesh with beliefs about curriculum and the other aspects of education we listed above.

From a curriculum perspective, it is important to note that what an individual or group of educators believes about curriculum is tied to beliefs about the other seven aspects of educational philosophy. If, for example, curriculum is believed to be principally an opportunity for students to grow in their humanity, it is likely that a more student-centered approach that considers individual learning needs and interests is reflected in beliefs about the purpose of education, assessment practices, instruction, the role of parents and guardians, organization of students for learning, and the materials that teachers and students use to facilitate learning. Contrast this with a belief that curriculum is the primary means by which to train students to fill jobs for the future workforce. We would expect the beliefs associated with this view of curriculum to be very different. What is most significant about this insight is that human beliefs drive human actions. This truth extends into all aspects of education, from the macrocosm of provincial or state legislation to the microcosm of the solitary classroom. What individuals or groups of people believe to be real, good, and true about teaching and learning will be a consistent predictor of educational action, including how school authorities envision and develop curriculum.

Two Philosophies of Education

To note historical developments, North American public education has been engaged for more than a century in a tug of war between several competing educational philosophies; the best known of these are progressivism and essentialism (Edmunds, Nickel, & Badley, 2015; Gutek, 2010). Each paradigm has taken a turn appropriating center stage only to recede again on the educational horizon, followed by a re-emergence. This swinging of the pendulum most often coincides with larger political and economic shifts and trends. Throughout the twentieth century and into the twenty-first, as economic prosperity has given way to economic restraint and back again to prosperity, there have been corresponding back-and-forth movements between progressivism and essentialism. In these shifts, the political and economic dimensions are consistently linked, with elected officials mirroring these trends as they grapple with the two classic questions of curriculum development: what should students learn and how should that learning be organized?

Progressivism

As an educational philosophy, progressivism evolved largely as a backlash against some prominent assumptions and beliefs of the later nineteenth century, including the image of the authoritarian teacher, reliance on the "great books" of the past, the view that students' interests and developmental needs were irrelevant, and the notion of fixed or permanent knowledge. Shifting from a European model of learning that focused on filling the mind rather than nurturing intellect, progressivists sought to draw meaning from students' experiences and to encourage students to demonstrate their understandings. Its formal beginnings as an educational philosophy in 1919 mirrored larger social, political, and economic changes in North American society following World War I. It would endure as the most influential philosophical force in education through the 1930s. The 1960s and the 1990s saw progressivist revivals, with another resurgence in the second decade of the twenty-first century.

Although John Dewey (1859–1952) is most often credited with fathering progressivism, it was in fact the earlier work of Horace Mann and Henry Bernard in the late nineteenth century that formed the initial foundations for this educational philosophy. The pioneering ideas and writings of these two men strongly influenced Dewey in his early career. Dewey's (1916) publication *Democracy and Education* outlined many of the crucial elements of progressivism in its infancy. As the title suggests, the primacy of democracy to education was a fundamental principle.

Dewey perceived that the beliefs and conventions associated with democracy could be successfully transplanted to a school setting. To him, this was a necessary step in helping students develop positive citizenship and problem-solving skills. This emphasis on democracy also contributed to a new political and economic identity for the United States following World War I, distinguishing it further from European counterparts.

Progressivism places an emphasis on understanding, as opposed to the strict memorization of content. Students are taught *how* to think as opposed to *what* to think. Critical and reflective thinking are encouraged. To that end, the progressive teacher is a facilitator or guide. As Cook and Doll (1973: p. 43) noted of the progressivist swell of the late 1960s, "The teacher is not to be a dispenser of facts, but a moderator or leader. He is not a promoter of a point of view ... teaching is more exploratory than explanatory." Flexibility and the attitude and aptitude to be able to respond to the range of students' needs and interests are key for the progressivist teacher. While traditional paper-and-pencil testing is not necessarily eliminated in progressivist classrooms, there is a greater emphasis on student demonstrations of learning. Products and the processes used to develop or arrive at them are often viewed as valid forms of assessment.

That theories of child development and the view that the needs and interests of children should be the basis for designing curriculum were novel concepts when this educational philosophy was first introduced. The progressive view of the child as a unique individual contributed to more student-centered practices, and individualized instruction and student choices regarding optional or elective courses became instructional features of progressivism later in the twentieth century.

Public perceptions of progressivism have varied and have sometimes been based on complete misapprehension. Dewey himself was critical of those who supported mistaken or misguided notions about basic progressive ideals, specifically in relation to overly romanticized perceptions of children and their needs for freedom. More recently, progressivism has been inaccurately lumped together with "discovery learning." That is to say that the trendy perception of "discovery learning" is that it is a kind of educational free-for-all in which students aimlessly muck about and eventually make intuitive leaps that lead to erroneous conclusions. Furthermore, the "discovery learning" teacher is often rendered as a kind of inverse Mary Poppins who has no plan and no control over the learning situation. By contrast, an effective progressive classroom requires teachers to have such a strong command of curriculum and such a depth of knowledge of their students that they can engage those students with a wide range of resources and help them to make meaningful connections as the learning unfolds. This process implies that students' questions are addressed within the context of the given teaching and learning moment. Richness of learning—not chaos—is the goal.

That it can be challenging to implement progressive ideals well has added fuel to the fires of those who attack progressive approaches. Criticism of progressivism often emerges during times of fiscal restraint and is typically followed by a shift to more essentialist practices. For example, the 1971 expiry of the 1944 Bretton

Woods financial and trade agreements between Canada, Western Europe, Australia, the United States, and Japan marked the onset of a period of economic decline in North America. This was followed by the 1973 oil crisis, a stock market crash in 1973–1974, and an economic recession through 1975. These economic shifts were followed and mirrored by a corresponding shift from progressivism to essentialism in educational practices across North America.

Essentialism

Historically, essentialism has had the greatest degree of influence within the North American educational system (Knight, 2008). First appearing in the 1930s as a pushback against progressivism and gaining strength toward the end of World War II, essentialism dominated education in the late 1950s and early 1960s as the Cold War escalated and the Russians launched the world's first satellite, *Sputnik*. The 1970s and the late 1980s through the early 1990s saw further essentialist revivals, followed by yet another wave in the early 2000s.

Essentialism has frequently been termed a "back to basics" or "3 Rs" movement. William Bagley (1874–1946), of the Teachers College of Columbia University, is credited with formalizing the essentialist perspective, with Arthur Bestor and Hyman George Rickover acting as major proponents in the 1950s and 1960s. Essentialism's initial evolution as an educational philosophy paralleled massive waves of immigration to North America. Its intent was to provide a basic education to the offspring of the working masses, with a strong focus on reading, writing, and arithmetic while preserving the social status quo. Bernal (1971: p. 1149) commented on this process at the onset of the revival of essentialism in the 1970s:

> the new working class needed enough acquaintance with the three R's to do their jobs properly, and provision for teaching them was reluctantly provided on the cheapest basis. But there was all the more reason for seeing that the education of the masses did not go too far, and that it introduced no unsettling ideas.

Thus, the original function of an essentialist education was to provide the future workforce with literacy and other necessary skills (with the exception of critical thinking, which was not encouraged) so that they could contribute to the developing economy.

A hierarchical class structure is frequently embedded and legitimated within essentialist education. Inequalities among students are seen as a function of genetics or other biological factors, and the ranking of students is viewed as a natural outcome. Rickover (1958: p. 61) illustrated this rather deterministic view when he stated, "For all children, the educational process must be one of collecting factual knowledge to the limit of their absorptive capacity." Quantity and rate of learning, therefore, are viewed as variable, and depth of learning is thought to be determined by student ability. Rickover (1958: p. 61) further noted, "The student must be made to work hard ... nothing can really make it fun." While a common curriculum exists for all, essentialists believe that latitude must be given, particularly to the gifted student. In a kind of educational Darwinism, the strongest and best students are traditionally encouraged to strive and grow beyond mere mastery of basics.

Of particular significance to the theme of this volume, essentialism often resurfaces in conversations about education when public education is under attack. Sometimes seen as a kind of panacea for educational ills and societal failures, its popularity often coincides with times of economic restraint, when some politicians attempt to make political capital out of attacking such "frills" as the fine arts.

The high profile of a US report, *A Nation at Risk* (National Commission on Excellence in Education, 1983), was largely responsible for essentialism's return to the educational spotlight in the late 1980s. However, in that decade and the 1990s, supporters' focus shifted slightly from an emphasis on minimal competence to one of increased achievement. This excellence-versus-adequacy mindset was consistent with an ethos of global economic competition. Like the previous great period of essentialism in the late 1950s and early 1960s—when North America was competing against the USSR—attempts were made to compare North American student achievement with achievement in Japan, Germany, and other countries. Themes of competition and survival in the international marketplace that pervaded newspapers, business reports, and educational journals have persisted to our own time. Schools are still viewed as pipelines to national economic prosperity and to international political power. The emphasis on international test results that rank students against those of other nations remains as strong as ever.

Comparing Progressivism and Essentialism

Following the premise that debate about curriculum is grounded in values, it becomes more apparent how these two paradigms reflect two sets of values in relation to what and how students should learn. However, in practice, the curricular relationship between progressivism and essentialism is not usually completely dichotomous; that is to say, curriculum in the twenty-first century is rarely purely progressivist or purely essentialist. Rather, it tends to be plotted somewhere on a continuum between the two.

Knowing where one is anchored along this continuum of progressivism and essentialism is critical if one is to avoid simply being swept up in the winds of change every time a new curriculum appears on the horizon. A change to provincial or state curriculum need not require us to abandon our corresponding beliefs about the purpose of education, assessment, instruction, the role of parents and guardians, the organization of students for learning, and the materials that teachers and students use to facilitate learning. Rather, the arrival of any new curriculum should be an opportunity to take mental stock of what we, as teachers, believe and value, and it should prompt us to remind ourselves about what fuels our passion for teaching. Herein lies the concept of joyful defiance.

Joyful Defiance

Joyful defiance is both an attitude and an action, grounded in conviction, determination, courage, and fortitude. It is about the teacher as quiet revolutionary—one who lives out his or her values and beliefs about teaching and learning with no need for a public platform or public praise. This is a teacher who finds satisfaction in doing the right thing to meet the needs of students and community while simultaneously honoring his or her own identity. Often this is a teacher who listens first, observes, and only contributes to collegial conversations when he or she has a comment or insight of substance to convey (as Sunshine Sullivan noted in Chapter 5). The quiet revolutionary considers the legal parameters of a given curriculum document and then works to bring that two-dimensional construct to life within the three-dimensional realities and needs of the classroom. In this process of curriculum animation, teachers draw from their own educational philosophy and consider the learning needs and community context of their students in order to inspire learning. As Albert North Whitehead noted in his seminal text *The Aims of Education and Other Essays*:

> The students are alive, and the purpose of education is to stimulate and guide their self-development. It follows as a corollary from this premise, that the teachers also should be alive with living thoughts ... The reason is that we are dealing with human minds, and not with dead matter.
>
> *(Whitehead, 1957: pp. v, 5)*

Curriculum documents are legislated policy documents, and policy rarely considers the ethos about which Whitehead wrote. In this vein, it is an illusion that teachers are constrained to follow the literal letter—rather than the spirit—of the law when it comes to curricular matters. Letting go of literality and considering teaching as an art form facilitates interpretation. It is the difference between a painting-by-numbers art project and a Rembrandt. Imagine if ballet dancers were so regulated that there could be only one interpretation of a piece of music, and that every dancer in a province or state was required to perform the same routine, year after year. How would that facilitate their growth as dancers? How fulfilling would it be for choreographers? Similar questions could be asked with regard to teachers interpreting curriculum.

The field of curriculum studies tells us that a high-quality twenty-first-century curriculum is not akin to a service manual for a vehicle. That is to say, a curriculum should not simply be a series of facts and figures combined with technical procedures to yield an efficient end product. As Whitehead (1957) noted, students are alive and their minds are not dead matter. A quality curriculum should have a logical vertical organization (the sequencing of content, skills, and processes for a given subject, spanning the kindergarten through high school student experience). This vertical organization reflects how learning is ordered, presented, and scaffolded over time. It allows for the incremental building of students' understanding over time, and it works to facilitate deep rather than surface learning. A quality curriculum should also consider horizontal organization (opportunities for interdisciplinary learning across the subjects a student encounters at a given grade level). Horizontal organization creates opportunities for students to transfer learning from subject to subject, across multiple subjects, and to real-world contexts. When combined, vertical and horizontal organization represent a map of learning that reflects developmental appropriateness based on an understanding of the nature of learning and the learner.

A high-quality curriculum includes learning outcomes that describe what students are expected to know, understand, and be able to do independently at the completion of a grade level. In the past two decades, many curricula also included learning outcomes that described dispositions or attitudes that were deemed to be socially important to cultivate within the student population. However, changes to assessment practices have challenged and are challenging that curricular practice, as teachers continue to find it difficult to make authentic and defensible judgments about the degree to which students have internalized or manifested these attitudes.

It should be noted that understanding is different from knowing. This is an important distinction, although the demands of living and working in the twenty-first century require students to have both. Furthermore, learning outcomes should capture the spirit and nature of the subject and underscore what is most important to know, understand, and be able to do in relation to that subject. Learning outcomes should also be sufficiently broad to allow for teachers' professional judgment and local decision-making based on students' needs and local context. As a collection, a suite of learning outcomes should reflect an appropriate balance of types and levels of thinking and performance that are required from students and should also be developmentally appropriate.

Finally, a high-quality curriculum considers load: the composite picture of all learning outcomes at a given grade level. The overall load must be sufficiently robust without overtaxing students, so that deep learning is possible.

In a best-case scenario, curriculum would always echo the above. However, as we noted earlier, politics and economics sometimes intervene. Teachers who are prone to joyful defiance may feel curricular inadequacies first at the intuitive level. But if we are to be true quiet revolutionaries, joyful defiance requires us to go further than instinct: it requires self-knowledge and self-reflection. That said, it thrives in the company of allies.

Self-knowledge and Self-reflection

Historically, the ancient Greek philosopher and educator Socrates has been credited with declaring that "an unexamined life is not worth living." In tackling a new curriculum, we, as teachers, are often constrained not by the policy document itself, but by our own lack of self-knowledge. If we are unaware of our beliefs and values in relation to education, how can we possibly approach curriculum in any manner other than through the literal letter of the law? How can we bring our living thoughts and our humanity to the task if we do not know who we are as human beings or as teachers? In this vein, self-knowledge is a prerequisite for joyful defiance.

Within the life of every teacher is a meandering narrative, a series of stories about significant events and people that shape values and perspectives. Encased within these critical incidents are the keys to what gives us joy as human beings and as teachers. Taking inventory is a starting point to developing greater self-knowledge. It begins with considering a series of questions. We have used variations of these questions with our own undergraduate and graduate students to prompt them to uncover their own beliefs about teaching and learning. Interestingly, the same themes have permeated many of our coffee conversations as we have continued to evolve in our thinking and teaching practices over the years.

- What and who have influenced my perspective on the purpose of education?
- How do I define "success" in educational contexts?
- What informs my thinking on what should be included and emphasized in the curriculum?
- Do I presume that each student is capable of learning? How have my interactions with my own teachers helped to shape this?
- Who are my role models and how have they influenced by understanding of my role as a teacher?
- How have my own experiences as a student impacted my thinking about organizing or grouping students for learning?
- How have my own academic successes and failures shaped my views on how student learning should be assessed?
- How have my own experiences influenced my views about the role parents should play in their children's education?
- To what extent do my own learning preferences influence how I choose curricular resources, including technology to support student success?
- How are my beliefs about what is real, good, and true about teaching and learning connected to what is important in my life?

A self-portrait is likely to emerge whenever a pre-service or in-service teacher responds to these questions. Joyful defiance implies commitment to one's beliefs and to the ideals that stem from those beliefs. However, it is very challenging to be committed to an ideal if one does not understand its personal meaning. Moreover, commitment is deepened when we grasp how that ideal came to have meaning. Finally, taking stock allows us to acknowledge the influential teachers of our individual pasts without impersonating them as a kind of default action. Every teacher is unique and must have the freedom and courage to bring that inimitable value to the particular educational context that they inhabit.

Knowing oneself sets the stage for self-reflection—taking time to contemplate how faithfully beliefs are acted upon in the day-to-day life of teaching. As teachers and professionals, we tend to believe in what we value and to value what we believe. This tenet nurtures optimism rather than pessimism, and joyful defiance is neither cynical nor peevish. Rather, it is about generating creative possibilities for living out one's beliefs as a human being and as an educator. When properly exercised, joyful defiance is never an affront to the school's authority or administration. Rather, it is about nurturing the growth of professional and personal identity. It is the embodiment of the classic maxim from Shakespeare's *Hamlet*: "to thine own self be true."

Taking time for self-reflection also fuels loyalty to ourselves and to our beliefs, rather than allegiance to a given curriculum as a gold-standard policy document. While it is true that we may see ourselves reflected in a curriculum, loyalty to self is a key element of joyful defiance.

Building Alliances with Joyful Defiance

What does joyful defiance look like in action? What does it sound like? From where do we get cues that others may share our quietly mutinous mindset? The answers to these questions help to inform the decision to be joyfully defiant.

Countless studies have found that speaking to one's beliefs as an educator is linked to effective teaching. But such articulation also lays the groundwork for identifying like-minded teachers and leaders who have the courage to analyze and challenge the premises of curriculum documents rather than simply accept them as foregone conclusions of policy. This is where allegiance to our beliefs and values meets allying with others.

The school staff room has long been a caffeinated sanctuary, a place of camaraderie, and a source of intelligence about what is transpiring in the school and the wider educational community. It can also be a professional battleground for dialogue and debate. Which teaching stories are colleagues sharing? Are they stories of hope or of pessimism? Are the words inspiring or self-defeating? Is there delight or resentment behind the words? A potential ally will speak about—and with—optimism, creativity, and gratitude. In order to attract such a collaborator, it is important to communicate in the same coded language. The segue to discourse about values and curriculum will then flow more easily.

Visiting colleagues' classrooms will provide visual cues about potential comrades (as Jay Mathisen pointed out in Chapter 8). The artifacts that appear on the walls, the arrangement of student seating, and the general atmosphere of the space will yield clues about how students are situated within the scheme of things. Are they central to the learning process or merely recipients of knowledge? What level of vitality seems to characterize the space? What is prioritized or at least considered? How effortless or challenging would it be to teach in this classroom? What is the general ethos or climate in the room? Because beliefs and values are often symbolically articulated in the physical spaces that we create and manage, the answers to these questions will yield much insight as to whether a colleague may be another quiet curriculum revolutionary.

Once kindred spirits have been identified, joyful defiance can begin with curricular conversations grounded in possibilities. Analyzing curriculum to discover both the hard boundaries and the more elastic elements allows the defiant revolutionaries to maintain fidelity to what is legally required, but also aids in identifying where there is room for creative interpretation. Where is the space for local decision-making? How might student needs and interests be incorporated? Planning together, sharing resources, team teaching on occasion, forming temporary learning groups that allow for students across classroom or grade-level boundaries to learn with and from each other—these are all manifestations of joyful defiance in partnership with others. It is in such conversations and actions that the spirit—rather than just the letter—of the curricular law emerges.

Joyful defiance also finds company in professional learning communities—at conferences and professional development sessions or in online forums. Joyful defiance is invigorated by the ideas of others, but also galvanized by opportunities to learn more. Recall Whitehead's insistence that "teachers also should be alive with living thoughts." One of the clear hallmarks of the joyfully defiant teaching life is that it is a career-long journey in learning, in questioning, and in seeking out possibilities.

Conclusion

As a provincially or state-mandated policy document, curriculum reflects the political and economic context in which it is cultivated. It is a reflection of broader societal values at a given point in time. The back-and-forth movement between competing societal values has historically been played out in shifts between progressivism and essentialism—two distinct educational philosophies that have dominated the North American educational landscape for more than a century. It can be challenging for teachers to navigate the ebb and flow of progressivism versus essentialism without getting lost or simply becoming exhausted. In order to weather these ideological and curricular tides, teachers must anchor themselves to two key premises. First, beliefs drive human actions, forming the foundation for why we act as we do; that is to say, we act in accord with what we believe. Second, as human beings, we all have ideas about reality, goodness, and truth. If this were not so, we would have no goals; and the world of teaching is chock-full of goals. Indeed, in large measure, they define the vocation of teaching. Without them, our work can easily drift to mindless activity.

Mindfulness is the converse of mindlessness. It begins with self-knowledge and with being self-reflective with regard to what one believes about high-quality teaching and learning. With this awareness firmly rooted, the arrival of a new curriculum can serve as an exhilarating challenge to be true to ourselves and our beliefs, and to live out that new curriculum in ways that honor ourselves as teachers and as human beings. Rather than simply accepting a new curriculum as *de facto* policy akin to a vehicle's service manual, its introduction should be seen as an opportunity to be joyfully defiant, to be a quiet and joyful revolutionary.

Joyful defiance is manifested in the exploration of curriculum in order to discover creative possibilities for bringing a two-dimensional document to life in ways that showcase the best of teaching and the best of learning. It is a way of approaching professional practice that taps into what fuels each individual's passion for being a teacher. It thrives in the company of like-minded teachers and leaders, and it flourishes in professional learning opportunities. Joyful defiance is an approach to our teaching life that carries us through the push and pull of progressivism versus essentialism and lands us on the comparatively tranquil shores of knowing that we have done our very best for our students, our communities, our profession, and ourselves, as teachers and as human beings.

References

Aristotle. (1999). *The politics*. Batoche Books.
Bernal, J. D. (1971). *Science in history*, volume 4. MIT Press.
Cook, R. & Doll, R. (1973). *The elementary school curriculum*. Allyn & Bacon.
Dewey, J. (1916). *Democracy and education*. University of Illinois Press.
Edmunds, A., Nickel, J., & Badley, K. (2015). *Educational foundations in Canada*. Oxford University Press.
Gutek, G. (2010). *Historical and philosophical foundations of education: A biographical introduction* (5th ed.). Merrill/Prentice-Hall.
Knight, G. (2008). *Issues and alternatives in educational philosophy* (4th ed.). Andrews University Press.
National Commission on Excellence in Education. (1983). *A nation at risk: The imperative for educational reform*. National Commission on Excellence in Education.
Rickover, H. G. (1958). European vs American secondary schools. *Phi Delta Kappan*, 40(2), 60–64.
Spencer, H. (1860). *Education: Intellectual, moral, and physical*. https://psycnet.apa.org/doiLanding?doi=10.1037%2F12158-001.
Whitehead, A. N. (1957). *The aims of education*. Williams and Morgate.

13

TEACHER–STUDENT RECIPROCITIES WITHIN THREE EDUCATIONAL MODELS

Daniel H. Jarvis and April E. Jarvis

Given this book's theme and title—*Joyful Resilience as Educational Practice*—our abundance of apposite memories, accumulated during 43 years of teaching practice, and our long-held desire to reflect jointly with our children on the past two decades of family schooling and related outcomes, we took the collective decision simply to chronicle and cross-examine these lived experiences. We are not entirely sure what readers will gain from this exercise, but we hope there will be moments of informative insight and/or meaningful inspiration.

By way of background, both Dan and April received undergraduate liberal arts degrees, followed by Bachelor of Education degrees, in Ontario, Canada. Given the scarcity of teaching jobs in Canada in the late 1990s, they decided to begin their careers as international school educators in Chiang Mai, Thailand. After returning to Canada in 1998, Dan began teaching secondary school math/art courses and pursued part-time graduate studies. Clara and Anna were born in 1999 and 2001, respectively, and in 2002 the family relocated to southern Ontario so that Dan could complete four years of full-time doctoral studies. April decided to begin homeschooling Clara in the fall of 2003. During the following two years, Clara attended public school, then did a year of homeschooling, then a third year of public school (along with her sister Anna) after the family's relocation back to North Bay, Ontario. Clara would later attend a local high school for grades nine and ten, but decided to switch to virtual learning for her final two years of secondary education. Three of her younger sisters have experienced homeschooling for the elementary grades, then virtual schooling from grade nine onwards. In summary, as documented in Table 13.1, the two oldest girls experienced all three models of schooling (homeschooling, classroom, and virtual), whereas the next two had, at the time of writing, experienced only homeschooling and virtual learning (two different types of the latter). At the time of writing, their youngest sister, 12-year-old Ella, had experienced only homeschooling.

DOI: 10.4324/9781003124429-13

FIGURE 13.1 Jarvis family teachers and learners (l to r: Dan, April, Clara, Thea, Ella, Anna, Rose)

Having moved ten times in ten years, we are happy to report that we have spent the past 15 years at our country home in the small village of Corbeil, just outside North Bay, Ontario, Canada. All five of our daughters (Figure 13.1) are currently studying within our home. The two university students—a future English teacher and a future nurse—are both undertaking online learning due to the global pandemic and the closure of their university campus. Our next two daughters are high school students; our youngest is homeschooled. We have semi-reliable internet connectivity, but easy access to nature walks and other outdoor activities.

In preparing for this chapter, we gave our oldest three girls a set of seven questions (see the Appendix at the end of this chapter) and asked them to respond in writing, so that we could capture their individual perceptions without the influence of their siblings. By contrast, we interviewed the two youngest sisters together, using a similar set of questions, then transcribed the audio recording. Dan also asked April to reflect, in writing, on her experiences as both a classroom teacher and a homeschooling parent. To all the above Dan added his own observations as an educator who has participated in all three forms of teaching. Finally, we divided the content into several thematic sections in order to highlight notable contrasts across the three schooling models.

Three Schooling Models in Context

In this section, we provide some contextual background regarding the three educational models of homeschooling, classroom-based schooling, and virtual schooling.

Homeschooling

Lawyer and author Michael Donnelly's contribution to the edited collection *Balancing Freedom, Autonomy and Accountability in Education* is simply titled "Homeschooling" (Donnelly, 2012). In summary, his chapter provides a thorough overview of the homeschooling tradition, including its definition, origins, legal recognition, parental motivation for its adoption, specific related structures and practices, and common parent and student outcomes. Donnelly (2012: pp. 199–200) comments:

> Although it is more established in English-speaking liberal democracies, particularly the United States, Canada, the United Kingdom, and South Africa, homeschooling is also catching the interest of parents in other countries as an educational alternative ... Depending on the philosophical underpinning, country of origin and other factors, homeschooling is also known as home-based education, home education, unschooling, home-centered learning, home instruction, deschooling, autonomous learning, and child-centered learning.

State support for homeschooling ranges from enthusiastic (with laptops provided and specialists visiting homes to discuss curriculum and assessment) to non-existent (e.g., it is illegal in Brazil and Germany).

With reference to parental motivation for homeschooling children, Donnelly (2012: p. 202) notes that "the decision is idiosyncratic at the individual family level, and depends on the individual needs and desires of the parents and children involved." Collum and Mitchell (2005: p. 277) report that "there is a general consensus among researchers that the decision to home school is motivated by four broad categories of concern"—namely, dissatisfaction with public schools, academic and pedagogical concerns, family life, and religious or moral values. Similarly, in her recent book *How to Homeschool in Canada: A Travel Guide for Your Homeschooling Journey*, homeschooling mom Lisa Marie Fletcher (2020: pp. 11–12) lists the following five reasons why families may choose the homeschooling option:

- to offer an education that lines up better with your religious or moral beliefs;
- disapproval of or dissatisfaction with the school system's curriculum, methods, agenda, environment, ability to meet your child's needs, etc.;
- bullying or other social challenges;
- medical needs or special needs such as illness, autism, allergies, ADD, learning disabilities, etc. that would be better handled from home; and
- lifestyle choices, such as travelling, sports/acting, or living in a foreign country.

Due to the popularity of the homeschooling movement in North America, ever more print, digital, and human (local groups/activities) resources are available to support this form of schooling. According to the Ontario Federation of Teaching Parents website (OFTP, n.d.):

Many home educating parents do not register with local school officials so an exact number is not known. However, it is estimated that approximately 1% to 2% of all school-age children are homeschooled in North America, which translates to around 20,000 to 40,000 children in Ontario. The number for Canada as a whole is estimated at approximately 47,500 to 95,000 homeschooled children. Estimates for the United States range between 1 million to 2 million children being homeschooled.

Clearly, homeschooling is increasing in popularity as a viable alternative to regular public schooling. Moreover, it seems likely that the COVID-19 pandemic, which forced many children to learn from home in 2020–2021, will have a longer-term impact, with many families choosing to continue with homeschooling once regular public education returns to normal.

Classroom Schooling

Unlike many other countries, Canada does not have a federal Ministry of Education, nor a mandated national curriculum. Rather, education is a provincial responsibility, with Ministries of Education in charge of public schooling in each of the ten provinces and three territories. Nevertheless, the various Ministers of Education from across the country are all members of the Council of Ministers of Education, Canada (CMEC). The CMEC regularly publishes, and makes available online, findings from its various research studies. For example, the recently released *Education Indicators in Canada: An International Perspective* (CMEC, 2020) was produced as part of the Pan-Canadian Education Indicators Program (PCEIP) and allows readers to compare data for the provinces and territories with data from other member nations of the Organization for Economic Cooperation and Development (OECD). This report highlights a number of issues relating to classroom-based learning:

- Education is compulsory up to the age of 16 in every Canadian jurisdiction, except for Manitoba, Ontario, New Brunswick, and Nunavut, where it is compulsory up to 18.
- In Canada, in 2018–19, the total cumulative intended instruction time in formal classroom settings was 11,081 hours on average, between the ages of 6 and 17 (this includes the primary, lower secondary, and upper secondary levels of education). By comparison, total intended instruction time for the OECD countries was 8,836 hours.
- In 2018–19, teaching hours of primary school teachers varied by province and territory, ranging from 700 hours in New Brunswick to 905 hours in Alberta.
- In 2017–18, expenditure per student ($14,253/$17,948) at the primary/secondary level was similar for Canada, other G7 countries, and the OECD average.
- For the university level, at US$28,747, Canada's figure [expenditure per student] was 64% higher than the OECD average of US$17,566, and was third highest in the G7.*(CMEC, 2020: pp. 109, 18, 17)*

To summarize, Canada generously funds all three levels of education (university study is partially subsidized, with students paying relatively low tuition costs in comparison with the United States), with each child receiving over 11,000 hours of "intended instructional time" from ages 6 to 17, and with teachers working in classrooms for approximately 800 hours per year.

In addition, and uniquely, Ontario has four different publicly funded school board systems based on language and religion (31 English public boards, 29 English Catholic boards, 4 French public boards, and 8 French Catholic boards), with each system responsible for its own administration, schools, curriculum (usually one of the two official language versions of the Ontario Curriculum), and policies. There are also ten school authorities (four geographically isolated and six hospital-based) and one provincial schools authority. As of 2018–2019, there were 3,948 elementary and 880 secondary schools in Ontario; 128,091 full-time equivalent (FTE) teachers; 7,436 administrators; 9,158 early childhood educators; and 2,040,432 students. The provincial government invested $26.5 billion in education in that school year (OME, n.d.).

Virtual Schooling

In Ontario, the Virtual Learning Centre (VLC) is run under the auspices of the Trillium Lakelands District School Board (TLDSB). Since its inception in 1997, the VLC has provided Ontario's secondary school students (grades nine–twelve) with a wide range of flexible and well-designed, accredited courses, which has enabled the province's homeschooling children to earn credits while studying at home or abroad (TLDSB, n.d.; VLC, n.d.). Although official statistics are not currently available, as parents of children who have taken VLC courses over the past seven years, we can safely intuit that the program has grown dramatically in that time, with an increasing number of courses, sections, teachers, and even extra-curricular initiatives (e.g., student government, yearbooks, clubs). Certified teachers, who are regulated by the Ontario College of Teachers (OCT), use the same Ontario Curriculum as is used in classrooms for grades nine–twelve. They are responsible for all learning experiences (with both synchronous and asynchronous components) and for student assessment. Courses (approximately 90 are currently offered) are free for all Ontario students, with a small deposit of $50 per course required from each new student (which is refunded after successful completion). Those registered as full- or part-time students with a publicly funded Ontario school are required to arrange for half of their government funding (approximately $775 per course) to be redirected to the TLDSB; non-Ontario students may pay tuition fees ($1,500 per course) to take courses as well. The VLC has made it a priority to host an annual graduation ceremony for its grade-twelve students, at which they have an opportunity to meet their teachers, administrator, and fellow students in person, often for the first time and sometimes having known and worked with them online for several years.

A number of other virtual learning organizations are licensed to offer Ontario secondary school credits. One such resource is the TVOntario Independent Learning

Centre (TVO ILC), which favors more of an online correspondence course approach. Because there are no scheduled synchronous ("live") sessions, students work independently, submitting assignments within a given timeframe. There is a small fee of $40 per course, and TVO ILC is open to students of all ages, including adults. It offers 144 courses and currently caters to over 20,000 students (TVO ILC, n.d.).

COVID-19 led to the sudden adoption at all levels of a compulsory and (for many educators) unfamiliar distance-learning model. The widespread lockdowns from March 2020 brought about abrupt and unexpected changes in how and where teaching would be completed for the remainder of the school year. Virtual schooling methods rapidly came to dominate the thoughts of countless administrators, teachers, and support technicians. Elementary and secondary schools faced the dual challenges of communicating effectively with parents and guardians and finding creative ways to maintain continuity in ongoing curriculum coverage and student assessment. At the university level, numerous institutions similarly found themselves scrambling to provide help and support for instructors in such areas as webinars, software training, drop-in sessions, peer mentoring, and links to online conferences. According to Leary *et al.* (2020: p. 271), "Despite the tremendous growth of online learning in both the K-12 and university settings, there appears to be slow growth for development and agreed upon best practices for online teacher professional development programs, instructors, and institutions." The pandemic, and the related surge of virtual schooling at all levels, no doubt exacerbated this problem.

Learning and Assessment

In this section, we present and discuss material from the questionnaire and interview with our five children. Specifically, we explore the three educational models' different approaches to learning and assessment. What do the teacher and students actually do during a given day, week, or term in each of these settings? This information will include learning activities as well as how assessment and evaluation are conducted. For each of the three models of schooling under discussion, we will present a summary of our older children's comments, followed (where applicable) by an excerpt from the interview with our two youngest children, and finally April's related thoughts as a certified elementary classroom teacher and seasoned homeschooler.

Learning and Assessment in Homeschooling

According to all five children, homeschooling involves learning that is primarily directed by the parent, especially during the lower elementary grades. It often involves lessons and direct instruction, reading books aloud to students, literature-based study, internet research, and a variety of projects that allow for cross-curricular connections. Beginning in approximately grades four–six, learning often becomes more self-directed than in public school, especially if there are several children in the home. If students fall behind or need more time to work through a particular topic, there are more opportunities to catch up.

With regard to assessment, the parent may periodically check or grade a child's work, but there is minimal emphasis on grades or marks. Homeschooling allows flexibility and encourages independent learning. Once learning is complete for the day—usually by noon in the lower grades, and by 2:00 or 3:00 pm in grades seven–eight—students have the rest of the day to pursue other activities. There is no homework, unless they wish to read a book related to the curriculum.

Ella on Homeschooling

During the interview, Dan specifically asked the younger girls about school reading:

DAN: In a regular classroom it's often something like, "Okay class, here's an hour for your reading." But in homeschool, if you really like a book, can you just keep reading it, for hours even?
ELLA: Yes, I finished a book in one day once.
DAN: In one day, wow! And we know that Ella likes to climb a maple tree behind our house, and she reads up there at high altitude. Do you read faster and better up there? (Figure 13.2)
ELLA: In the summertime, yes.

FIGURE 13.2 Ella in her independent reading-time tree

April on Homeschooling

In a homeschool setting, students can go through their work at their own pace, sometimes going quickly through topics and other times slowing down if they need extra teaching to get a firm grasp on the content. Homeschooling will look different in the varying homes that implement their children's schooling in this way. There are always monetary, time, and employment considerations regarding homeschooling. Teaching your own children can cost varying amounts, from a little to a lot. Choices abound as to curriculum, manipulatives, extra-curricular activities, and students' interests. We have found that there was an initial cost with the first child but as the years went by and each of them "graduated" to high school, we reused almost all of our curriculum and books for the subsequent children. New workbooks and writing materials may be the only ongoing costs. There are also multiple avenues by which used materials can be acquired. This can happen through used-book sales at homeschool conferences, homeschool swaps, online groups, Kijiji, Facebook, and other venues. There are many expensive options, but a family that really wants to homeschool should not feel that they cannot afford it. We know of several families who access free curriculum online for all of their homeschooling. Children at public school also often require money for field trips and extra-curricular activities, so there is not much of a difference there.

Assessment is a one-on-one experience, where the homeschooling parent is aware of the progress of their child and can teach with this in mind at all times. For example, with a daughter who struggled with reading for understanding, the reading was done by the homeschooling parent at times, so that the child could focus on the topic instead (e.g., reading the math problem for them while they did the math). The most important quality for a successful homeschooling experience is a parent who is dedicated to consistent instruction and wishes to instill a love of learning in their child or children. This method is supported by a well-chosen—or well-assembled—curriculum. The option to draw from different sources in different subject areas with regards to a child's individual learning needs (e.g., *Nelson Mathematics* for math, *Abeka* for language, *Sonlight* for literature) can be viewed as another benefit of homeschooling.

Learning and Assessment in Classroom Schooling

According to our daughters, public school learning (i.e., classroom schooling) is directed by the teacher, who, for the majority of the school day, engages the students with prepared lessons and instruction, sometimes supplemented with independent work time and/or collaborative group activities. During a regular day at public school, the teacher will begin with a particular subject, such as math. After teaching that lesson, and possibly facilitating some practice activities related to the topic, they will move on to the next subject, and so forth throughout the day. This block format is generally followed each day, every day, with a set schedule that comprises, for example, math, followed by writing, followed by social studies, with very little deviation. In general, the teacher is readily available to provide one-on-one help for any concerns or problems that arise during class time. They are also usually able to identify each student's level of comprehension based on their facial expressions and comments.

Assessment in public school is almost always conducted by the teacher, unless an activity has a self-assessment or peer-assessment component. Because the teacher presents all of their instructions for each assignment or test to the students in person, they are usually able to outline their expectations clearly. Therefore, during assessment, there is a particularly strong emphasis on examining each student's ability to listen to, understand, and follow the teacher's instructions.

April on Classroom Schooling

There are three main advantages of classroom schooling: it helps students to keep pace with their classmates; each student gets to know their classmates and their teacher very well; and learning is the main goal. The primary means of assessment are tests and report cards.

Learning and Assessment in Virtual Schooling

Our daughters explained that the VLC uses *Canvas* software as its Learning Management System (LMS) platform. There are usually two structured, 75-minute classes per course each week, wherein the teacher presents new material and answers questions. The rest of the learning is completed independently by the student. These courses prioritize flexible learning, with each online lesson recorded for students to watch (and pause or rewind, as necessary) at their leisure. This accommodating feature facilitates learning among students with other commitments, such as work and extra-curricular activities, and eliminates the problem of timetable clashes. Learning is often done through PowerPoint slideshow presentations, poll questions, online quizzes, discussion posts, breakout rooms, and a large number of assigned textbook readings. Because deadlines are often very strict, good time management skills are essential.

Student learning is evaluated by means of a percentage grade for each course, similar to those used in public schools. In the VLC program, there are normally three elements in each course grade: term work (60%); Independent Study Unit (ISU; 10%); and final examination (30%). In addition, students receive mid-term reports, which provide helpful, specific feedback, as well as a final report card. Both of these are usually sent to the student by regular mail (or via email attachment during the pandemic). Teachers also make themselves available online at Open Office times, usually on Fridays, for one-on-one advice.

In general, there are no scheduled classes and no online peer-discussion forums for the TVO ILC courses, and assignments must be completed within ten months. Most of them are provided through the *Desire to Learn* (D2L) platform, where all of the content is available to students. Interestingly, our fourth daughter, Thea, preferred these less structured courses to the VLC program, since they gave her more freedom to schedule her time and projects.

Thea on Virtual Learning

With online schooling, you do your work, but you're never really done because you keep having more assignments to do. So, you don't really get to stop and have a break. You don't see anybody else doing work, so you don't really feel like you want to do work all the time. Also, for TVO ILC, it's harder to get good marks because I think the longest course has six assignments and the shortest one has four, so, if you do one really bad one, it can be worth 25 percent of your whole mark.

April on Virtual Learning

Virtual schooling is very different from homeschooling, although it usually takes place in the home. (It can be mobile, wherever there is wi-fi connectivity.) The parent's role is very different in this context, as the scheduling and teaching cease; however, support is needed for discussion, study help, help with editing, and occasional direction as to project choices and course selection. We know a family that used virtual schooling while both parents were working full-time. Their child ended up using this method for only a year, possibly in part because of being alone all day. This method of distance learning would work differently for each family, depending on the nature of the child, the program, and the technology.

Teachers and Teaching

In this section, we focus on teachers and teaching in relation to the three educational models. Again, we will present a summary of the older children's comments, followed (where applicable) by an excerpt from the interview with our two youngest children, and finally April's reflections on each of the three models.

Teachers and Teaching in Homeschooling

Our children explained that the homeschooling parent/teacher may face a number of challenges, including: combining the two roles of teacher and parent; frustration when they cannot understand the content; balancing home duties with education;

TABLE 13.1 Student experiences within the three different educational models

Schooling context	Homeschool	Classroom school	Virtual school
Clara (age 22)	JK, Grades 2, 4–8	SK, Grades 1, 3, 9, 10	Grades 11–12
Anna (age 20)	JK, SK, Grades 2–8	Grade 1	Grades 9–12
Rose (age 18)	JK, SK, Grades 1–8	—	Grades 9–12; 2 ILCs
Thea (age 16)	JK, SK, Grades 1–8	—	Grades 9–10; 6 ILCs
Ella (age 12)	JK, SK, Grades 1–6	—	—

and anxiety over whether they are educating their children adequately. On the other hand, they may gain great satisfaction from: playing a direct role in facilitating the growth and learning experiences of their own child; observing the student's struggles and subsequently adapting their teaching style or content accordingly; providing opportunities for self-directed learning; and identifying subjects that are of particular interest, or in which the student excels, and pursuing further study or activities in those areas.

Our daughters suggested that the best homeschooling teachers enjoy sharing learning with their students, maintain loving and nurturing relationships with their children while guiding them toward educational goals, and care deeply about their students' overall success in life, rather than just their ability to absorb and recite information. In contrast, the worst homeschooling teachers devote insufficient effort to trying to understand the curricular content, treat schoolwork as a chore rather than an opportunity for fun and exciting activities, and place undue trust in their students to do everything on their own, with little or no guidance.

Thea and Ella on Homeschooling

THEA: Well, homeschool teachers work with the same kids every day, then through all the grades.
ELLA: If they're busy with other stuff, they might get frustrated if they don't want to be teaching right then.
THEA: And they have to read the same books over and over again.
ELLA: Yes, the same book five times with different kids.
THEA: Since it's their own kids, I mean, they're not going to treat their mom in the same way as they might treat a teacher at school. Maybe they'd show less respect to them sometimes.

April on the Benefits and Challenges of Homeschooling

The first benefit that comes to mind is friendship with the children. So much time is spent together reading, in nature, and in learning new things that a special bond develops through this time spent together. A homeschooling family knows each other in a way that isn't possible when the children are absent from home for 30-plus hours a week. This extended time together could be a difficult scenario in an unstable or stressful home situation, but our experience has been a very positive one. As a parent who is their teacher, and who has a vested interest in their becoming responsible and contented adults, moral teaching is much more than a character curriculum with ten chapters to get through. It's a daily-lived life of making good choices and doing the next thing ... sometimes with joy and excitement, and other times just because it's a school day, and that's what needs to be done. In the words of English educator and reformer Charlotte Mason (1925/1954: p. 118), "Every day, every hour, the parents are either passively or actively forming those habits in their children upon which, more than upon anything else, future character and conduct depend."

The teaching parent is also keenly aware of learning capabilities, including struggles. With this information gleaned from daily interaction, lessons can be repeated, done in several new ways, and returned to whenever needed. The student can also progress rapidly through material of which they have a quick and firm grasp. This is rewarding and encouraging for both the teacher and the student (parent and child). In addition, a schedule can be developed that is beneficial and enjoyed by the family. This may include different school breaks than the public school. For example, our family works through local school Professional Development Days and Snow Days (school cancellations), then takes equivalent breaks at later dates (e.g., to enable a visit to the children's grandparents). The increased time at home also means there is more time for other pursuits, such as music, painting, exploring outside, and developing a keen awareness of nature ... really anything that parents would like to encourage their children to do and learn, as well as pursuits for which the children have a natural bent. A homeschooling community or group within a given area is another benefit. This may be a formal cooperative that offers shared instruction or extra-curricular sports or activities for the local homeschooling population. For example, North Bay's homeschooling cooperative organizes tennis, skating, gymnastics, skiing, swimming, and nature walks throughout the year. Moreover, it is often able to secure significant group discounts for paid activities as homeschoolers are able to attend during low-traffic times of day.

As one might expect, homeschooling presents some challenges, with the time involved perhaps being the greatest. In general, homeschooled children spend roughly the same amount of time in lessons as their counterparts in public school (although they may begin each day earlier or later, as there is a lot of freedom regarding scheduling). So, the teaching parent has to commit a large part of each day to teaching. Keeping a schedule functioning around family life (e.g., new baby, toddlers, sickness) can be challenging. At times, respect for the parent/teacher may be lacking, and unwillingness to complete schoolwork may come into play as well. Another consideration for the teaching parent is that homeschooling will inevitably restrict their employment opportunities. It is almost impossible to engage in full-time work while homeschooling, but the teaching parent may find it necessary and/or desirable to take on some part-time work, either inside or outside the home. In such situations, any required teaching of new material or written guidance regarding assigned work that needs to be completed while the parent will be absent or working should be done or prepared, respectively, in advance.

Teachers and Teaching in Classroom Schooling

With public or classroom schooling, our children noted that the teacher may have insufficient time and/or energy to give each individual student the attention they need, may be unable to understand and address the requirements and/or abilities of each student (i.e., provide support for weaker students and challenge their stronger classmates), and may have trouble dealing with behavioral issues. On the other hand, they may be able to facilitate the growth of an entire classroom of students, learn about the abilities/struggles of a wide variety of students and plan their lessons accordingly, see and interpret students' reactions to learning experiences, and help students in person.

Our daughters suggested that the best kind of classroom teacher not only puts effort into their lessons and tries to make learning fun and engaging, but also strives to develop personal and meaningful relationships with their students. In contrast, they felt that the worst kind of classroom teacher puts little effort into preparation, teaches with minimal enthusiasm, and shows little interest in their students' lives outside of school.

April on Classroom Schooling

Classroom schooling offers a number of benefits for both teachers and students. Schoolteachers are encouraged when they see progress in their students. This is especially true in classrooms where the children engage in group work, observe their classmates' progress, and learn together. Teachers prepare and deliver lessons that provide in-depth instruction, following provincial curriculum guidelines. Students can build friendships and enjoy learning opportunities that they may not have in a homeschool setting. The bond between teacher and student may be very strong and often provides encouragement to both. A daily schedule of learning may also benefit the children, especially those who need more structured routines.

There are also some drawbacks to classroom schooling. For instance, trying to meet the needs of 30-plus students, with their wide range of aptitudes for learning, is always a challenge. In addition, an individual student's (or group of students') behavioral issues may be detrimental to other students' learning, and repeated interruptions of the school day may impede consistent learning. Collaborative group work can be challenging too, especially if expectations and the students' roles are not clarified from the outset. Students may also bring emotional issues they are facing at home into the classroom, and these can affect their—and potentially their peers'—ability to concentrate and learn. Clearly, then, meeting all of the students' needs while providing quality instruction can be very difficult.

Teachers and Teaching in Virtual Schooling

With regard to virtual (online) schooling, our children highlighted the teacher's inability to converse with students in person, internet connectivity issues, difficulties identifying students who are either falling behind or not participating, low attendance rates during live class sessions, the need to condense curriculum content into just two weekly lectures, and inadequate answers to questions posed by email as some of the main challenges. On the other hand, this form of schooling allows the teacher to work within a more flexible schedule, use multi-media resources by means of posted files and the internet, and encourage students to become self-directed learners.

Our daughters characterized the best kind of virtual schooling teacher as one who engages frequently with their students (e.g., by regularly checking and replying to emails), is available to provide extra help on a weekly basis (and encourages students to take advantage of this support), presents well-prepared lessons, including slideshows and/or videos, plans interesting activities, such as breakout-room discussions and guest speakers, returns graded assignments promptly so that students can learn and improve from the feedback provided, and displays real enthusiasm while teaching. By contrast, the worst kind of virtual schooling teacher rarely uses their camera during live sessions, answers emails sluggishly, seems rigid or stern when answering questions about assignments or exams, and has little interest in getting to know their students.

Thea on Online Schooling

DAN: Do any of the students have discussions with the teacher that aren't exactly to do with the lesson? Is there a friendship created between your teachers and you in the VLC program?

THEA: Well, it really depends on the teacher. Some teachers really don't want to share anything about their personal life, but others will share about what they did the past week. One teacher starts class ten minutes early each day, so she can play music, and everyone chats in the box about stuff, and she has a puzzle on the screen. But then another teacher I have says things like, "I'm not here to make friends, I'm here to make 'mathletes'—to get you to the top of the class in grade eleven."

DAN: So, you kind of have both extremes there.

THEA: Yes, the only personal thing about her that I know is that she has a dog, and her husband collects birds. But I do think she's a good teacher.

Clearly, teachers in the virtual schooling context had employed a variety of relational approaches.

April on the Benefits and Challenges of Virtual Learning

One of the main benefits of virtual schooling is that it allows a family to be mobile. This means that visits to friends and extended family, or even trips abroad, can be undertaken with no interruptions to the children's schooling. We have made full use of this. For instance, one year we took a vacation to the coast and our two teenage daughters brought their high school classes with them, to be done in the early morning and evening—before and after our holiday activities. Of course, every virtual school will have its own individual characteristics, but the two that our daughters enrolled in (VLC and TVO ILC) offered rigorous, academic study as well as friendly, well-organized, and competent teachers. In addition, some students prefer the self-directed and solitary nature of virtual learning, while others enjoy cultivating online friendships. If a student misses a class, for whatever reason, they will generally have an opportunity to catch up via an online recording of the lesson in question. Finally, many virtual schooling students benefit from supportive interactions with family members throughout the school day.

Among the challenges of virtual learning are disagreements over whether pyjamas should be worn all day and confrontations over piles of dirty dishes in bedrooms. In addition, students may find it difficult to get to grips with the unconventional deadlines, such as 6:00 p.m. or even midnight for assignments, and a few hours to a few days for tests.

The Jarvis Family's Schooling Preferences

When asked independently about their schooling preferences for elementary and secondary school, our five daughters shared a variety of opinions.

Clara on Her Preferred Mode of Schooling

Clara, who experienced all three forms of schooling, expressed a preference for homeschooling in the lower grades and for virtual schooling (specifically VLC) in grades nine–twelve.

> I most prefer the homeschool system for JK–grade eight ... because I believe that homeschooling offers benefits that are specifically advantageous to this age group, in terms of opportunities or situations that are not generally applicable or possible in the public-school setting. These benefits include: academic flexibility (especially critical, as all children begin their learning journey at differing rates); more efficient learning (low student–teacher ratio, with little wasted time); meaningful learning (the ability to closely monitor a student's progress and change a teaching/learning approach accordingly); encouragement of independence and autonomy from an early age (developing intrinsic motivation and a love for learning); fostering a reduced dependency on peers; and allowing time for the activities that the student truly loves (playing outdoors, initiating and pursuing projects, picking books to read, practicing cooking or crafts). I most prefer the virtual (online) learning system for grades nine–twelve ... because I believe that virtual learning offers benefits that are specifically advantageous to this age group, and that are not generally applicable or possible in the public-school or homeschool setting. Such benefits include: encouragement of self-motivation and self-direction (preparation for future education in the university or college setting, or for a continued ability to be disciplined and motivated); training students to be technically efficient (to learn how to access various online resources, to conduct research efficiently, and to operate and understand how to use various computer programs); and allowing flexibility in schedules for extra-curricular activities.

Anna on Her Preferred Mode of Schooling

Anna, who also experienced all three forms of schooling, preferred homeschooling for the elementary years but found it difficult to identify the best option regarding secondary.

> I thoroughly enjoyed being homeschooled from grades two to eight because it allowed me to develop lasting relationships with my sisters, it forced me to learn how to manage my time, and I was able to develop time management skills that have served me well in high school and beyond ... I don't think it's fair to say that there is a better or best system. I believe public school, homeschool, and virtual school all have their strengths and weaknesses, and in the end, all lead to further learning and growth for the student. It really depends on the student's attitude towards learning, and how one is able to challenge oneself to make the most out of any of these systems.

Rose on Her Preferred Mode of Schooling

Rose, who has experienced homeschooling and two types of virtual schooling (VLC and TVO ILC), expressed a preference for the former during the elementary years and the latter (specifically VLC) for high school.

> I preferred homeschool for JK–grade eight because it allowed me to spend more time with my sisters, to be less stressed out, and to learn with my mom. I like how you get to finish at a certain time and then are free to spend the rest of the day doing fun things such as spending time outdoors. For grades nine–twelve, I have enjoyed online learning because I can still be at home, but I can also be taught by teachers who have advanced education in specific curricular areas. Online learning is very independent, and I think that will be important when moving forward into post-secondary studies because you get the idea of what it is like to have a variety of teachers, and you gain an understanding of the dedication needed for self-directed learning.

Thea on Her Preferred Mode of Schooling

Thea, who has experienced homeschooling and two types of virtual schooling (VLC and TVO ILC), expressed a preference for homeschooling for the elementary grades but suggested she may have enjoyed classroom schooling because of the sports and extra-curricular activities. She favored virtual schooling for high school, and specifically TVO ILC rather than VLC, due to the former's less rigid structure, lack of synchronous class sessions, and more flexible deadlines.

THEA: I would pick homeschooling, because I feel like you can learn better.
DAN: Would you prefer to homeschool from JK all the way to grade twelve, or just up to grade eight?
THEA: Just to grade eight, I think, then online after that.
DAN: You've never had a classroom experience, so maybe it's hard for you to compare?
THEA: I would probably like on-site learning too, but I would still prefer to be at home for one–eight.

Ella on her Preferred Mode of Schooling

At the time of writing, Ella was in grade six and had known nothing other than homeschooling. Nevertheless, we sought her opinion on which of the three options she favored, based on her knowledge of each of them.

ELLA: Well, I've never went to a public school.
DAN: But your best friend … goes to public school, and she chats with you all the time.
ELLA: Well, every day they get each lesson done, because everything is timed in their classes. Sometimes, for homeschooling, if it's summer or spring, you can go work on stuff outside, too.
DAN: So, given they both have benefits, which of those two models do you think you would prefer?
ELLA: Homeschooling, probably.

April's Concluding Remarks on the Three Modes of Schooling

In summary, all five girls indicated a preference for homeschooling during the elementary grades, and most of them favored virtual schooling (either VLC or TVO ILC) during the high school years. As a family, we have preferred homeschooling for the elementary level (JK–eight), although our first two children attended public school for a few years as well. Teaching them how to read and being able to read wonderful literature to them, or with them, while they were young have been highlights of our homeschooling time together. But there are many advantages in switching to online schooling for grades nine-twelve, so that has proved a good choice for our girls thus far.

Dan's Reflections on Reciprocities

At the time of writing, I was in the middle of a period of sabbatical leave that allowed me to pursue a number of research and writing projects, including the following reflections on homeschooling, classroom teaching, and virtual schooling.

Like so many colleagues and friends during this pandemic, I am able, and temporarily required, to work from a home office space. This has meant that I've had the wonderful opportunity to live daily among our children and not only help them with their numerous and sundry educational pursuits, but also spend quality time with each of them in various contexts and activities. For example, last summer, with help from all our daughters (e.g., carrying, measuring, framing, drywalling, painting, building, tiling), we transformed an old storage shed by our pond into an insulated, furnished, woodstove-heated cabin (Figure 13.3). Throughout the subsequent fall and winter months, this became a favorite retreat where one could bunk overnight, play games, read books, observe birds and animals, work on one's laptop, warm up while skating

FIGURE 13.3 Cabin renovated as collaborative family learning project during summer 2020

or skiing, or sample hot chocolate and cinnamon beaver tails. This serves as just one example of how homeschooling can allow families to seize on opportunities to explore cross-curricular projects, to collaborate, and to "provoke the creation of curriculum that is … engaging and meaningful" (Efford & Becker, 2017: p. 34).

This special time at home has thus allowed me to observe directly and purposefully the homeschooling and virtual schooling contexts. Having taught in classrooms and online for more than 20 years, and having watched the homeschooling program develop over that same time period, I feel like I have a fairly good sense of what each of these three systems has to offer.

As April stated earlier, homeschooling has been an excellent choice for us. Several of Fletcher's (2020) five forms of parental motivation came into play in our decision to homeschool all of our children during the elementary school years (kindergarten to grade eight). During my first decade as a university instructor, I traveled a great deal due to research projects and conferences, and thus was sometimes absent for long periods of time. April liked to have the ability to pack up and head to one of the grandparents' homes (both long journeys) to visit and for support. This was made possible by a mobile schooling option. One daughter experienced some light but physical bullying from a classmate in her senior kindergarten year; then her grade-one teacher left abruptly mid-year and her learning suffered as a result. Another was diagnosed with a relatively rare brain condition that we were told could lead to reading and communication difficulties (and potentially even blindness). After a series of hospital visits and a neuropsychological assessment, a specialist informed us that the homeschooling option would be beneficial for her. We are thankful that she has made excellent academic progress through the years. Finally, we appreciate having the ability to assemble a curriculum that includes a faith-based component that aligns well with our moral values and beliefs.

I realize that we are both certified educators, and that we live in a rural setting with direct access to nature—two factors that have no doubt helped us to create and implement this kind of program. However, a number of family friends who are not certified teachers, and who reside in more urban settings, have found equal joy and success in pursuing their homeschooling journeys. Online, multi-media resources (e.g., simulations, clubs, podcasts, blogs, vlogs, digital libraries) abound for both the homeschooling parent and their child. Books such as *What Tree Is That?* (Arbor Day Foundation, 2018) and *The Stargazer's Guide to the Night Sky* (Lisle, 2012), interactive websites such as *Animals* (National Geographic, n.d.), and educational video games such as *Walden* (Fullerton, 2017) all serve to promote the exploration of nature from within the home, if and when direct access is not possible. In other words, location and lack of training are not prohibitive factors when deciding whether to homeschool one's child.

In contrast to some other jurisdictions, it should be noted that homeschoolers in Ontario do not receive any funding from the provincial or federal government. As Donnelly (2012) notes, some countries, states, and provinces operate a voucher-based system that allows parents to spend a schooling allowance on their choice of educational model, including private and homeschooling options. Some of these systems even provide parents with laptops for each child, and dispatch curriculum experts from the local school board to meet and discuss curricular and assessment strategies with them in their own homes. In Ontario, we are required to pay regular school taxes *and* cover all of our own homeschool-related expenses (supplies, books, software, internet access, sports equipment, field trips, etc.). In the case of the VLC online learning system, because the courses are freely offered to Ontario residents and taught by fully qualified Ontario certified teachers who implement and assess the provincial curriculum, Ontario parents who choose this option do benefit directly from public funding. Meanwhile, TVO ILC is generously subsidized, which means that Ontario residents are charged only $40 per course.

Perhaps the most common criticism leveled at homeschooling families is that this method often leads to antisocial behavior and narrow thinking. This may be true in some cases, but we can describe only what we have implemented and observed in our own context. We have made a concerted effort to involve our girls in a number of extra-curricular activities in the knowledge that this is important for their social development. For instance, they have all participated in a weekly, church-based children's program and youth group, a drama club that performs annual musicals, and the local community youth orchestra, where they each play a stringed instrument. In addition, we have pursued activities such as skating, swimming, tennis, film studies, and gymnastics with other homeschooling families. Our children visit regularly with their cousins and friends both in person and online; they have all participated in summer camp adventures; and we have taken a number of family road trips to explore interesting parts of Canada and the United States. After grade twelve, our eldest, Clara, ventured (on her own) to the Philippines, where she taught at an international school for one year prior to beginning her university studies.

Given the nature of the literature-based program we have used, and our encouragement to discover titles beyond the prescribed curriculum, each of our girls will have read (or will have had read to them) hundreds of books by graduation. We regularly discuss current events, including controversial issues, and encourage debate, research, and family sharing on any topic, including recent readings that may have captured their interest. Due to the one-on-one nature of the instruction, the close monitoring of learning needs, and the consistent correcting of spelling and grammatical errors, all five girls have excellent writing and comprehension skills. We share all this to support our claim that our children do not appear to be in any way maladjusted, either socially or intellectually.

I began as a teacher in 1997 and have now taught several thousand students and teacher-candidates in classroom settings. There is nothing quite like being among a group of students to experience engagement and the freedom to interact and observe small but important details. The dramatic actor in every teacher is perhaps also best liberated and encouraged within a live classroom setting. Like many teachers, I enjoy decorating and organizing a classroom to make it both inviting and manageable. In my mathematics and visual arts classes, I have found that creativity springs best from a well-organized and regularly inventoried set of classroom materials. As a teacher-educator, I believe that all classroom learning—even in mathematics—can and should be exciting, especially when one follows Einstein's challenge to awaken "joy in creative expression and knowledge" as the supreme art of teaching (quoted in Calaprice, 2011: p. 99). Personalized learning, universal design, STEAM, problem-based math, integrated and cross-curricular projects (Jarvis & Naested, 2012) and many other teaching ideas can be brought to bear on a rich and wonderful classroom experience.

Despite being somewhat suspicious of the overall quality of virtual learning when I began teaching online courses in 2002, I soon became convinced that my assessment of students at both the undergraduate and graduate levels was actually better than when teaching on-site classes. My reasoning here is threefold. First, it involved more regular and detailed feedback on assignments. Second, it provided me with a permanent record of all student input, most of which was usually lost—or at best vaguely recalled—by end of term within an on-site classroom context with 20–40 students. Third, students who do not like to speak spontaneously in a classroom setting will often contribute more meaningful thoughts and peer responses in an online forum, as long as they are given sufficient time to read and reflect.

Finally, as mentioned earlier, our fourth daughter, Thea, prefers the TVO ILC system to the more structured VLC approach, especially for visual art courses, as the former allows more time for project completion. In other words, even in virtual schooling, one or a combination of several different options can usually be found to cater to each student's individual learning preferences.

Conclusion

It has been our goal in this chapter to provide readers with meaningful insights into the lived experiences of students and teachers vis-à-vis three different schooling contexts. All three of the models described within this chapter—homeschool, classroom, and virtual—enable a caring, creative, and committed teacher to provide students with high-quality educational experiences. While each has its own benefits and challenges, a teacher can expect to derive personal fulfillment from any one of them.

We trust that the thoughts we have shared here will encourage joyful resilience among all teachers as they seek to cope with—and even capitalize on—current COVID-19 circumstances and the world of teaching once the pandemic ends. Robert Frost defined education as "the ability to listen to almost anything without losing your temper or your self-confidence" (quoted in Ratcliffe, n.d.). With that definition in mind, we hope we can grow and expand our own teaching repertoires, effectiveness, and knowledge with joyful resilience.

Appendix: Questionnaire/Interview Questions

Compare and contrast homeschool, classroom school, and virtual school experiences.

Learning and Assessment

1. Describe generally how the learning and assessment work in all three models.
2. What are the benefits and challenges in teacher-directed versus self-directed learning?

Teachers and Teaching

1. What challenges/frustrations do you think the teacher experiences in all three learning models?
2. What positive highlights/joys do you think the teacher experiences in all three learning models?
3. The best and worst kinds of teachers in each of the three models are those who …

Model Preference

1. Which of the three models do you prefer most and why? For which ages/grades?

Other

1. Are there any other comments you wish to make about comparing the three models?

References

Arbor Day Foundation. (2018). *What tree is that? A guide to the more common trees found in North America*. https://arborday.org.
Calaprice, A. (Ed.). (2011). *The ultimate quotable Einstein*. Princeton University Press.

Collom, E. & Mitchell, D. E. (2005). Home schooling as a social movement: Identifying the determinants of homeschoolers' perceptions. *Sociological Spectrum*, 25(3), 273–305.

Council of Ministers of Education, Canada. (2020). Education indicators in Canada: An international perspective. www150.statcan.gc.ca/n1/en/pub/81-604-x/81-604-x2020001-eng.pdf?st=eBStLHcS.

Donnelly, M. P. (2012). Homeschooling. In C. L. Glenn, J. DeGroof, & C. Stillings Candal (Eds.), *Balancing freedom, autonomy and accountability in education*, volume 4 (pp. 199–220). Wolf Legal Publishers.

Efford, K. E. & Becker, K. (2017). Home-schooled students and their teachers: Provoking curriculum together through child-driven learning. *Journal of Unschooling and Alternative Learning*, 11(22), 34–52.

Fletcher, L. M. (2020). *How to homeschool in Canada: A travel guide for your homeschooling journey.* https://thecanadianhomeschooler.com/how-to-homeschool-in-canada-book/.

Fullerton, T. (2017). Walden, a game [video game]. www.waldengame.com/.

Jarvis, D. H. & Naested, I. (2012). *Exploring the math and art connection: Teaching and learning between the lines.* Brush Education.

Leary, H., Dopp, C., Turley, C., Cheney, M., Simmons, Z., Graham, C. R., & Riley, H. (2020). Professional development for online teaching: A literature review. *Online Learning Journal*, 24(4). https://olj.onlinelearningconsortium.org/index.php/olj/article/view/2198.

Lisle, J. (2012). *The stargazer's guide to the night sky.* New Leaf Publication Group.

Mason, C. M. (1925/1954). *Home education*, volume 1: *Training and educating children under nine.* J. M. Dent and Sons.

National Geographic. (n.d.). Animals. https://kids.nationalgeographic.com/animals/.

Ontario Federation of Teaching Parents (OFTP). (n.d.). Homeschooling FAQ. https://ontariohomeschool.org/about-homeschooling/homeschooling-faq.

Ontario Ministry of Education (OME). (n.d.). *Education facts, 2018–2019.* www.edu.gov.on.ca/eng/educationFacts.html.

Ratcliffe, S. (Ed.). (n.d.). *Oxford essential quotations* (4th ed.). Oxford University Press. www.oxfordreference.com/view/10.1093/acref/9780191826719.001.0001/q-oro-ed4-00003970.

Sarajlic, E. (2019). Homeschooling and authenticity. *Theory and Research in Education*, 17(3), 280–296.

Trillium Lakelands District School Board (TLDSB). (n.d.). Virtual Learning Centre. www.tldsb.ca/schools/virtual-learning-centre/.

TVOntario Independent Learning Centre (TVO ILC). (n.d.). Why TVO ILC? www.ilc.org/pages/why-ilc.

Virtual Learning Centre (VLC). (n.d.). Parent information. https://virtuallearning.ca/parent-information/.

14
UNCOVERING JOYFUL RESILIENCE

Ken Badley and Michelle C. Hughes

After years of talking about teaching's reciprocities and rewards, we were finally able to put pen to paper alongside a talented group of friends and colleagues to collectively address joyful resilience. The distinct commonality among all this book's contributors is that we, a diverse group of 13 authors, are all practitioners. We are all teachers who love teaching's challenges, celebrate our students, and embrace the business of education. We still get our fingernails dirty on the classroom carpet as we read children's literature to kindergartners, create new exit activities for seniors in high school, hook middle school students into learning with powerful questions, help pre-service teachers find their way into teaching, and guide in-service teachers toward life-sustaining practices. We relish creating routines and designing review games to reinforce curriculum content, and feel satisfied when we call home to discuss a student whose participation was notable in some way. We dig deep, are committed, and continue to pick ourselves up and dedicate every day and every academic year to the business of students, learning, and education.

Whether we deal directly with students in the classroom (Chapters 2, 3, and 13), with curriculum (Chapter 5), with theory or practice (Chapter 6), or with textbooks (Chapter 4), we continue to show up. We show up for our students, their families, and our larger school communities. We show up believing that our daily efforts will help our students realize their potential and thereby make a difference to their future plans and career trajectories. We show up to build their confidence. And we show up to honor relationships, specifically the teacher–student relationship.

Our work and skills take us into unique contexts that extend far beyond our classrooms and students. In Chapters 7, 8, 9, and 10, our contributors highlight teachers' relationships with colleagues, supervisors, families, and our own educational histories. Each of these chapters supports the view that relationships showcase the impact that authors and readers alike can have on an educational community in a given academic year or across the arc of a whole career.

DOI: 10.4324/9781003124429-14

Chapters 11, 12, and 13 underscore some of the tensions we experience—from internal doubts to dissonance and disillusionment—and address issues relating to the political, financial, and ideological contexts in which we work. Notwithstanding these tensions, we, as teachers, remain reflective, dedicated, and open to personal and professional growth. As a representative sample of educators from around the United States and Canada, we all share the view that teachers can work with resilience from day to day and year to year. Furthermore, we believe that joy emanates from that resilience. Whether a given day sails by or becomes a slog, educators can always find joy in their work. We trust that we and our colleagues who have contributed to *Joyful Resilience as Educational Practice* have demonstrated that teachers are fearless and that they are willing to take risks and deal with school and district policies in ways that maintain our own mental health and facilitate our students' learning.

Teachers find hope in the struggle. We face challenges in the daily work of planning, instruction, and assessment. We experience both heartache and joy in our professional relationships, in our dealings with what we often call "the system," and even in events in our own classrooms over which we have no control. To be fully transparent, we know that most teachers have times when they consider leaving, quitting, walking away. The emotional toll of teaching can be exhausting and overwhelming. Still, day after day, through all the routines, quizzes, assemblies, and grading, not to mention natural disasters and even pandemics, we muster the courage to head back into the classroom for our students. The connections with colleagues in decision-making and curricular discourse and the new ways of thinking we learn from our students keep us going. Those students surprise us, overwhelm us, bring us to tears, and sometimes make us scream (to ourselves) in frustration. Yet, we keep showing up. We go to bed exhausted but somehow wake up the next day with a rejuvenated spirit of commitment and care, ready to tackle the day ahead.

So, what are the big ideas that we hope our readers will take away from this book? What are its *ah-ha* or *rainbow* moments? What are its lessons? Well, we hope it provides reasons not simply to keep working in education, but to reframe our educational work so we notice more readily the many ways in which that work gives back to us. In short, we want to shine a spotlight on the gifts we receive from teaching.

Building Bridges Between Ideas and our Students

Nestling somewhere in the foundations of every chapter in this volume is the conviction that teachers focus on their students' learning. We share this conviction with most teachers around the world. None of the contributors to this book is an armchair observer of education systems, schools, universities, or classrooms. All of us spend our days working with and on behalf of living, breathing students. We deal every day with the challenges we have written about here. We ask every day what is best for students (and many of us wake up in the middle of the night thinking about the same question).

All of us have taught students who represent each of Schlechty's five levels of engagement (see Chapter 6). And we all know the kinds of challenges that more resistant students can present. As several of our contributors have noted, most teachers enter this profession for the best of reasons—what we call humanistic reasons. We teach because we want to work with ideas, yes, but we also want to work with students, building bridges they can cross so they can enjoy ideas, too. That building work may be difficult, but it is also highly rewarding, especially when students are willing to make the crossing.

Without implying a gram of judgment toward those who enter professions that offer greater monetary rewards, we note teachers' typical responses to the question, "Why do you do it?" Some of the more familiar answers are: "I love how their eyes shine when they get it"; "I want to make the world a better place"; "I want to help my students find their way"; "I love it when things click"; and "I know my effort was worth it when they come back to my room years later and tell me they first learned this or that in my class." These are just a handful of teaching's non-monetary rewards.

With our book's title—*Joyful Resilience as Educational Practice: Transforming Teaching Challenges into Opportunities*—we have tried to underscore the truth that teaching is hard but rewarding work. Specifically, we all know that we will have some challenging students in our classes. But those challenges can be transformed into opportunities for professional growth and even joy. With the smallest hint of irony, we note that challenging students help us build resilience, so they make us stronger educators and better people.

The Teaching Journey

After a particularly hard Alberta winter, Ken was about to dig out a rose bush and toss it into the green bin for composting. To echo a *Monty Python* sketch about a parrot, he believed the rose bush to be dead. From eye level, it certainly looked dead. But as he was about to drop it into the bin, he noticed one tiny leaf near the base of the main stem. So, he dug a hole in a sunnier spot in the garden, filled it with water, soil, and fertilizer, and transplanted the bush. Within weeks, it was blossoming as if it had never had a near-death experience.

We assume that the rose pictured on the front cover has never received the kind of attention Ken lavished on that bush, but both of them illustrate this book's main thesis: on the teaching journey, teachers are repeatedly pruned, much like rose bushes. We are cut back and we try again. Perhaps we move to a new location. We reflect, we adjust, we redesign, and we start anew. We revise, add to, subtract from, supplement, strengthen, and improve. Growing in our professional practice—remaining curious and reflective—motivates us, inspires us, and keeps us going.

Why We Chose to Teach

Various contributors to this volume have noted that most educators follow their vocation because of some driving sense of the greater good. They want to give back, do meaningful work, make a difference. This great and noble vision helps to sustain teachers when they face the day-to-day challenges of teaching. But therein lies a tension. Faced with a resistant student, an intimidating stack of grading, or a hostile parent, a teacher may lose sight of that initial noble vision. In the back-and-forth—or sometimes the ups-and-downs—of a typical teaching day, the individual educator may forget the big picture of a changed world or the greater good. All the contributors have had up-and-down days, and we have all experienced moments (or hours, days, weeks, or months) when we have lost sight of the larger vision, yet we wrote the words in this book because we all believe there is still joy to be found in teaching, and we want to encourage our colleagues everywhere to carry on.

Teaching is Soul Work, Not Solo Work

On the opening page of *The Courage to Teach*, Parker Palmer (1998: p. 9) writes: "teaching engages my soul as much as any work I know." In his body of writing about the vocation of teaching (Palmer, 1998; 2000; 2004), he repeatedly insists that teaching is soul work. By this he means that teaching has to arise out of the deepest part of the self, what he calls the teacher's "identity and integrity." As he says, "good teachers share one trait: a strong sense of personal identity infuses their work" (Palmer, 1998: p. 10).

Palmer (2004: p. 172) also emphasizes that honoring the soul can strengthen our capacity to serve and do the work. He argues that good teaching can touch our students' souls. By contrast, bad teachers are all the same, as one disgruntled student points out: "their words float somewhere in front of their faces, like the balloon speech in cartoons" (Palmer, 1998: p. 11). We tried to resist, but here we must refer to the famous "Anyone? *Anyone?*" scene in *Ferris Bueller's Day Off* (Hughes, 1986). Ben Stein, as Ferris's unnamed economics teacher, perfectly encapsulates the kind of teacher whose words float somewhere in front of his face. On the other hand, we could list what some call *reel teachers* (Nederhouser, 2000; Shaw & Nederhouser, 2007) in both documentaries and feature films who beautifully personify Palmer's ideal.

Palmer (1998: p. 11) notes, "The courage to teach is the courage to keep one's heart open in those very moments when the heart is asked to hold more than it is able." We wholeheartedly agree that teaching takes an emotional and physical toll on us every day, yet we choose to persevere, to find more personal grit, and to develop greater resilience. In Chapter 11, Carrie R. Giboney Wall concedes that the day-in, day-out grind of the teaching profession often fosters doubts, dissonance, and disillusionment. This is our professional reality. Yet, through all the challenges and continual self-reflection, even when things don't connect, our joy of teaching is renewed.

On Palmer's telling, there is one final reason why we should regard teaching as soul work: our students' responses to our work touch our souls. Of course, at the level of instruction and instructional improvement, we reflect and revise as we teach and note our students' learning year by year. Most users of the popular phrase *assessment for learning* imply that the purpose of assessment is not simply to produce a grade … that is, our students learn by means of our assessment of their work. Ideally, we learn too. By assessing our students' work, we discover how well we have taught a particular section of the curriculum. For most teachers (including, we suspect, anyone who has read this far), this learning from assessment is standard practice. But Palmer points to a parallel process at the deepest levels of every teacher's self: our students' responses to our teaching confirm and disconfirm our conceptions of the teaching vocation. Of course, they may lead us to revise a particular unit or assignment, but they also nudge us to look deep within and reflect on why we do what we do, as well as how we do it. As we say in the title to this section, teaching is not solo work. Moreover, as Tiana Tucker argues convincingly in Chapter 7, we most need our colleagues—and they most need us—when teaching becomes most challenging.

We enthusiastically agree with Palmer's assertion that teaching is soul work. And we hope, as you finish this book, that you remember it is not solo work and now feel a stronger sense of camaraderie and collegiality.

Each contributing author hopes you find encouragement here, and that you know that your daily work and professional journey are recognized and valued. So we offer *Joyful Resilience as Educational Practice* as a love letter, an affirmation of the teaching vocation, with all the challenges and risks it entails, and all the strength it requires.

References

Hughes, J. (Director) (1986). *Ferris Bueller's day off*. Paramount.
Nederhouser, D. D. (2000). Reel teachers: A descriptive content analysis of the portrayal of American teachers in popular cinema. Doctoral dissertation, Northern Illinois University.
Palmer, P. (1998). *The courage to teach*. Jossey-Bass.
Palmer, P. (2000) *Let your life speak: Listening for the voice of vocation*. Jossey-Bass.
Palmer, P. (2004). *A hidden wholeness*. Jossey-Bass.
Shaw, C. C. & Nederhouser, D. D. (2007). Reel teachers: References for reflection for real teachers. *Action in Teacher Education*, 27(3), 85–94.

INDEX

Page references in *italics* refer to figures and **bold** refer to tables

abilities 35
academic performance 104–5
access to nature 154
accountability 9, 76–7
action-research paradigm 70
adolescent learners 28
agency 48–9, 94–5
Aguilar, E. 15
Ahearn, L. M. 48
The Aims of Education (Whitehead) 42, 130
Alberta 42
ancient Roman and Greek education 102
Antayá-Moore, Dana 38–9, 74
antisocial behavior 154
"the apprenticeship of observation" (Lortie) 107–8, 117
Aristotle, *Politics* 124–5
asking questions 76–7
assessments 143–4
assets-based instruction 107
Athens 102
attrition 3
authority 60–1
autobiographical reflections 98

"back to basics" 128–9
Badley, Ken 19–20, 38–9, 108
Bagley, William 128
baseline theory 61
behavior 29–30, 31, 108, 114, 148, 154
behavioral approaches 59, 61

Benson, Jeffrey, *Hanging In* 28–9
Bernal, J. D. 128
Bernard, Henry 126
Bestor, Arthur 128
body language 29
Brannon, D. 105
Bretton Woods agreement (1944) 127–8
Brown, B. 16
Brown, Mildred 90, 91, 95
building trusting and caring relationships 35
burnout 3, 48, 106

calling to teach 3–5, 9, 20–1
Canada: Departments of Education 39–40; provincial responsibility for education 139–40; trade treaties 1–2; universal, state-funded education 102–3
Canvas software 144
care 31–2, 85
care for students 16–17, 35, 53, 146
caring for ourselves 33, 36
Carrington, Jody 34, 35
celebrating successes 33, 34–5
Chadwick, Joy A. 26
challenges 1–9, 26, 31, 48–51, 61, 98, 141
challenging students 27
Chenoweth, K. 104
"child-centeredness" 97
child development theories 127
China 102, 107
choosing to teach 20–2

classical education 102
classroom challenges 31
classroom community 13
classroom contexts 51, 82, 85, 94, 112, 131–2, 151, 159
classroom experiences 34
classroom management 59–61
classroom schooling: Canada 139–40; decorating and organizing 155; improving practice 17–20; learning and assessments 143–4; responding to situations 29; teachers and teaching 147–8; visiting 68, 82, 133
Cobb-Roberts, D. 113
cognitive disequilibrium (Piaget) 112, 113
cognitive dissonance (Festinger) 112, 113, 115–16
collaboration 68, 75–6, 78–9, 104
collaborative relationships 75
collective agency 86–8
collegial exchange 76–9
collegial interdependence 77
collegiality 71–2
Collom, E. 138
community of practice 50–1, 53
community with a cause 85, 87–8
conceptual change (Strike and Posner) 113
"conduits" (Klabnik) 64
"contextual dissonance" (Rosenberg) 112, 114, 118–21
continuous improvement 72–3
conversations with colleagues 34
Cook, R. 127
core content 77
Cornett, C. E. 14–15
Council of Ministers of Education, Canada (CMEC) 139
counter-mentors/models 92
The Courage to Teach (Palmer) 49, 161
COVID-19 pandemic 4, 21–2, 84, 137, 139, 141, 144
Critical Friends Group 53–4
critical thinking 127
cross-curricular projects 152–3
Csikszentmihalyi, M. 20
Cuban, Larry 91
curricula: being told to follow 47; core content 77; and educational philosophy 125–6; joyful defiance 130–2; learning outcomes 131; legislated policy documents 130; organization 130–1; progressivism and essentialism 129; reflecting societal values 134
"curriculum-instructional gatekeepers" 94
curriculum studies 130

custom-published textbooks 44
custom-written texts 45

"Daily 5" framework 74
Davies, B. 48
Davis, H. A. 12, 13
decisions to teach 20–2
Democracy and Education (Dewey) 126–7
Departments of Education: Alberta 42; contracting for textbooks 39–40
Desire to Learn (D2L) platform 144
Dewey, John 49, 55–6, 126–7
dialogical stance 50
differentiation 63–4, 115–16
direction-planning 86
disabled students 27
disaffection 3
discouragement 115
"discovery learning" 127
disgruntled parents 106
dispositions 8, 13, 15, 131
dissonance 65, 111–21
distance-learning 141
diversity 35–6
Doctor Who 44
Doll, R. 127
Donnelly, Michael P. 138, 154
Doty, Tammy 83–4, 85
Drive (Pink) 81
Dweck, Carol 13, 109

educational identities 92
educational jargon 97
educational philosophy 125
education field experience reflective journal assignment 52
Education for All Handicapped Children (1997) 26
Education Indicators in Canada (CMEC) 139
education professors 68
educator dissonance 113–14
educators 16
effective progressive classrooms 127
electronic media 105–6
electronic textbooks 38
elementary education 90–1
"ELL/ESL students" 27
An Elusive Science (Lagemann) 99
emotional buckets 33, 35
emotional dissonance 112, 114–15
emotional exhaustion 33
engaged and responsive educators 50–1
engagement: classroom management 61; levels of 59–60, *60*
English learners 27, 116

essentialism 128–9
Evans-Palmer, T. 13, 15
Every Child Succeeds (2015) 26
examining the self and the inner life 15
excellence-versus-adequacy mindset 129
"existentialism" 97
Expressions of Faith (Badley, Antayá-Moore, & Kostelyk) 38–9
extra-curricular activities 154

families 101–9
Farrell, T. S. C. 15
fear of failure 28
Fecho, B. 50, 56
Feldman, Kevin 82–3
Ferris Bueller's Day Off (film) 161
Festinger, L. 111–12, 113
Finn, P. 48
Fish, Stanley, *Is There a Text in This Class?* 40
fixed versus growth mindset 109
Fletcher, Lisa Marie 153; *How to Homeschool in Canada* 138
"flow" (Csikszentmihalyi) 20
formative educational influences 93
framing and reframing problems 49
France, P. E. 12
Freire, P. 48
French Impressionism 44
friendship with children 146
Frost, Robert 156
frustration 31, 32
Fullan, Michael 82
funny and happy stories 13
Furlong, J. 117

Galman, S. 112, 114, 116, 118
Garcia, A. 56
Germany 102
gifts: teachers appreciating 108; textbooks giving teachers 43–5
gifts from supervisors 80–8; collective agency 86–7; community with a cause 85, 87–8; getting better 81–3, 87–8 *see also* reciprocity
Gill, M. G. 115
Glasser, W. 59
Goodwin, B. 21
Greene, Ross 30
greeting students 20
growth mindset 29, 34, 109, 115
Gustavsen, Bjorn 66, 69, 70

Hanging In (Benson) 28–9
Hardin, C. 115

Harlem Children's Zone Schools 105
Harlem Village Academies 105
Hattie, J. 35
helping colleagues 74–5
hidden roles and influences 92
A Hidden Wholeness (Palmer) 5, 51
Hill, L. 113
Hinchion, C. 118
Hollingsworth, S. 113
homeschooling 138–9, 151–2; common criticisms 154; costs 143; COVID-19 pandemic 139; cross-curricular projects 152–3; discussing current events 155; extra-curricular activities 154; friendship with children 146; home life 147; learning and assessment 141–3; lower grades 150; multi-media resources 154; neuropsychological issues 153; reading 142, 143, 154–5; state support 138, 154; teachers and teaching 145–7; working at own pace 143
homeschooling community 147
"Homeschooling" (Donnelly) 138
hooks, B. 50
How Full is Your Bucket? (Rath, Reckmeyer, & Manning) 32
"How It's Being Done" schools 104–5
How to Homeschool in Canada (Fletcher) 138
Hughes, Michelle C. 30, 36, 103, 104
"humanistic education" 97
humor 13–15, 81
"humorless" teachers 14

identity dissonance 112, 116–18
identity formation 116
impact on students 20, 35
implementation gap 73
Impressionism and Post-Impressionism course 44
improvement of others 72
improving classroom practice 17–20
inappropriate behavior 14, 29–30
Independent Study Unit (ISU) 144
indirect mentoring 92
individual agency 98
individual professional judgment 95
"inner landscape of the teaching self" (Palmer) 51
inner work within the community 15
"inside-out" reflection (Korthagen) 121
instructional choices 28
instructional theory 63
intellectual growth 113
intentional listening 15–16
investing in relationships 15–16, 19
"IPP/IEP students" 27

Israel 102
Is There a Text in This Class? (Fish) 40

Jackson, Philip 91
Jarvis, Anna 136, *137*; schooling context **145**; schooling preferences 150–1
Jarvis, April E. 136, *137*; classroom schooling 144, 148; homeschooling 143, 146–7; schooling preferences 152; virtual schooling 145, 149–50
Jarvis, Clara 136, *137*, 154; schooling context **145**; schooling preferences 150
Jarvis, Daniel H. 136, *137*
Jarvis, Ella 136, *137*; homeschooling 142, *142*, 146; schooling context **145**; schooling preferences 152
Jarvis, Rose *137*; schooling context **145**; schooling preferences 151
Jarvis, Thea *137*; homeschooling 146; schooling context **145**; schooling preferences 151; virtual schooling 145, 149, 155
John Paul II (Karol Wojtyła) 97
Johnston, P. 48
joyful defiance 130–5; building alliances 133–4; commitment to beliefs 132; curricula 131; exploration of curricula 134–5; professional learning communities 134
joyful resilience 1, 158–62
joy of teaching 92

K-12 education 39, 95, 106
K-12 schools 42
Kenny, Deborah 105
"kids do well if they can" (Greene) 30
kid watching 34
kindness 84
KIPP Academies 105
Klabnik, Steve 64, 65, 70
knowing one's students 55
"knowing thy impact" (Zierer & Hattie) 35
Kohl, H. 35–6
Kohn, A. 59
Korthagen, F. A. J. 113–14, 118
Kostelyk, A. 38–9

labeling students 27
Lagemann, Ellen Condliffe, *An Elusive Science* 99
landscape of practice 50–2
Latunde, Y. 109
laughter 13–15, 36
leading students towards learning 59
"leaning in" to a student's story 30

learning and assessments 141–5; classroom schooling 143–4; homeschooling 141–3; virtual schooling 144–5
learning from mistakes 73–4
learning gaps 77, 116
Learning Management System (LMS) 144
learning outcomes 131
learning patterns 67
learning to read and write 90
learning-to-teach journey 116
Leary, H. 141
legal contracts 2
legal reciprocity 1–2
levels of student engagement 50, 59–60, 159
Levin, B. 116
Lewis, C. S. 98
lifelong learners 56
listening to students 15–16, 19, 54
"look-fors" (points of emphasis) 83
Lortie, Dan 107–8, 117
loss of control 31

maintaining energy and stamina 36
Mann, Horace 126
Manning, M. J., *How Full is Your Bucket?* 32
Mason, Charlotte 146–7
Mason, J. 63
Massachusetts 103
math concepts 28
Mathisen, Jay 96
Maynard, T. 117
McFalls, E. L. 113
mediating artists 70
meeting expectations 26
mental health 1, 4, 16, 159
mentors and mentoring 16, 91–3, 95–9
Minchew, S. S. 14
mindfulness 63, 134
mindsets 29; collegiality 71–2; teachers and parents 108–9
missing the story 31
mistakes 73–4
Mitchell, D. E. 138
mobile schooling 149, 153
moment-to-moment experiences 28
moral companions 12
moral rewards 21
motivation 12, 17, 20–2, 95, 114, 150
Mullen, Andrew 90
multi-media resources 154
Murdock, J. 27
mutual relationships 11–12
My Place in the World (Badley, Antayá-Moore, & Kostelyk) 38–9

narrow thinking 154
National Commission on Excellence in Education, *A Nation at Risk* 129
Neal, Joanne 74
negativity 34
Nelson, John 93
neurodiversity 27–8
neuropsychological issues 153
new teachers 21, 105
New York 103
Nichols, Morgan Harper 109
Ni, Y. 107
No Child Left Behind (2001) 26
Noddings, N. 17
non-intimidating communications 105
nonverbal responses 29
North American public education 126
North Bay's homeschooling cooperative 147
no-such-thing-as-perfection-in-teaching caveat 72
novice teachers 78

observing and assisting colleagues 83
observing students 53
observing teaching 76
O'Donnell-Allen, C. 56
O'Flaherty, J. 118
O Gallchóir, C. 118
O'Keefe, T. 34
one-size-fits-all approaches 26
Onion Model (Korthagen) 114, 118
online gaming 105
online schooling 148–50
Ontario: homeschooling 154; school board systems 140; Virtual Learning Centre (VLC) 140
Ontario College of Teachers (OCT) 140
Ontario Curriculum 140
Ontario Federation of Teaching Parents (OFTP) 138–9
open-mindedness 15, 56
Organization for Economic Cooperation and Development (OECD) 139

Palmer, Parker 4, 11, 15, 20, 34, 55, 56, 94, 161–2; *The Courage to Teach* 49, 161; *A Hidden Wholeness* 5, 51
Pan-Canadian Education Indicators Program (PCEIP) 139
pandemics 4, 21–2, 84, 137, 139, 141, 144
paper texts 38
parental motivation 153
parent councils 106–8
parents 101–9; educational ideals 101–2; gifts 108; historical perspectives 101–2; involvement in education 103–6; mindsets 108–9; as teachers 146–7
parent–teacher–school relationships 104–5
passionate teaching 17
patience 32, 35
Pay it Forward (film) 2
"pedagogical fruit" 20
pedagogical strategies 113
pedagogical theories 63
perfection 72
The Perfect Wrong Note (Westney) 73
personal and subjective challenges 4
personal growth 16
personalism (person-centeredness) 97–9
philosophical paradigms 59
philosophy of mistakes 73
philosophy of teaching courses 63
Piaget, J. 113
Pine, G., *Teacher Action Research* 69–70
Pink, Daniel, *Drive* 81
Politics (Aristotle) 124–5
poor attendance records 16
Pose, Wobble, Flow (P/W/F) framework 56
positive feedback loops 33
Posner, G. J. 113, 116
Postman, Neil 105–6
preparation 55
prescribed curricula 48
pre-service teachers: cognitive disequilibrium 113; contextual dissonance 119; pedagogical strategies 113; self-reflection 132; tensions with theories 66
primary teachers 30–1
prior knowledge 61–2
problem-setting 49
professional autonomy 95
professional community of practice 53
professional development 68, 75
Professional Development Days 147
professional growth 16, 72
professional improvement 81–2
professional independence 77
professional mentors 92
professional reciprocity 72
professional rewards 22
professors 6, 38–41, 59, 68, 95–9
progressivism 126–8, 129
promoting collegial exchange 76–9
public education 126
public school learning 143–4

Ramirez, Mr (teacher) 19, 20
Rath, T., *How Full is Your Bucket?* 32
Ray, Paige A. 50

reading 90, 142, 143, 154–5
rebellion 60
reciprocity 1–2; building a productive classroom 63; gifts 80; mutual relationships 11–12; of sharing leadership 87; teacher–student relationship 17, 20; textbooks 39 see also gifts from supervisors
"Reciprocity Treaty 1854" 1–2
"Reciprocity Treaty 1875" 1–2
"Reciprocity Treaty 1911" 1–2
Reckmeyer, M., *How Full is Your Bucket?* 32
recognition by students 17–18
recognizing failures 55
recursive feedback 68
recursive relationship 67, 67
reflection-in-action 49, 53
reflection-on-action 49, 53
reflective action 49, 55–6
reflective journal assignment 52
reflective practice 48, 49–50, 56
reflective thinking 127
'relatedness' 17
relational work 20
relationships 11, 21–2
religious groups 102
remote learning 21–2
resilience 13, 15, 31
resource vocabulary 43
responding to classroom situations 29
retreatism 60
Rhoades, Bill 86
Rickover, Hyman George 128–9
ritual compliance 60
Robinson, Ken 11
role models 92–3
role-play 30
Rome 102
Rosenberg, M. 114, 118
routine actions 49
Royce, Josiah 99

Santoro, D. 106
Saskatchewan 107
scaffolding 78, 113, 130
Schlechty, P. C. 59, 60
Schmidt, M. E. 105
Schön, D. A. 49, 50, 53
school communities 85, 105
schooling preferences 150–2
school leadership 84, 105
"scrub-ins" 83
Segal, S. 67
self-awareness 16

self-discovery 116
self-improvement 72
self-knowledge 131–3, 134
self-reflection 76, 131–3
sense of community 84
shared experience of grief 104
"shared leadership" 86–7
shared responsibility 74–5
Skinner, B. F. 59
Smith, David 91
Snow Days 147
social Darwinism 124
Socrates 131
Sparta 101–2
special education classroom 54–5
Spencer, Herbert 124–5
staffrooms 34, 133
Standing in the Gaps 63–5
state-funded schools 103
Steeg Thornhill, S. M. 19–20
Stein, Ben 161
strategic compliance 60
strength-based approaches 26
strengths 34
Strike, K. A. 113, 116
student achievement 104–5
student assets 107
"student-centeredness" 97
student engagement 50, 59–60, 60, 159
student feedback 34
student resources 43
students: accessing prior knowledge 61–2; focusing on outbursts 30; frustration and loss of control 31; parent involvement 105; recognition by 17–18; role-play 30; teachers as models for 32; telling us about themselves 28; uniqueness 27; watching teachers 17, 30–2, 35; working at own pace 143
students on the margins 26–8
student teaching placement 53
Sullivan, Sunshine R. 74
supervision of student teachers 98
supervisors 80–8; gifts 87–8; and professional improvement 81–2; visiting classrooms 82; workplace culture 85
sustainable teaching 47–56; personal journey 52–6; teacher agency 48–9, 94
sustaining reflective action 55–6

"tact" 20
taking work home 32–3
Teacher Action Research (Pine) 69–70
teacher agency 48–9, 94

teacher-as-conduit 70
teacher authority 60–1
teacher burnout 48
teacher-candidates 99
teacher education programs 66
teachers: autobiographies 92; best/worst kind 148; communicating about help needed 105; "curriculum-instructional gatekeepers" 94; as educators and mentors 16; fear of failure 28; focusing on negativity/strengths 34; laughing at themselves 13–15; making a difference 160–1; as mediating artist 70; meeting the needs of students 148; mindsets 108–9; model for students 32; moral companion 12; observing students 53; perception of parents 108–9; perceptions of themselves 27; as quiet revolutionary 130; reading aloud 41; reasons for teaching 21; relational and interpersonal 12; as resources 77; sharing parents' concerns 107; wise advice from colleagues 74
teacher–student relationships 12–13, 17
teacher-to-teacher relationships 79
teaching: about the business of students 11; as an art 64; classroom schooling 147–8; the curriculum 28; homeschooling 145–7; interpersonal activity 12; isolating profession 71; as a moral practice 21; reciprocal rewards 21; as a science 64–5; as soul work 161; virtual schooling 148–50; as a vocation 20–1
teaching against the text 43
teaching from the text 41
teaching journey 121, 160
teaching plans 29
teaching to the text 43
teaching with the text 42–3
technology 105–6
tension: as a discipline 69–70; as a feedback loop 65–7; in teaching 1; theory and practice 50, 64, 65
text-based instruction 62
textbooks 38–46; how teachers use 40–3; packages 41–2; production 39–40; saving time 44; student resources 43; teachers' postures 40–3
theoretical responses to crises and rapid change 62
"Theory and Practice: The Mediating Discourse" (Gustavsen) 66
theory–practice tension 58–70; closing the gaps 64, 68–9; disjuncture 62; non-reciprocal relationship 59; recursive feedback 68; recursive relationship 67; vision of resolving 68
"3 Rs" movement 128–9
Ticknor, A. C. 118
time investment 75
tolerance for ambiguities 113
Tomlinson, C. A. 13
transformational change 112
Trillium Lakelands District School Board (TLDSB) 140
trusting and caring relationships 13, 22, 35, 59–60, 105, 109
Tucker, Tiana 53, 71
tutors/tutoring 102
TVOntario Independent Learning Centre (TVO ILC) 140–1, 144, 145, 154, 155

unconventional deadlines 150
"undivided life" (Palmer) 51
unexpected professional rewards 18
United States 1–2, 26, 102–3
Universal Design for Learning (UDL) 107
universal, free education 102–3

Vanderwater, E. 105
van Manen, M. 20, 28
vertical colleagues 78–9
video resources 62
virtual learning 155
Virtual Learning Centre (VLC, Ontario) 140, 144, 154, 155
virtual mentoring 92
virtual schooling 140–1; COVID-19 pandemic 84; grades nine–twelve 150; learning and assessment 144–5; mobility 149; teachers and teaching 148–50; unconventional deadlines 150
vision-setting 86
visiting classrooms 68, 82, 133
vocations 1–5, 20–1, 50–1, 68, 112, 134, 160–2
vulnerability 16

Wall, Carrie R. Giboney 65
Wandersee, J. W. 14
Waywood, A. 63
Weddell, H. D. 85–6
Wei, F. 107
Weinstein, C. S. 113
Wells, G. 51
Wenger-Trayner, B. 50–1
Wenger-Trayner, E. 50–1
Westney, William, *The Perfect Wrong Note* 73

Whelan, Michael ('Professor Whelan') 95–9
Whitehead, Alfred North 134; *The Aims of Education* 42, 130
Who am I? (Badley, Antayá-Moore, & Kostelyk) 38–9
Wojtyła, Karol (John Paul II) 97
working at own pace 143
working authentically 74

working independently 74
work–life balance 32–3
workplace culture and climate 85
Worldviews, Contact and Change (Antayá-Moore) 39

Zierer, K. 35
Ziv, A. 13

Printed in the United States
by Baker & Taylor Publisher Services